Copyright 2018 Sebastian De Angelis
ISBN: 978-0-9679947-1-0
What Is It Series start date: 11-26-2001
Book (2) revised on: 07-19-2018

Description: What Is It Book 2, Drawings 251 to 500
eBook ASIN: B07FMQB367, ISBN: 978-0-9679947-1-0

The What Is It Series of Books is a compilation of over a thousand drawings by Sebastian De Angelis. The drawings are interesting, fascinating and sometimes humorous. They're in black & white and are available in paperback. The whole family should enjoy hours of viewing these detailed drawings. De Angelis' unique, unusual style will leave you wondering What Is It?

Although there doesn't seem to be a rhyme or reason as to what the artist is drawing, small creatures appear randomly throughout the books. These humanoid looking beings (unnamed or purpose described) come in all shapes and sizes. They typically are involved with things of a malicious nature, throwing levers, pressing buttons and all-out getting in the way of normality.

So where do all the wild ideas come from that sets the artist's pen in motion? Most of the work tells me that De Angelis is delivering a message that life is not as perfect under the facade surface as we imagine. And that situations in the world around us are a lot more ironic then we assume. The nuts & bolts, chewing gum & duck-tape that holds it all together is the World's way of evolving. Then the practicality fades due in part to those pesky humanoids! So be careful (xiao xin) out there, it's much more precarious then you think! Heee heeee…

Books in the What Is It Series

Book (1) Drawings 1-250
Book (2) Drawings 251-500
Book (3) Drawings 501-750
Book (4) Drawings 751-1000

What Is It

Book 2

Drawings 251 to 500

Sebastian De Angelis

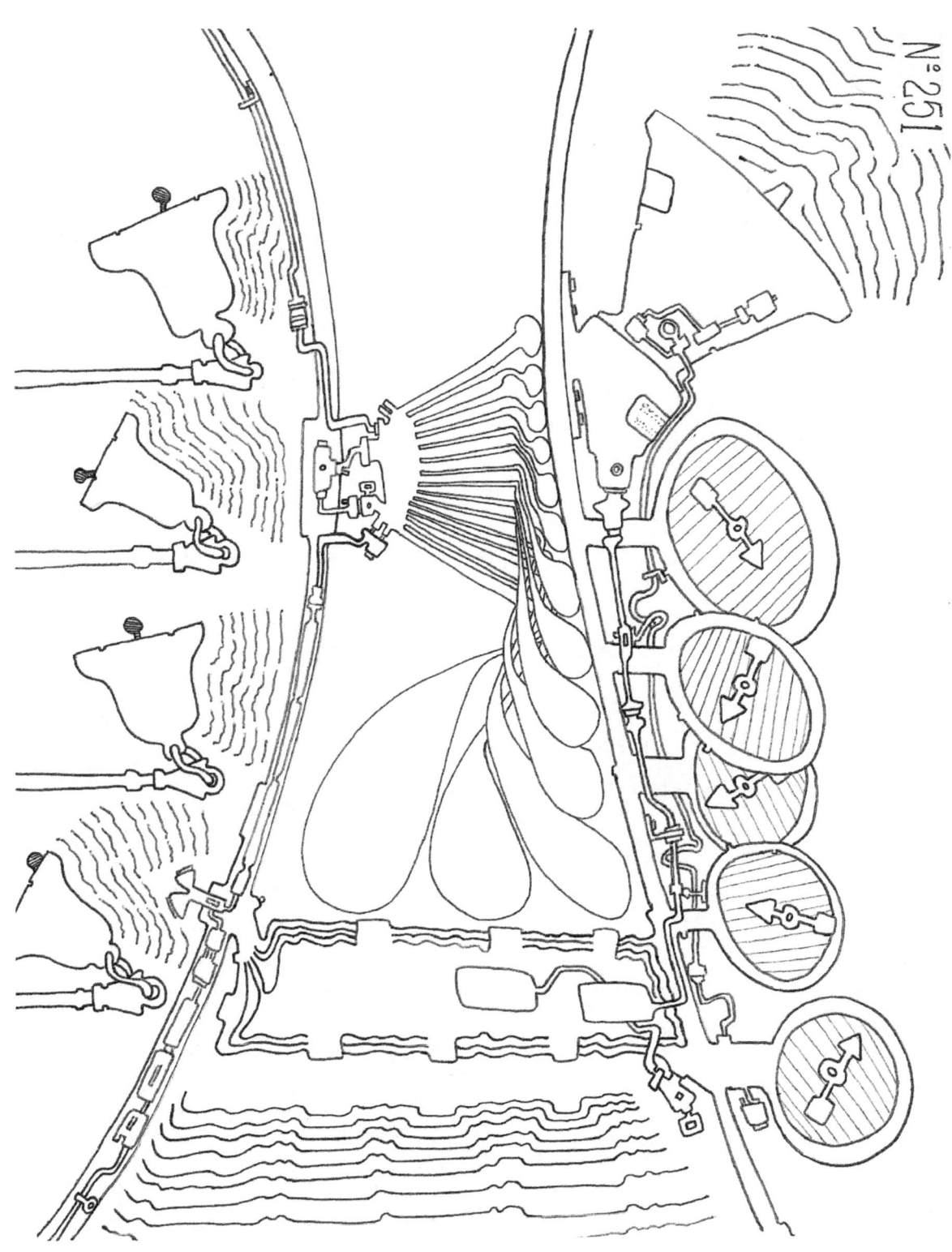

N° 251

N° 252

N° 253
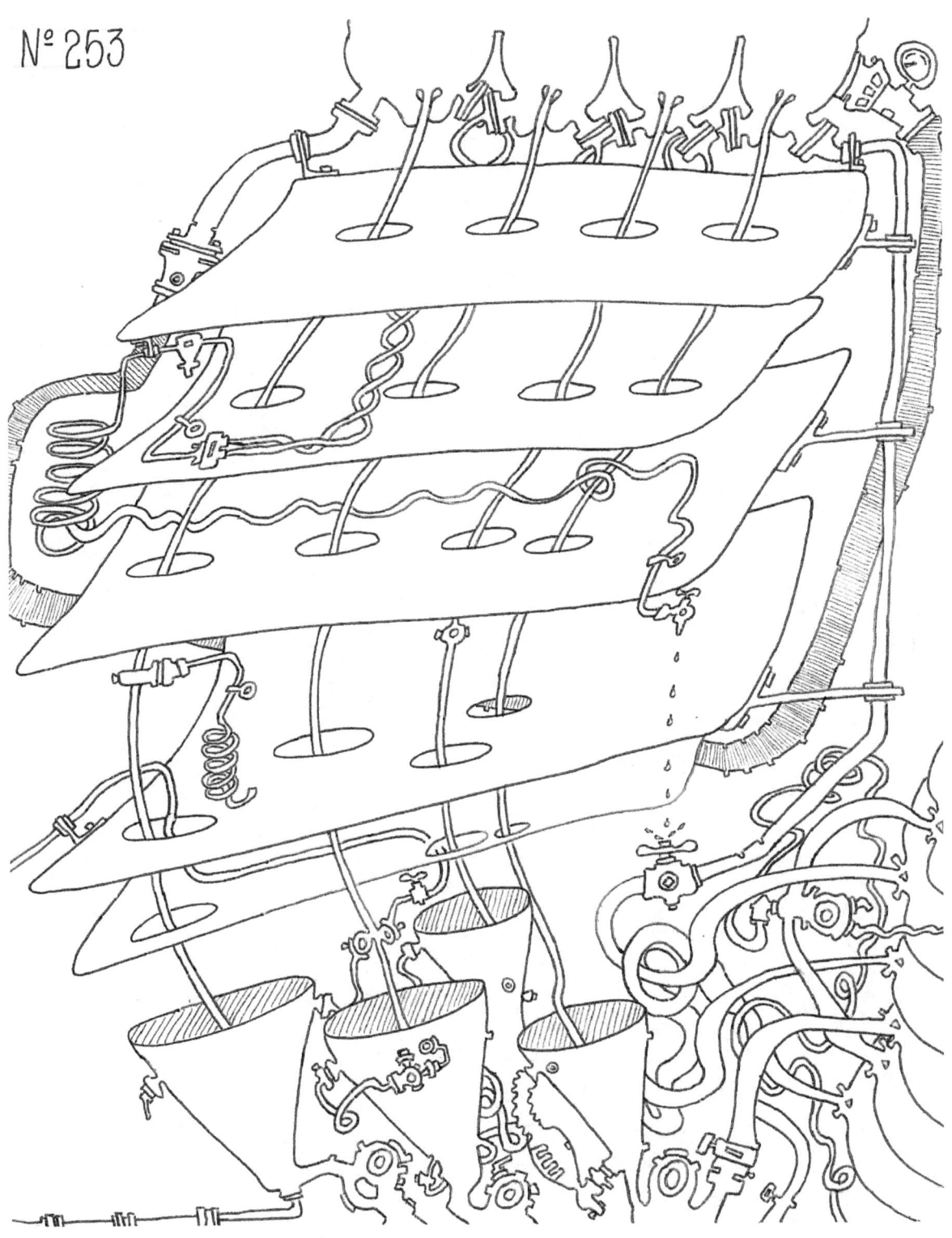

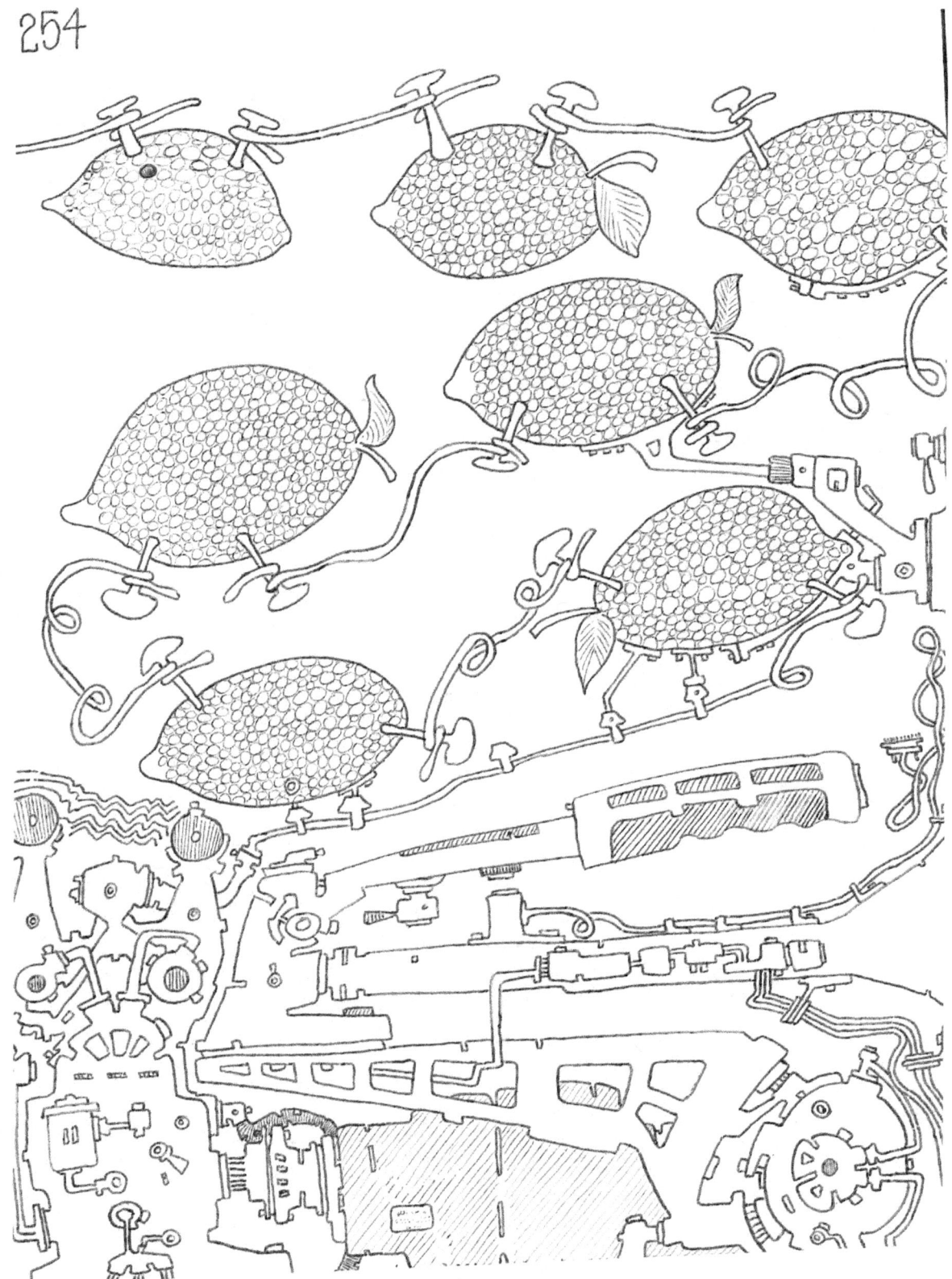

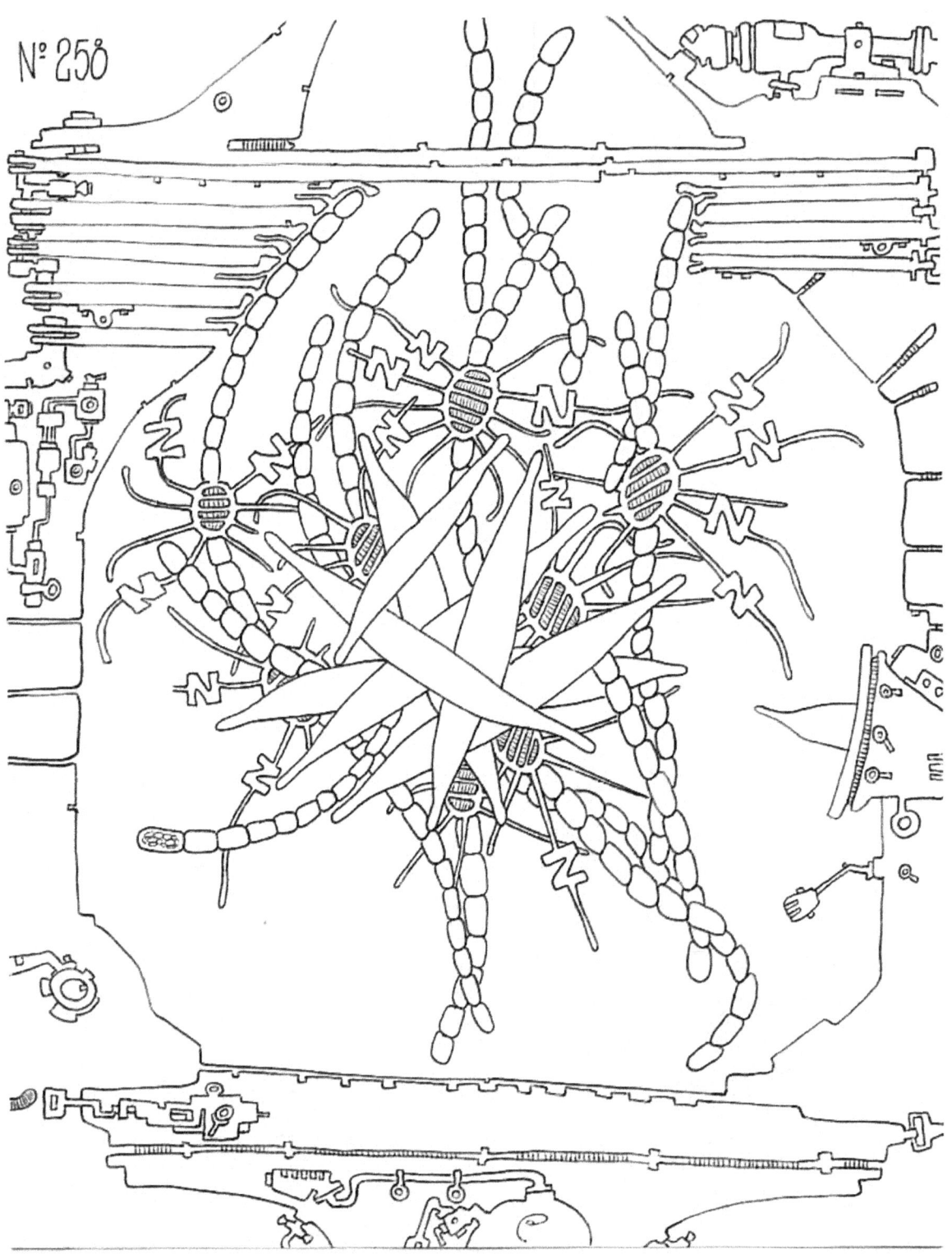

N° 261

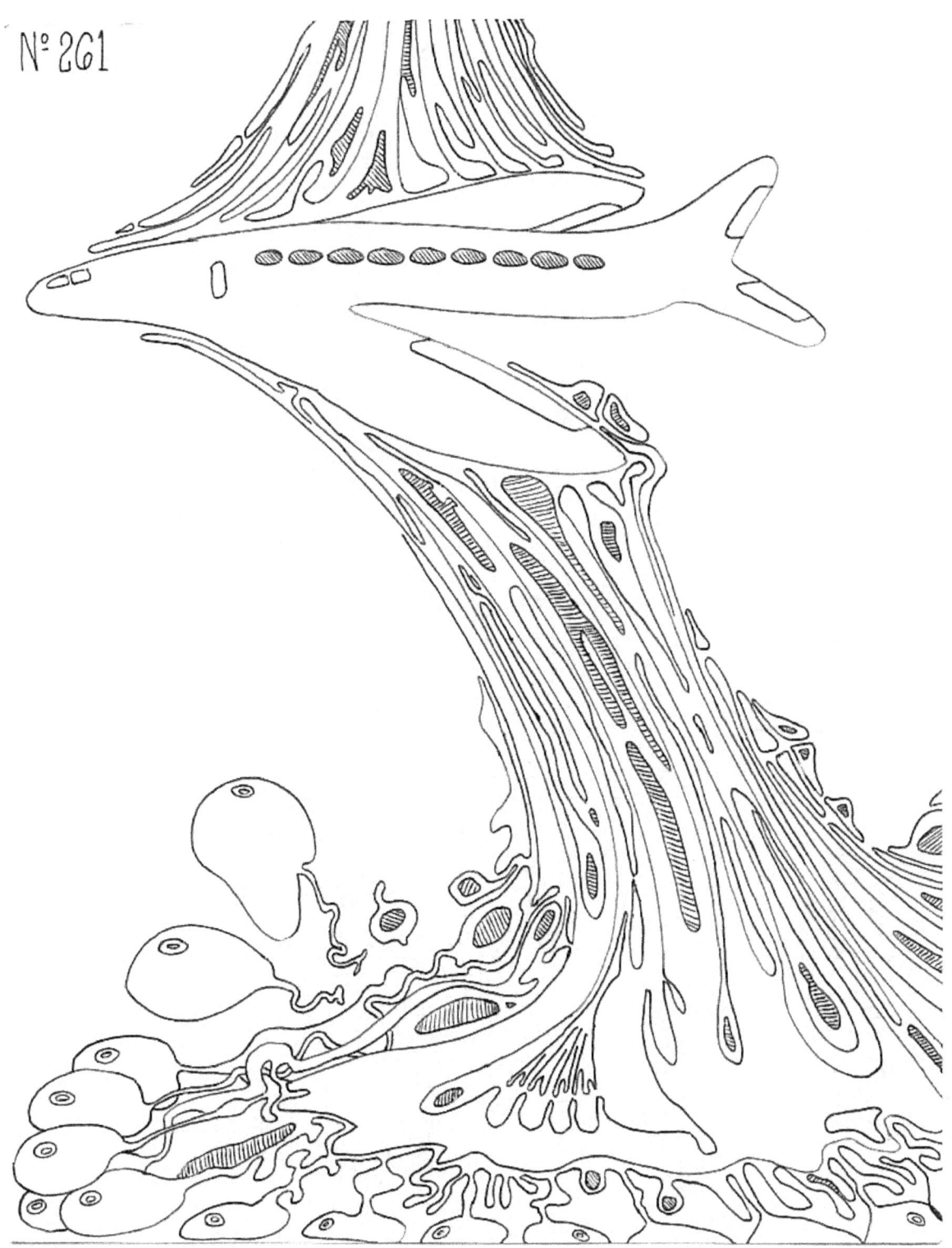

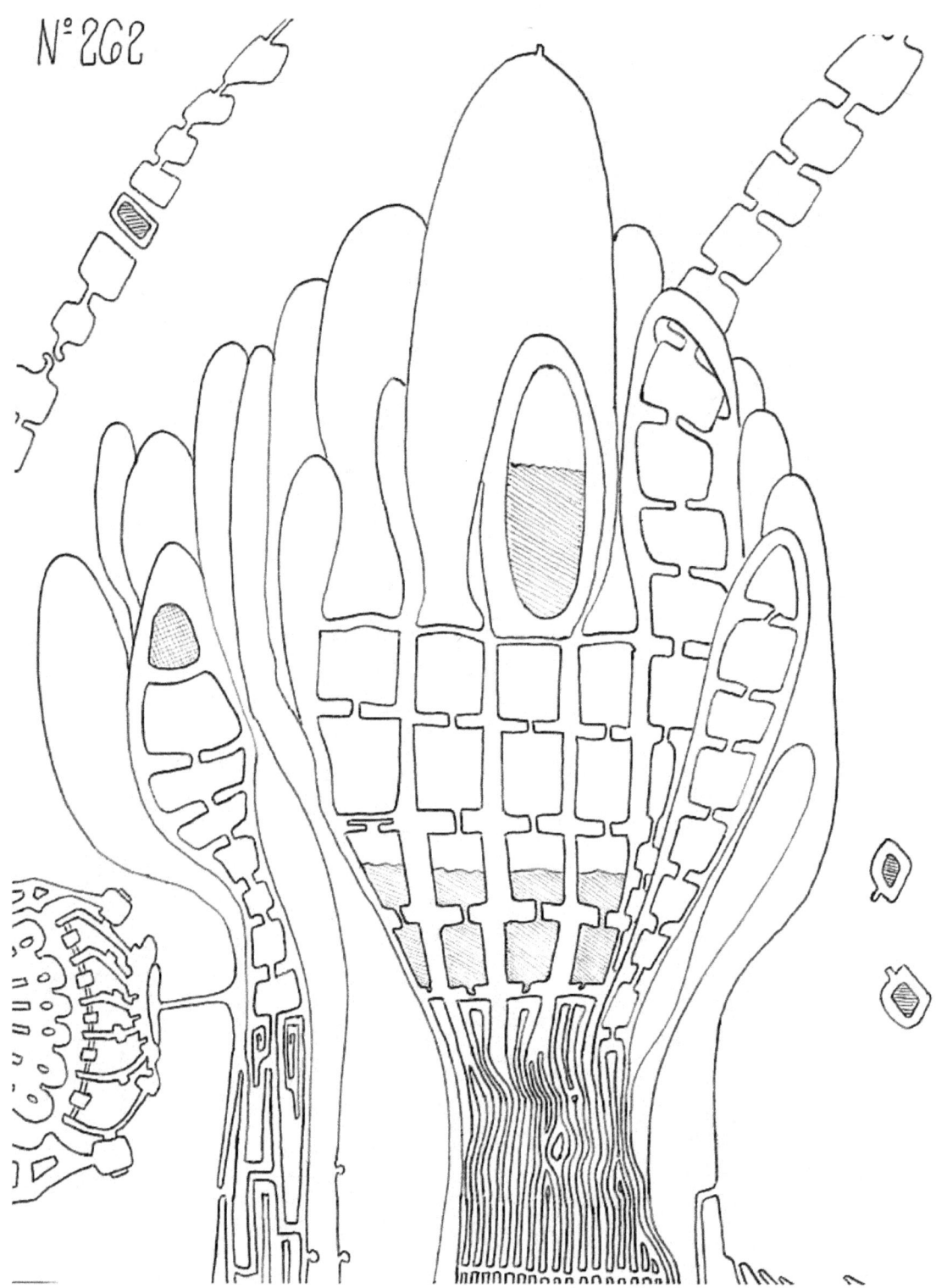

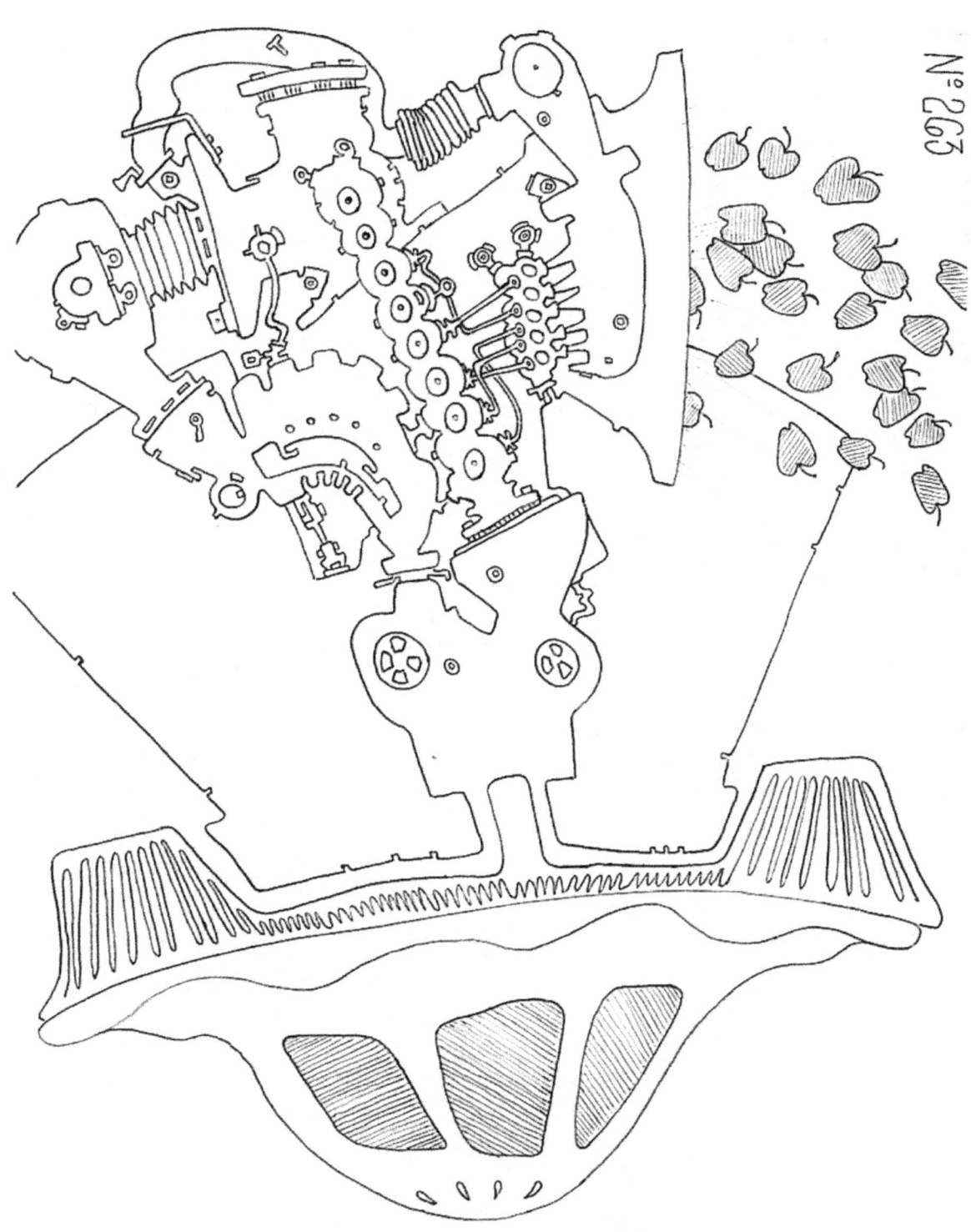

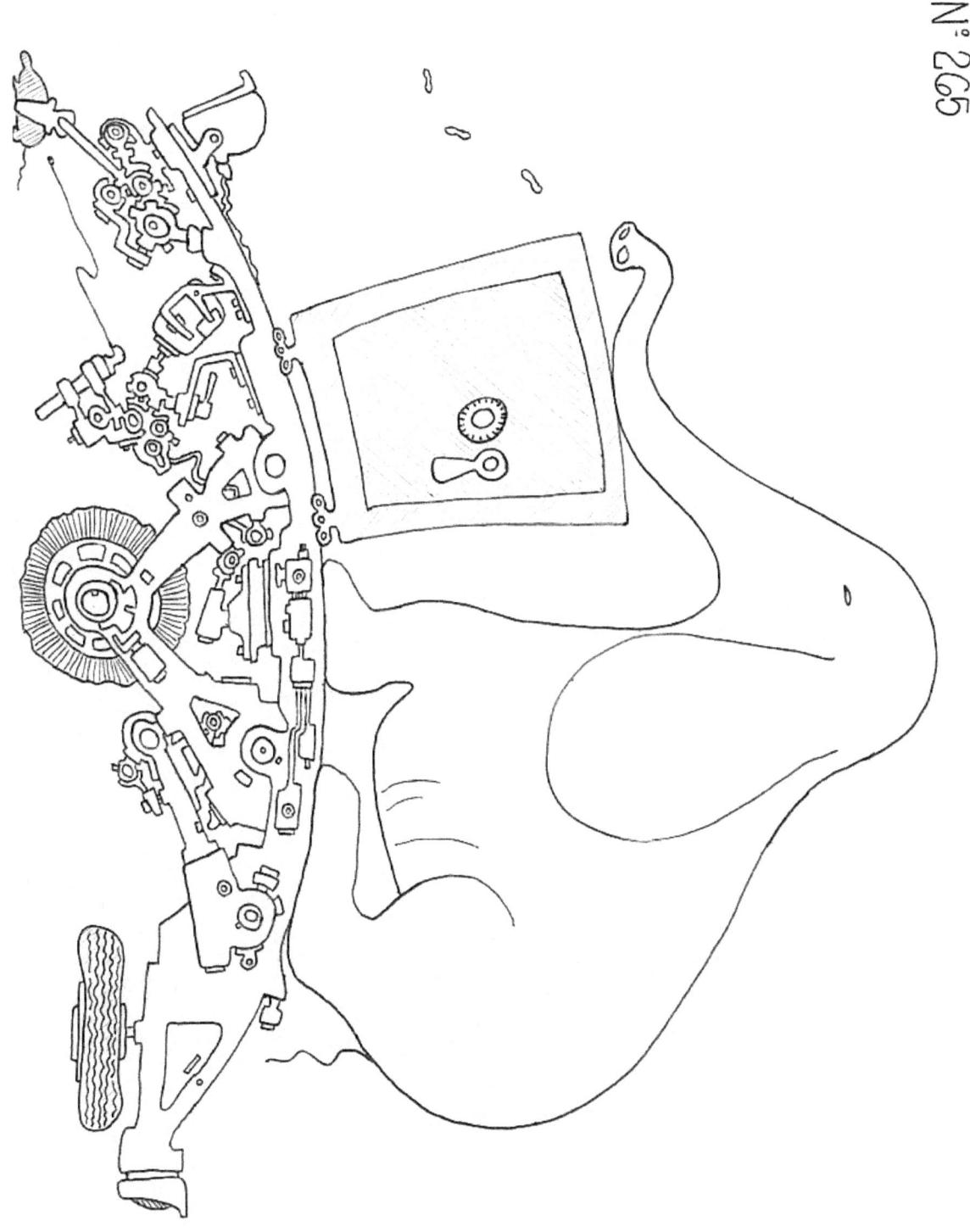

Nº 265

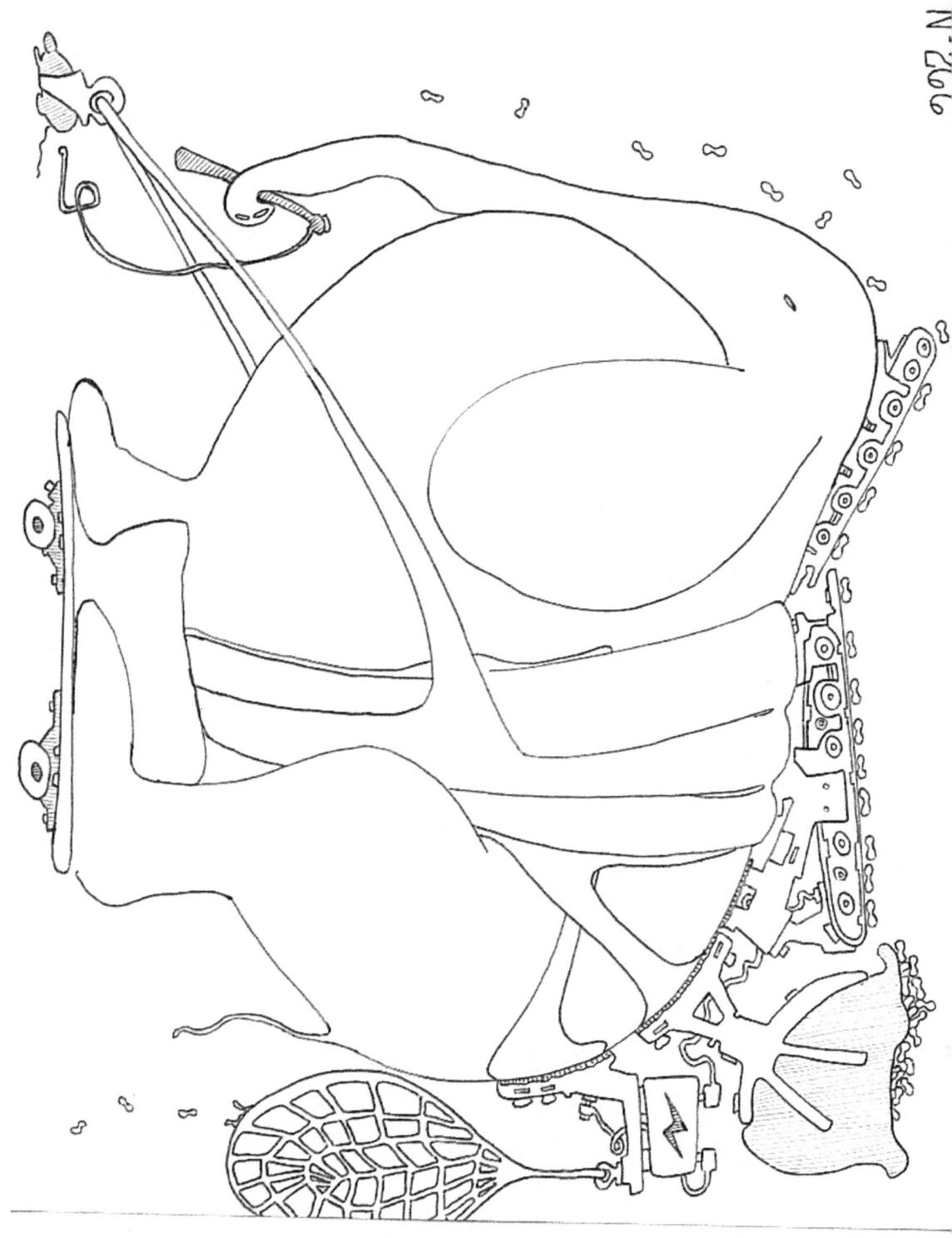

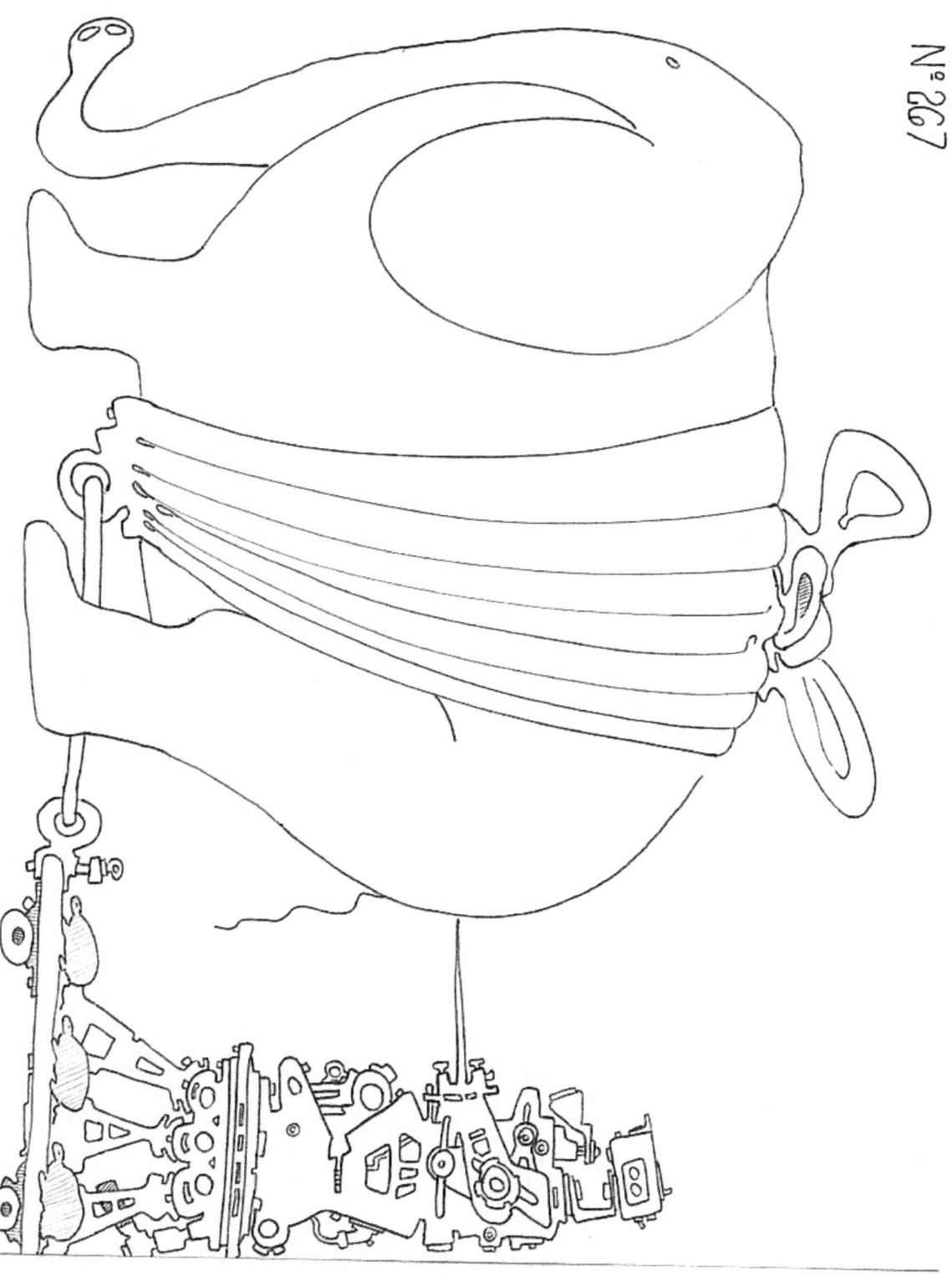

N° 267

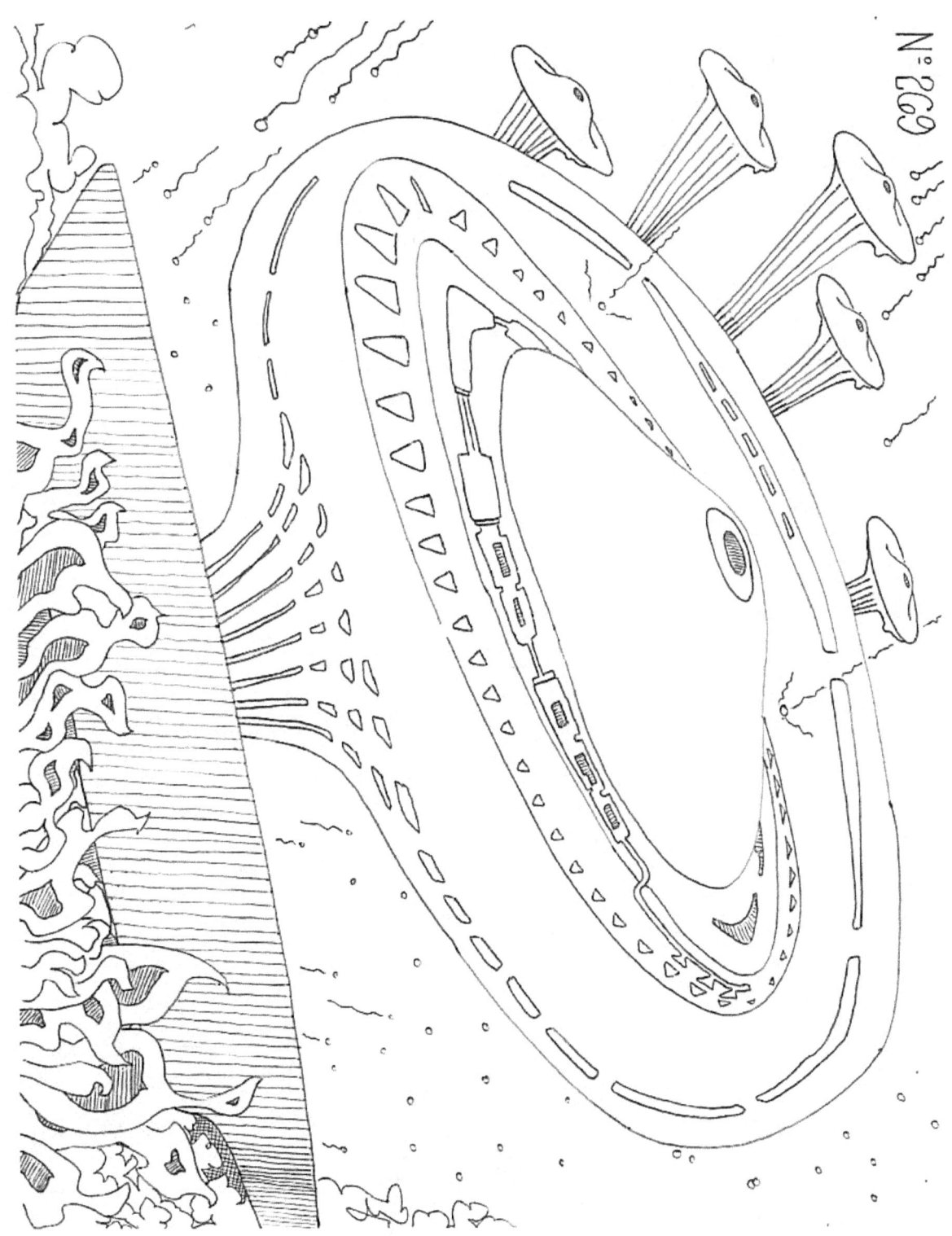

N° 271

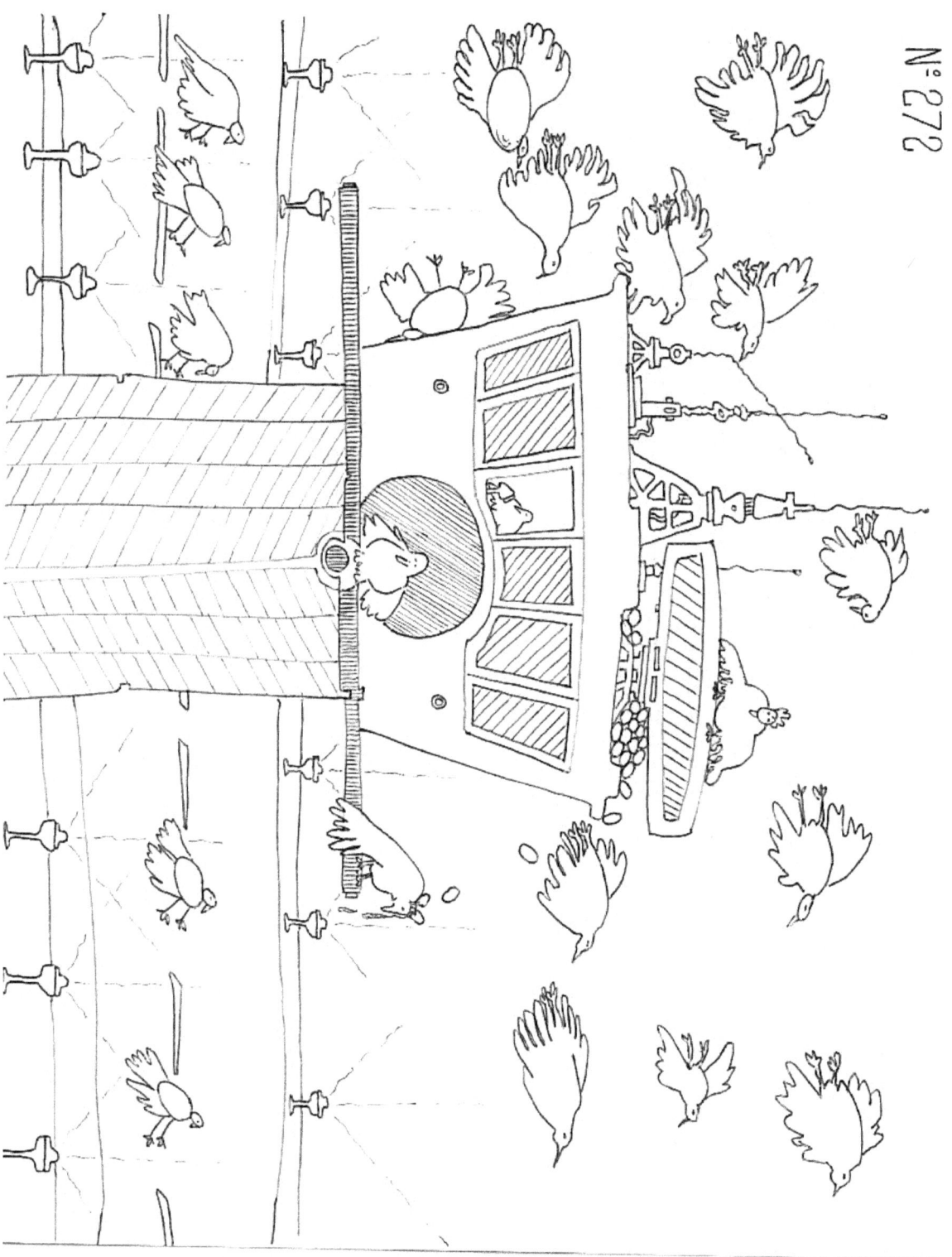

N° 274

N° 276

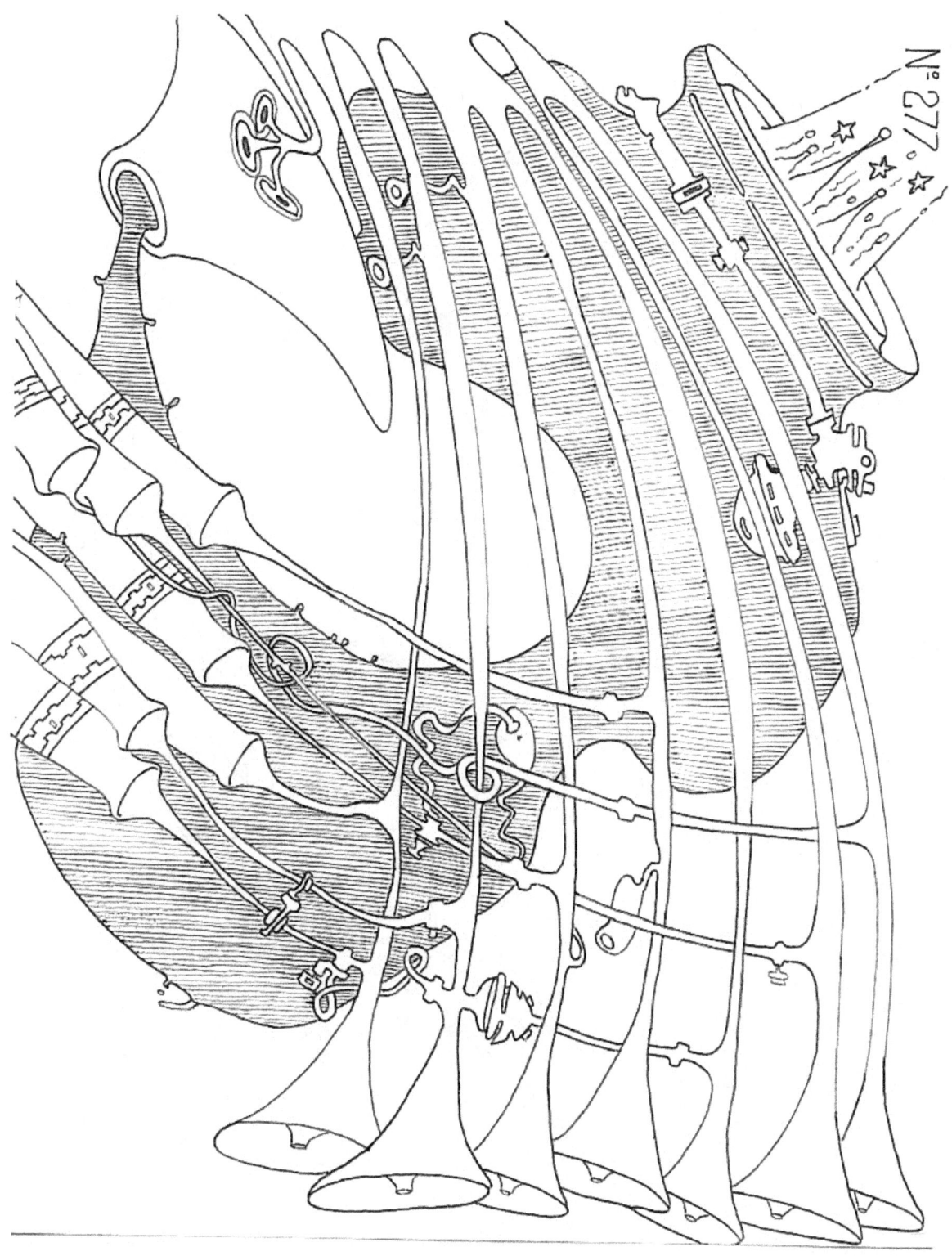

Nº 279

N° 280

Nº 281

Nº 282

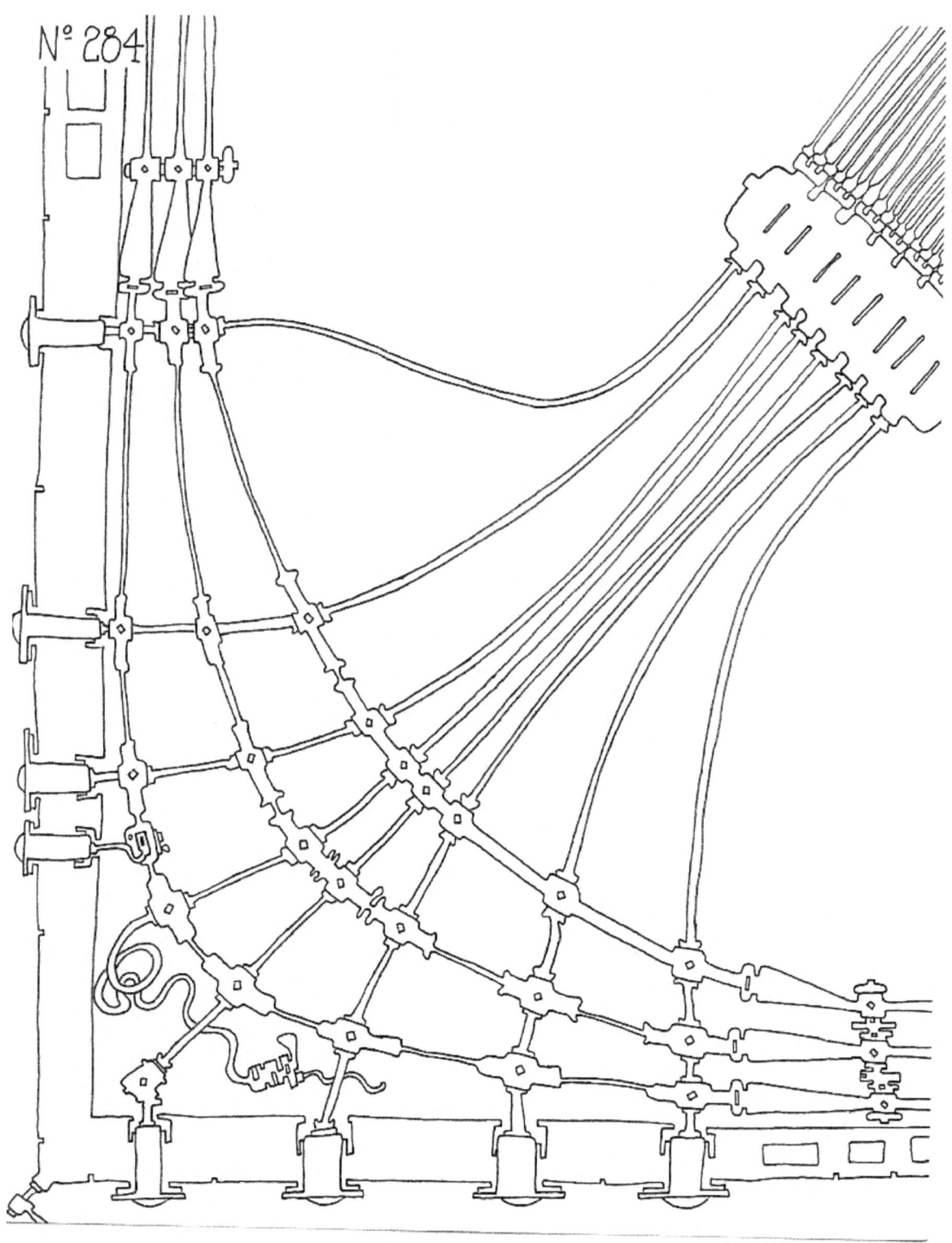

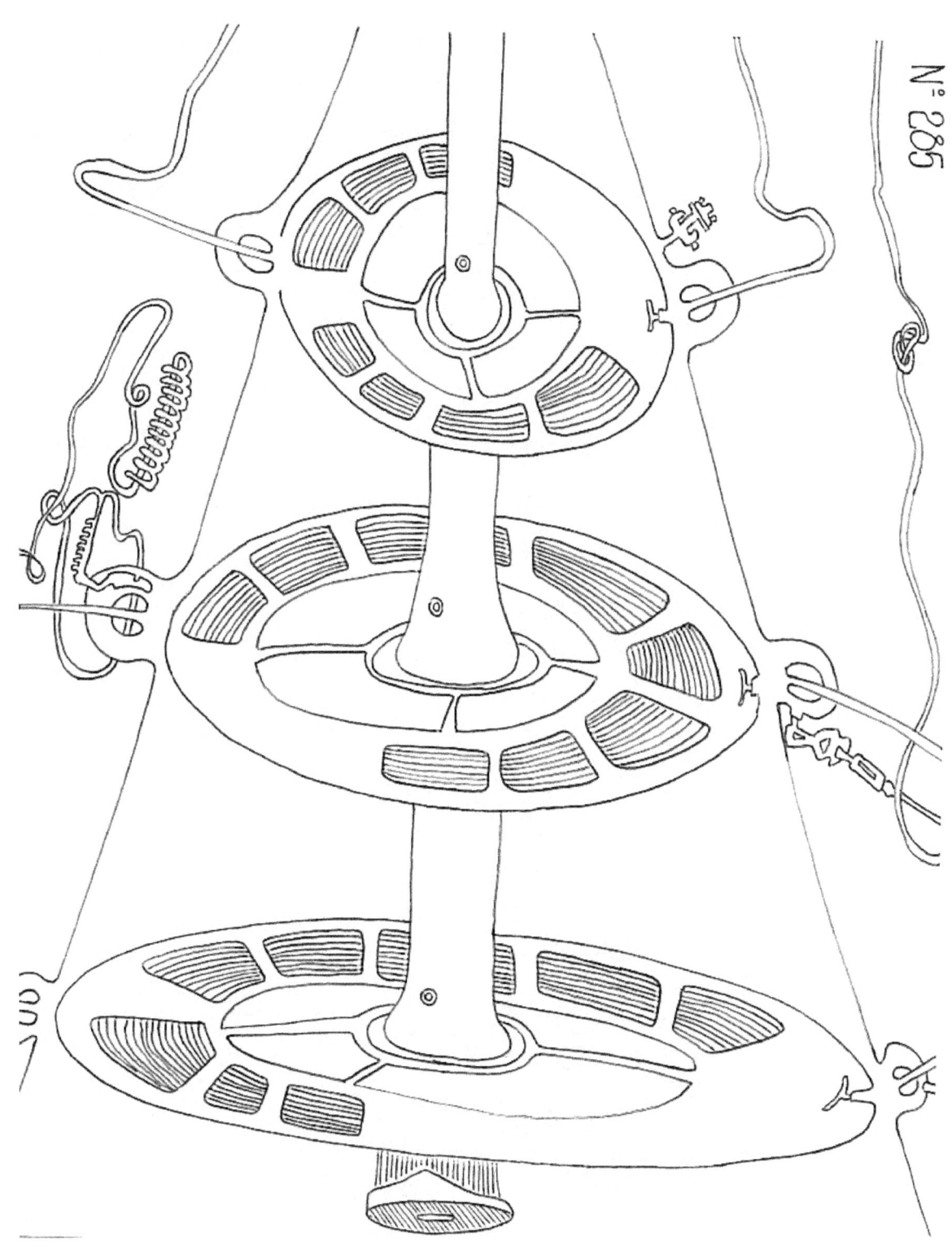

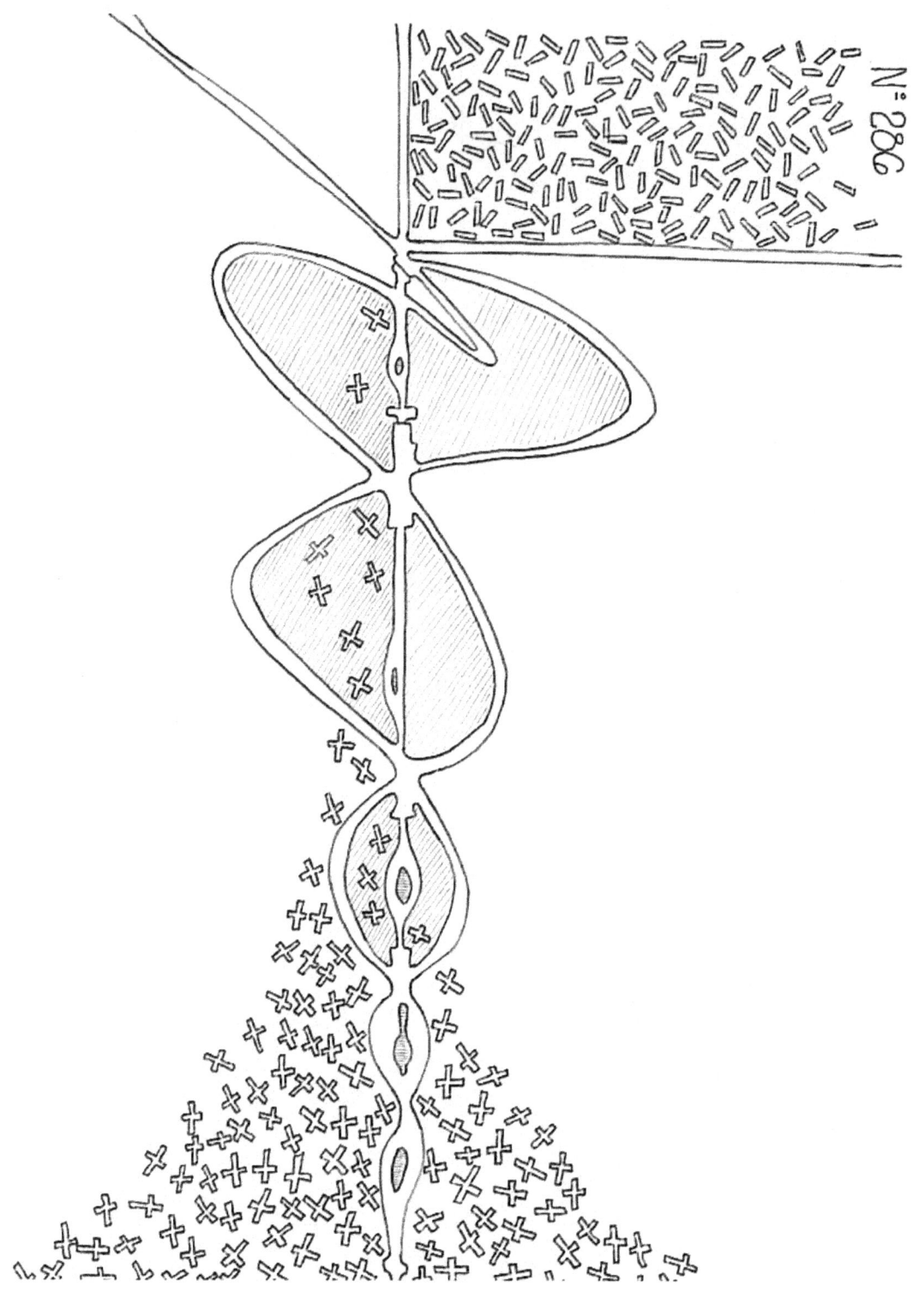

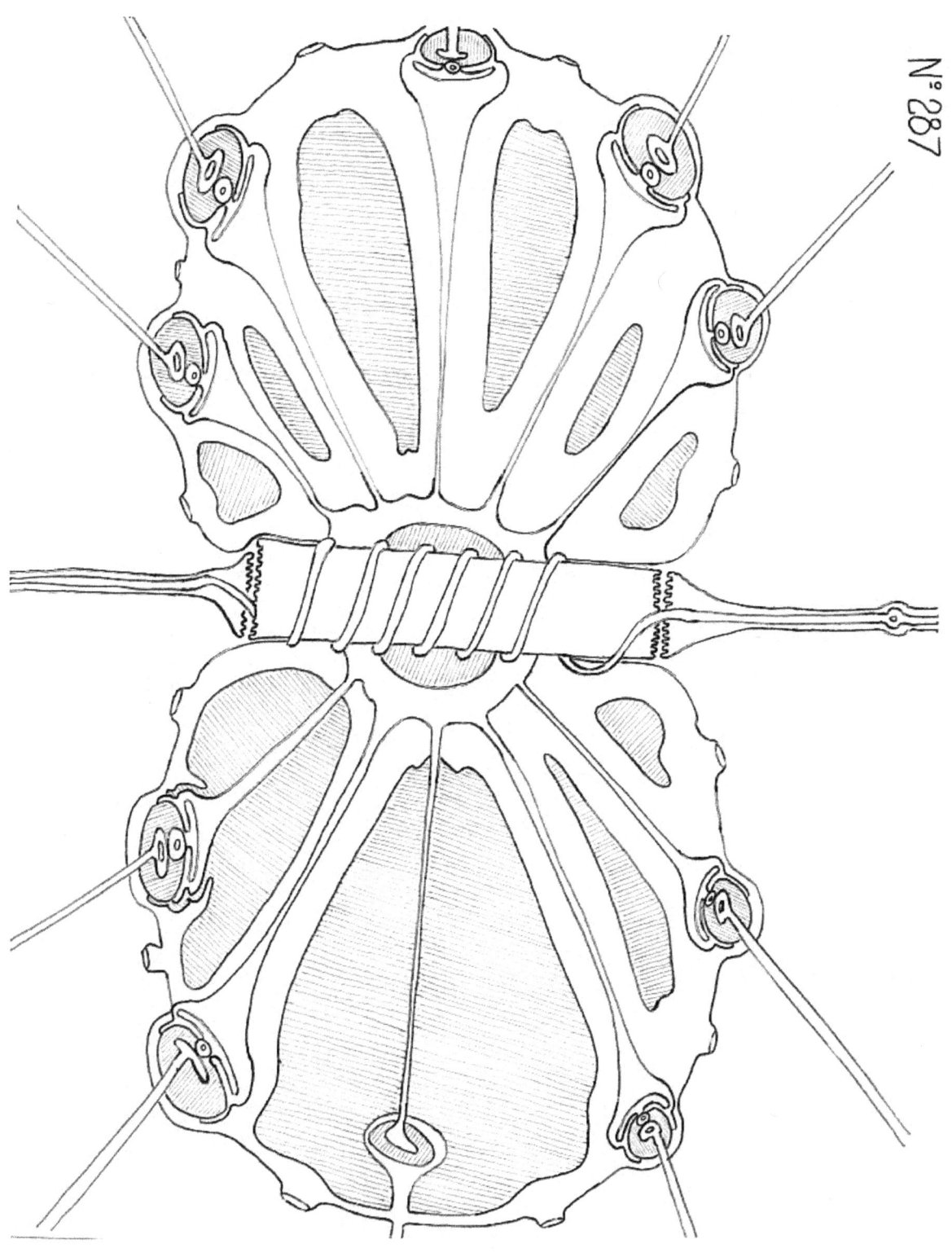

Nº 287

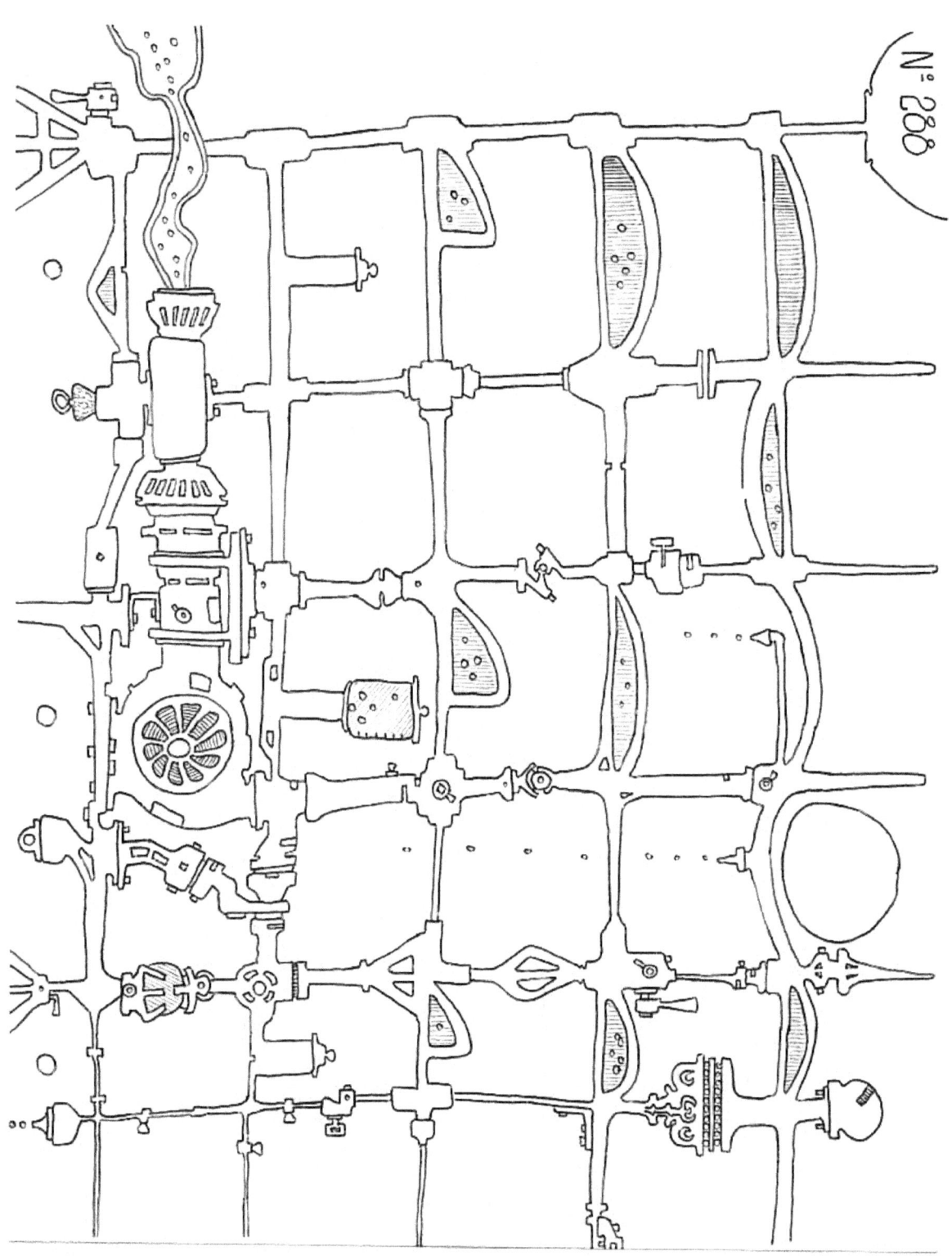

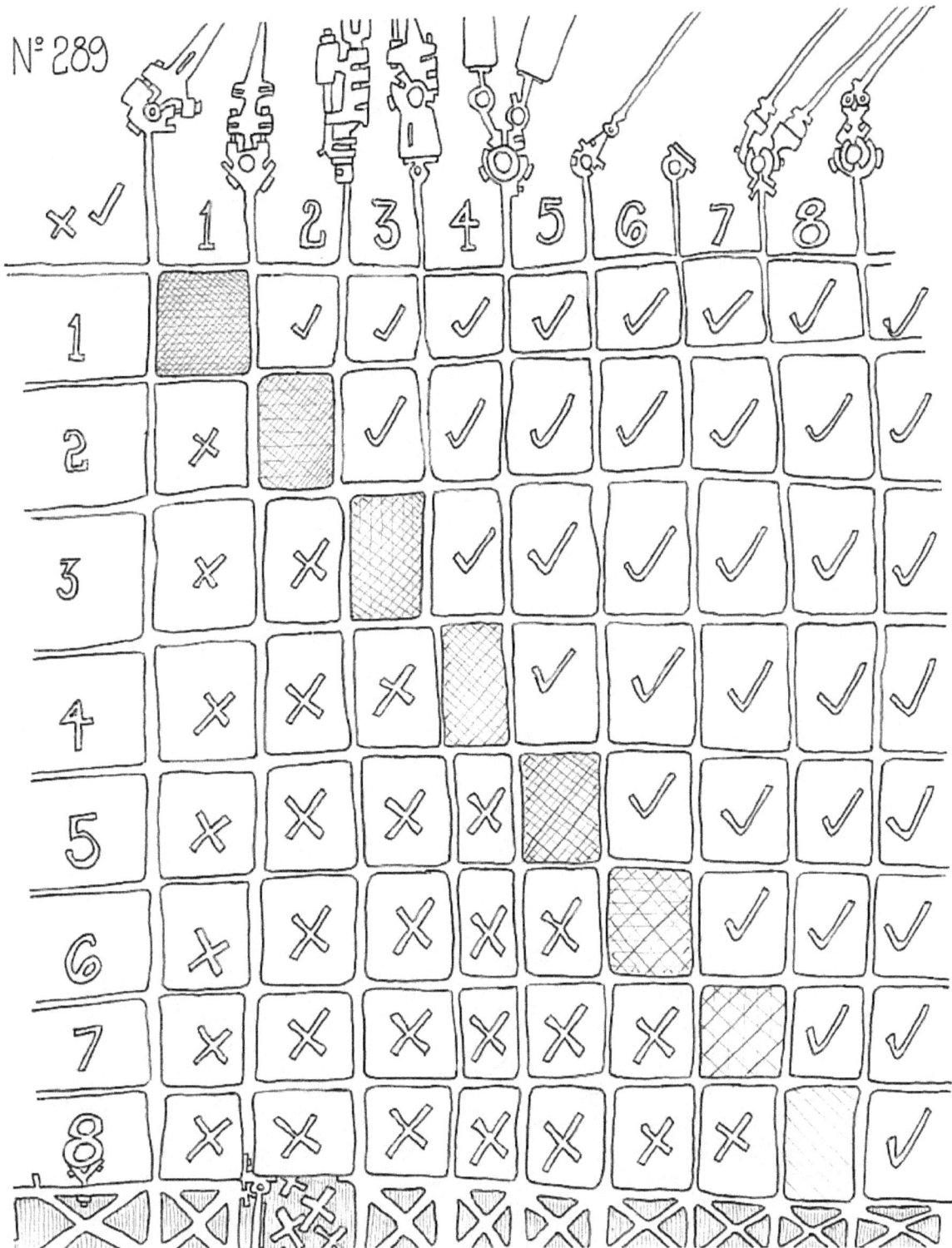

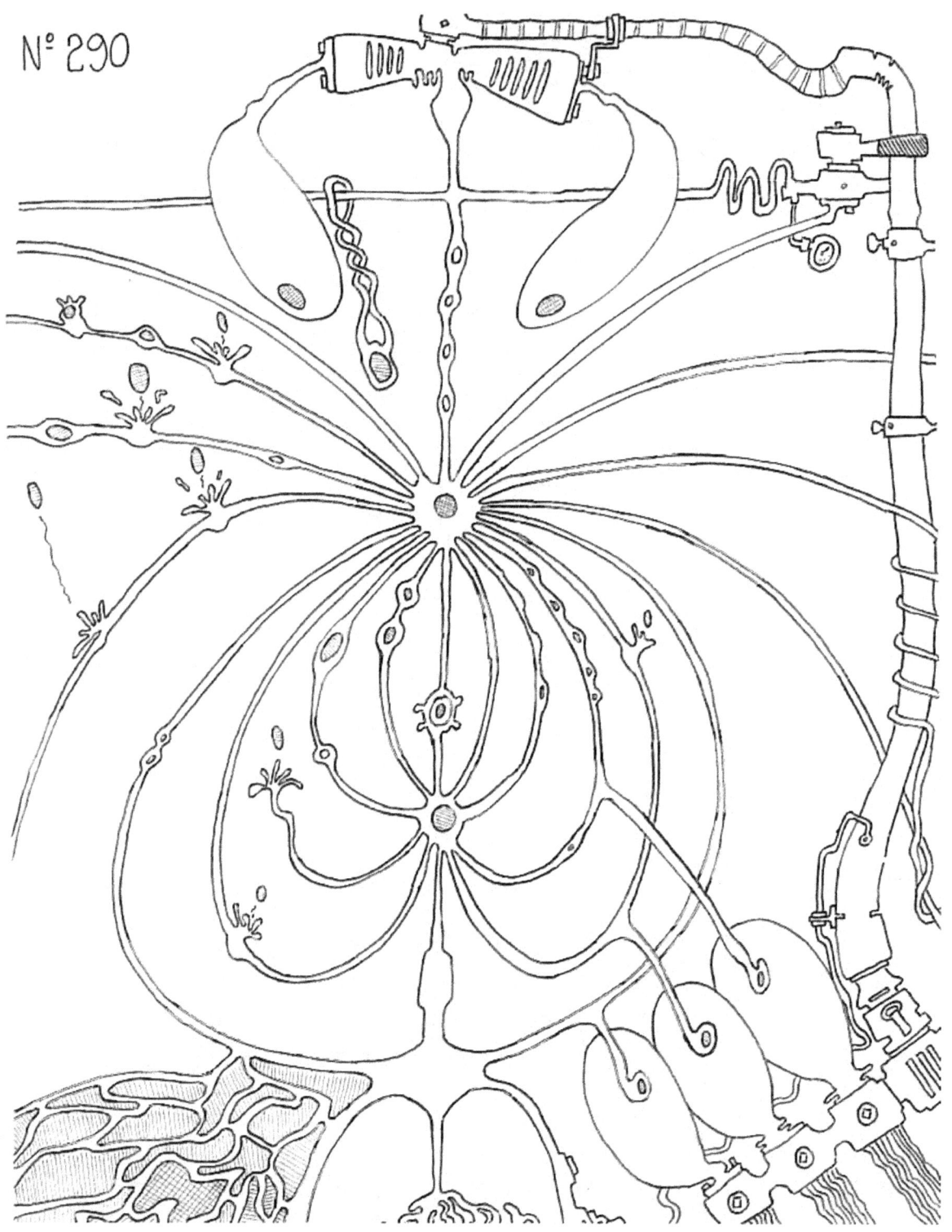

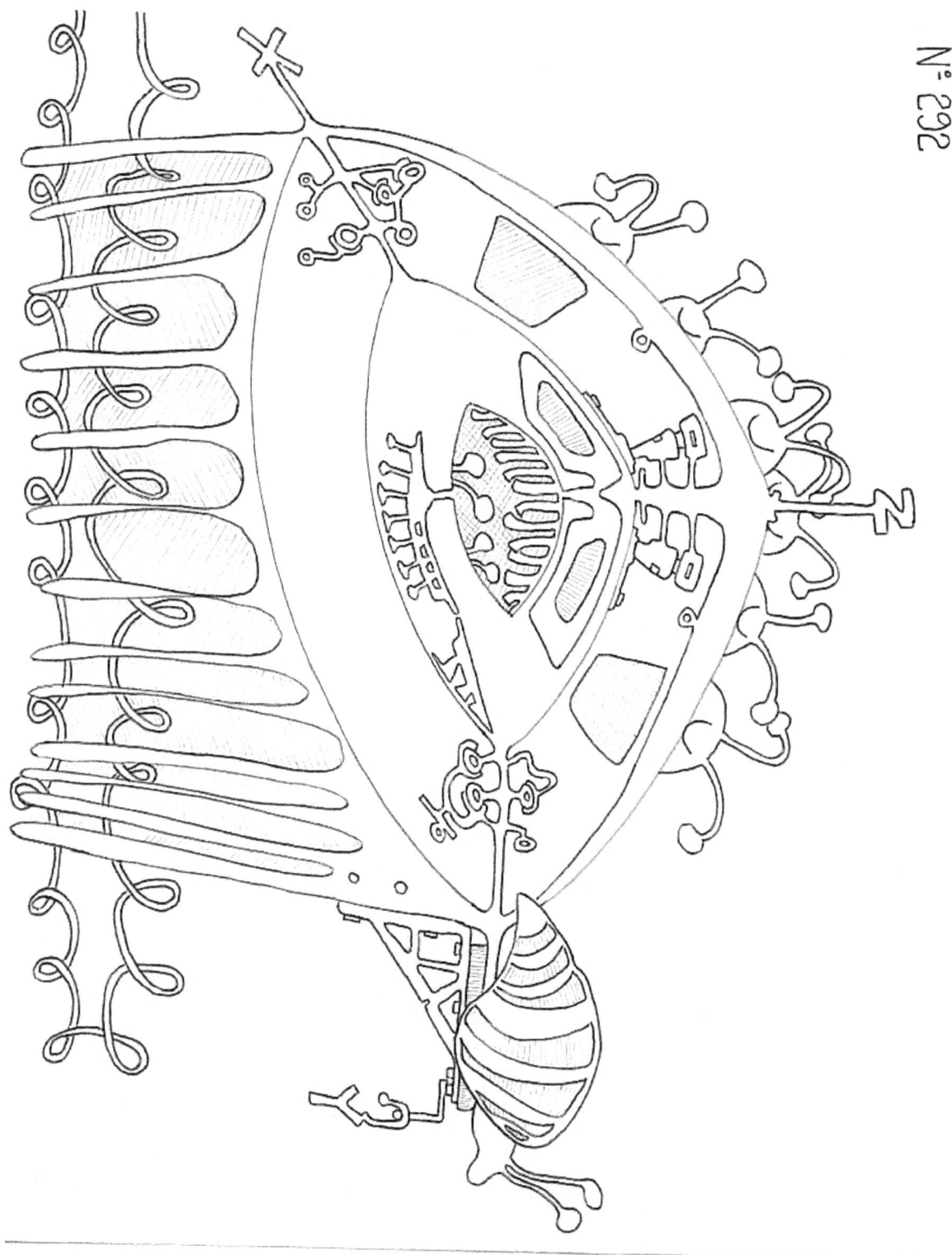

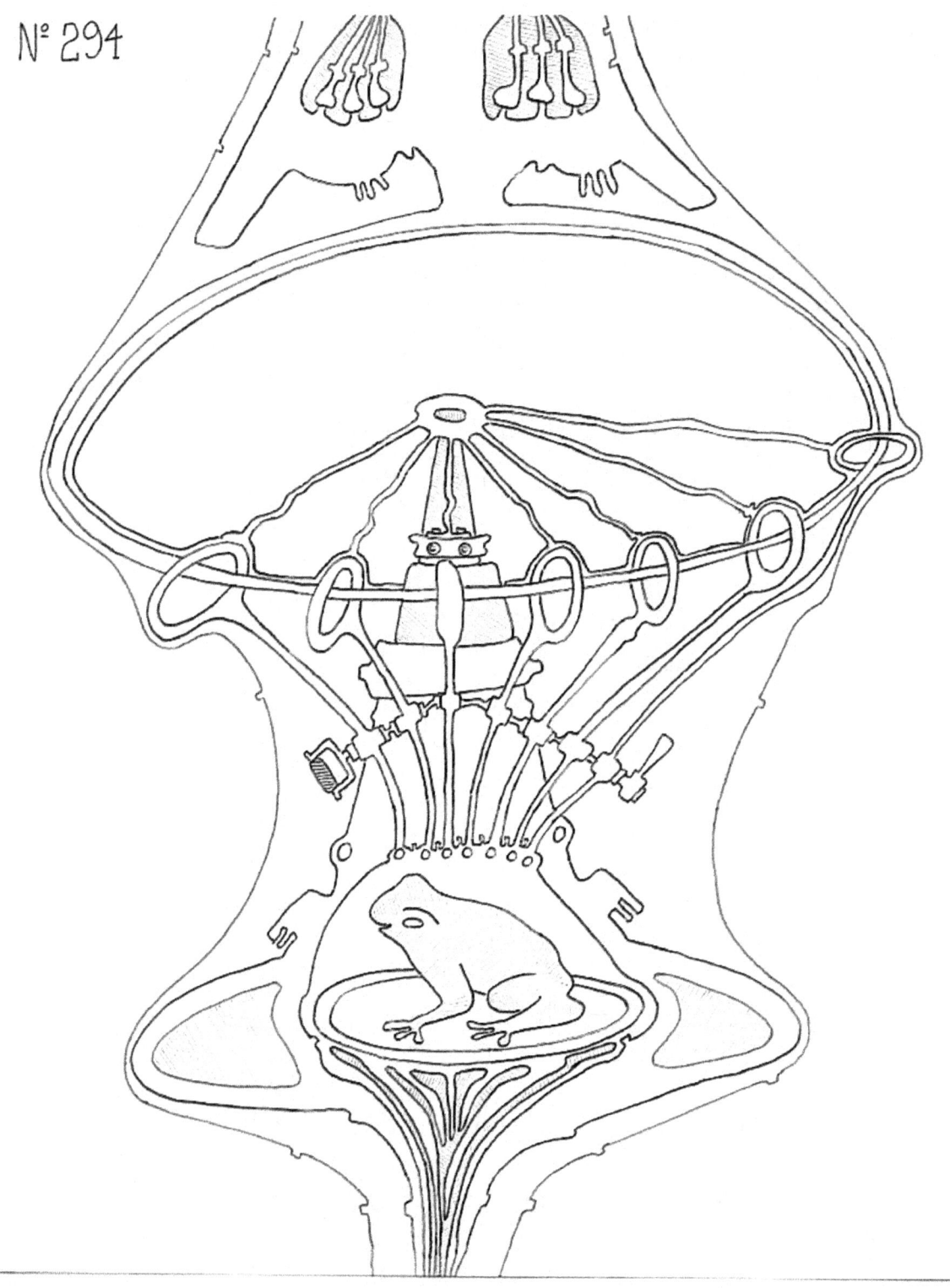

N° 295

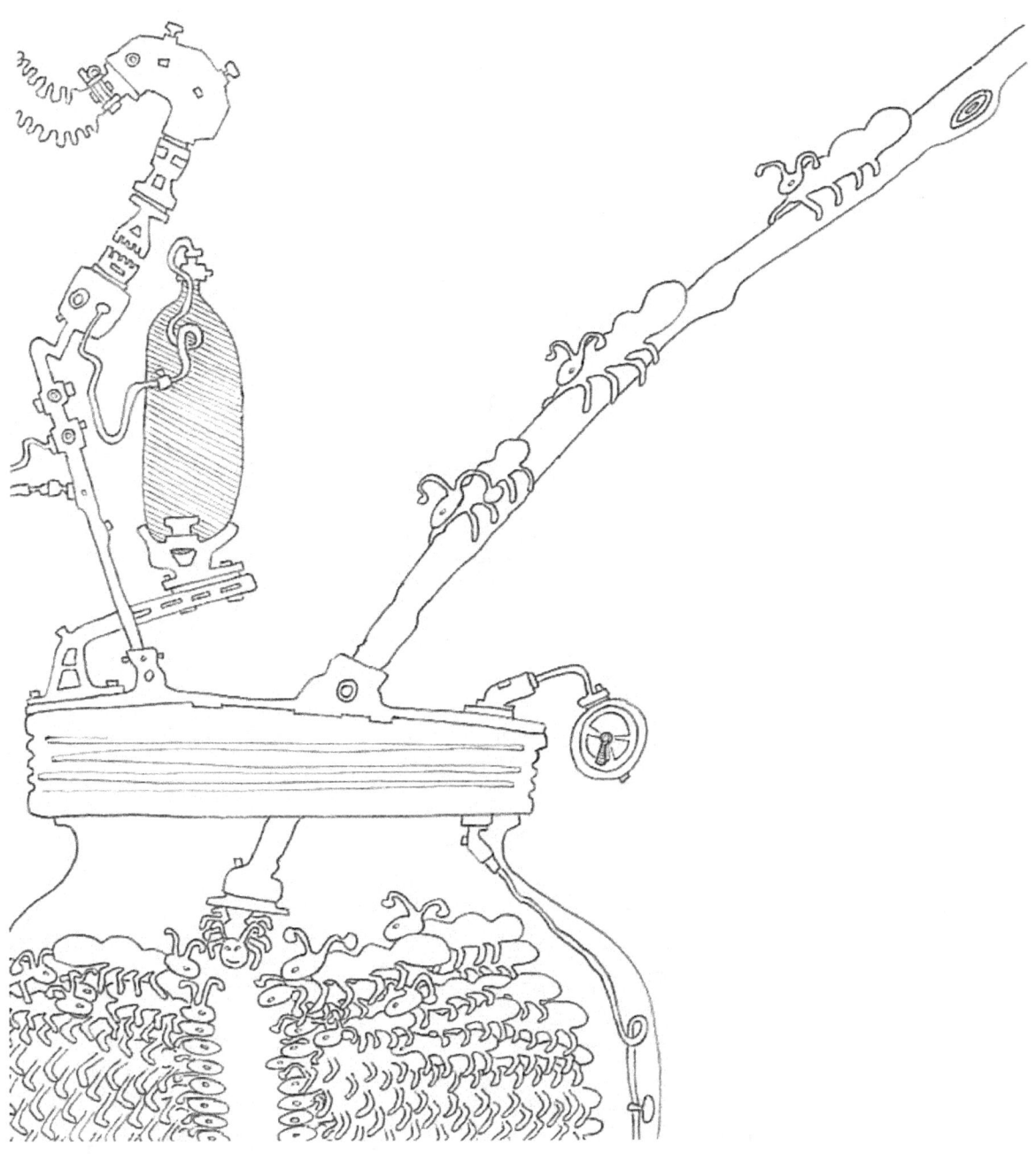

N° 296

N° 297

N° 298

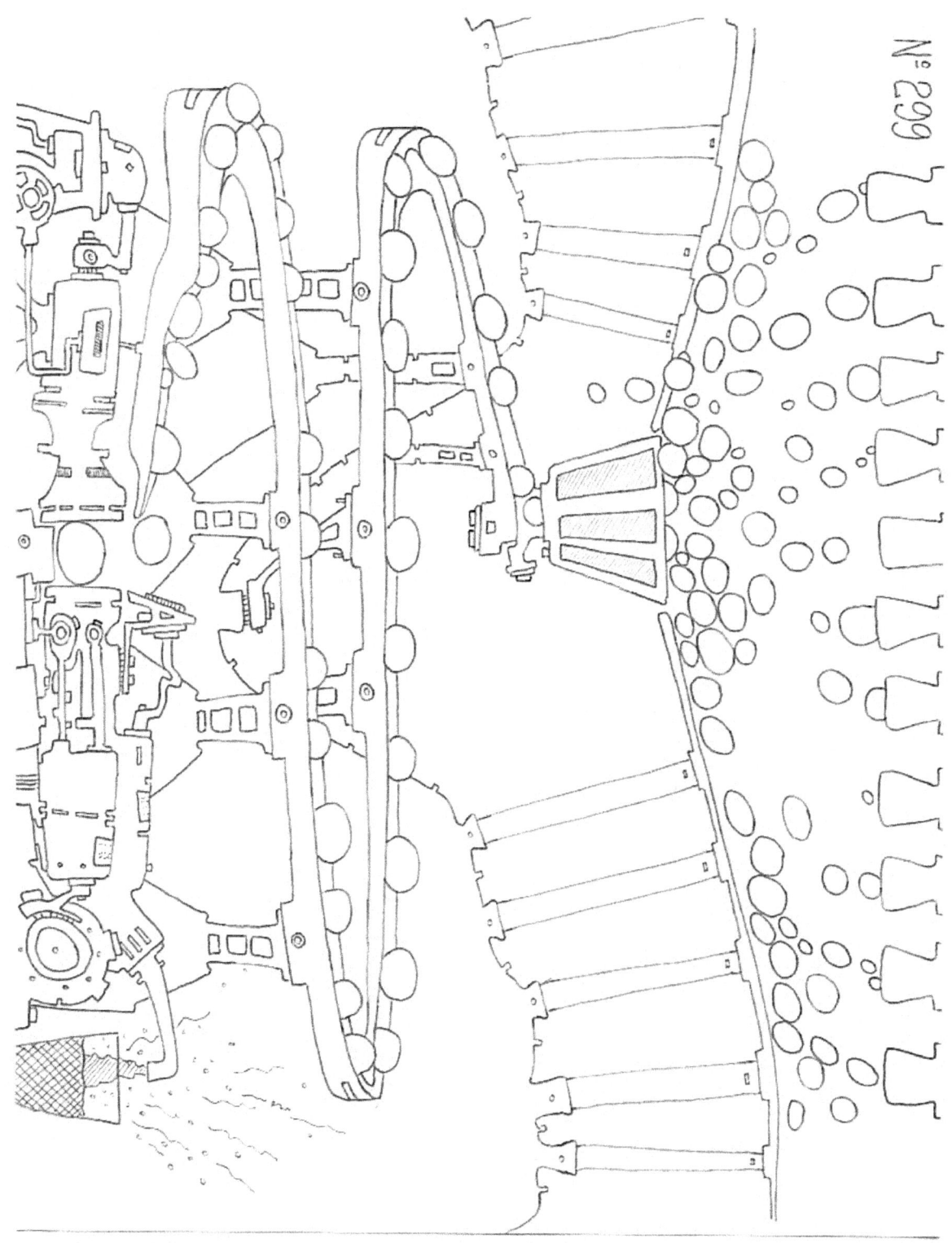

Nº 299

N° 301

N° 303

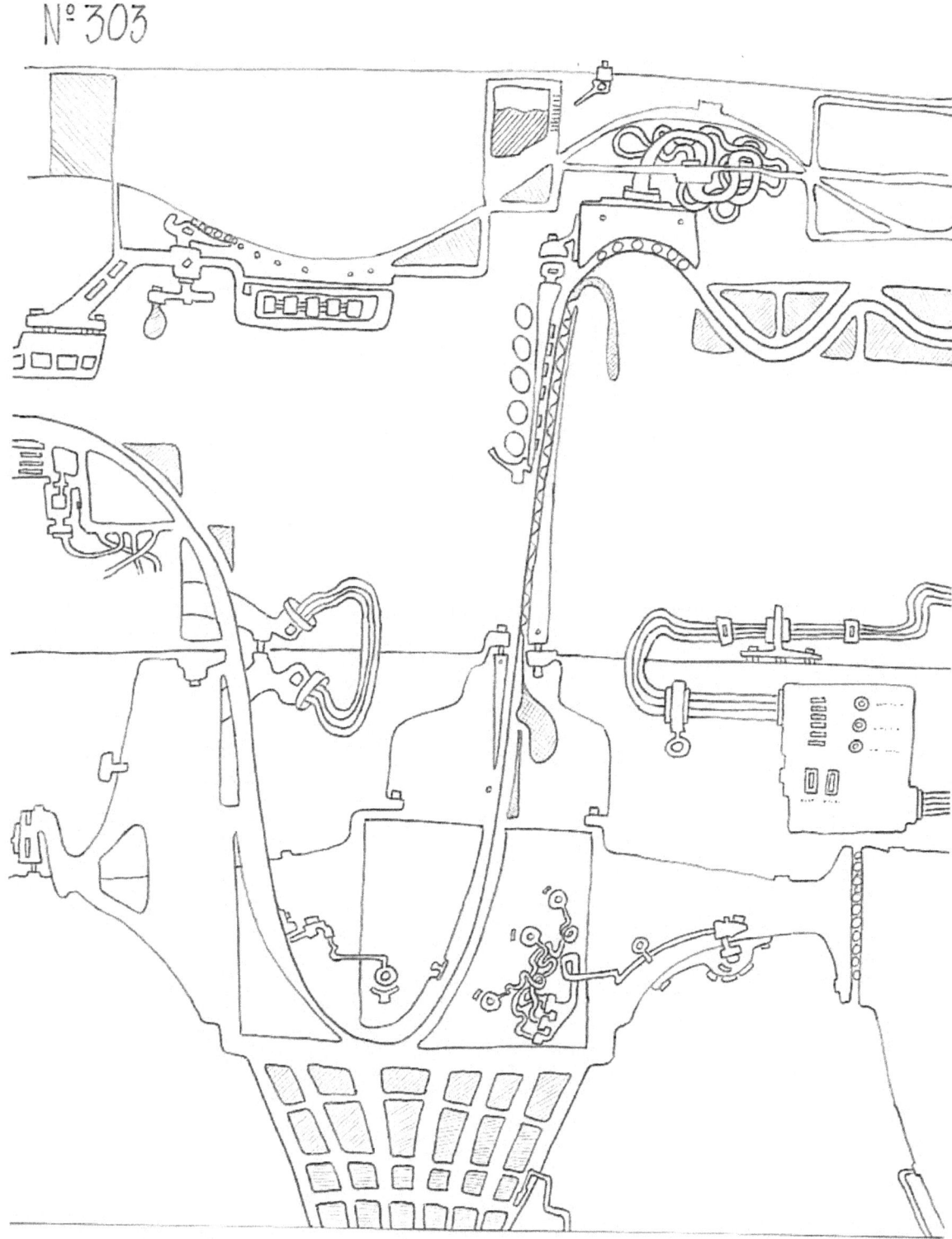

Nº 505

N° 306

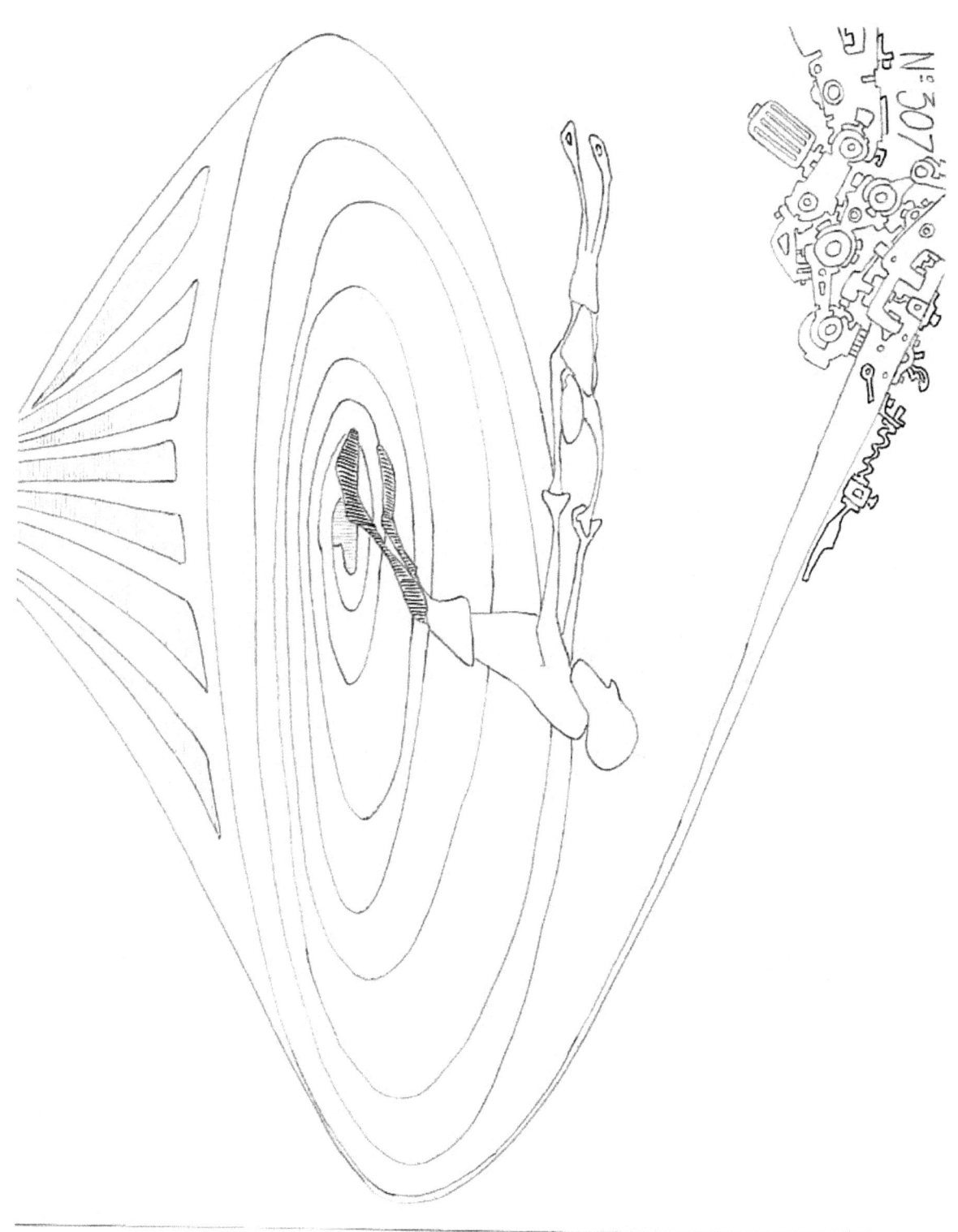

N° 309

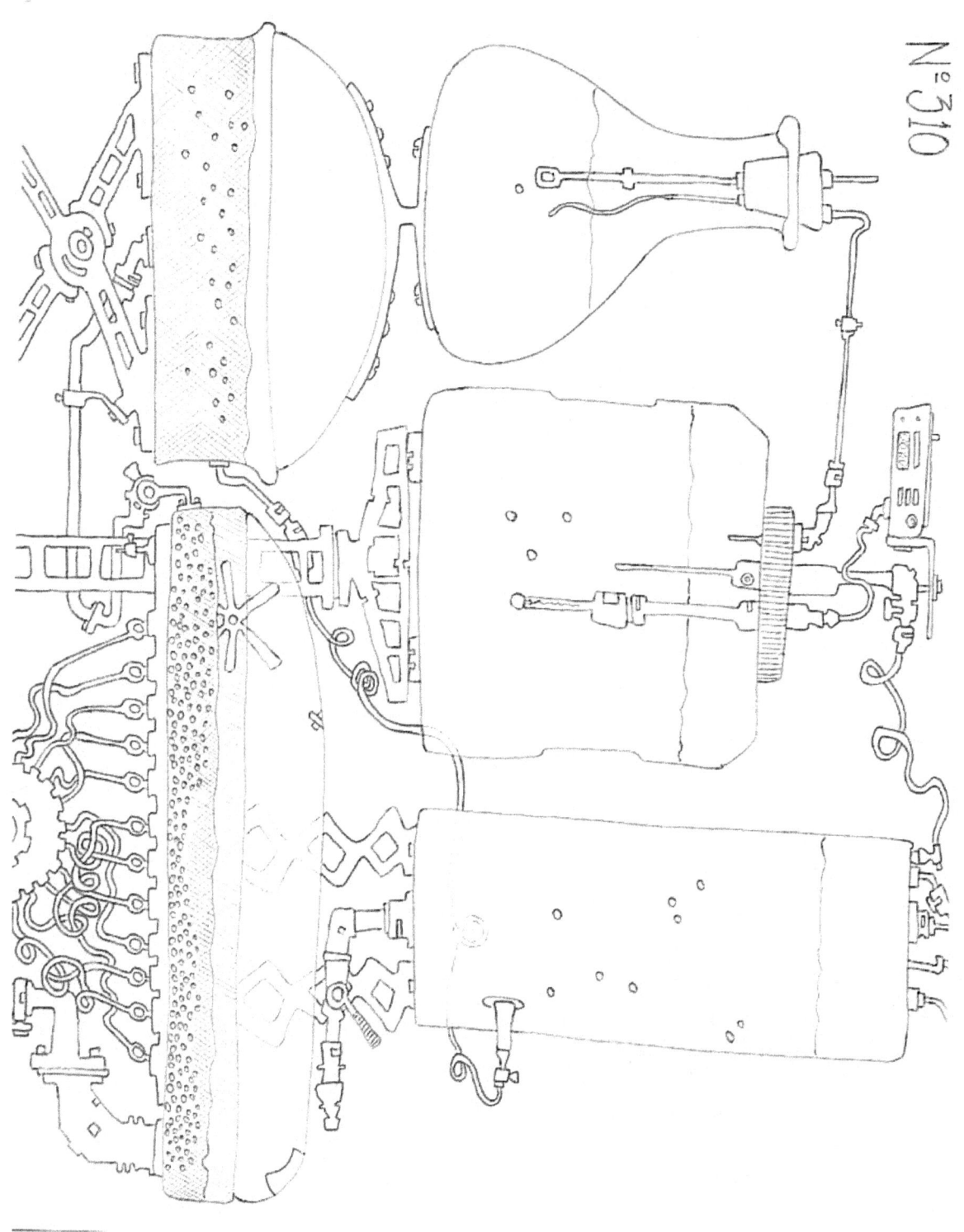

N° 310

N° 311

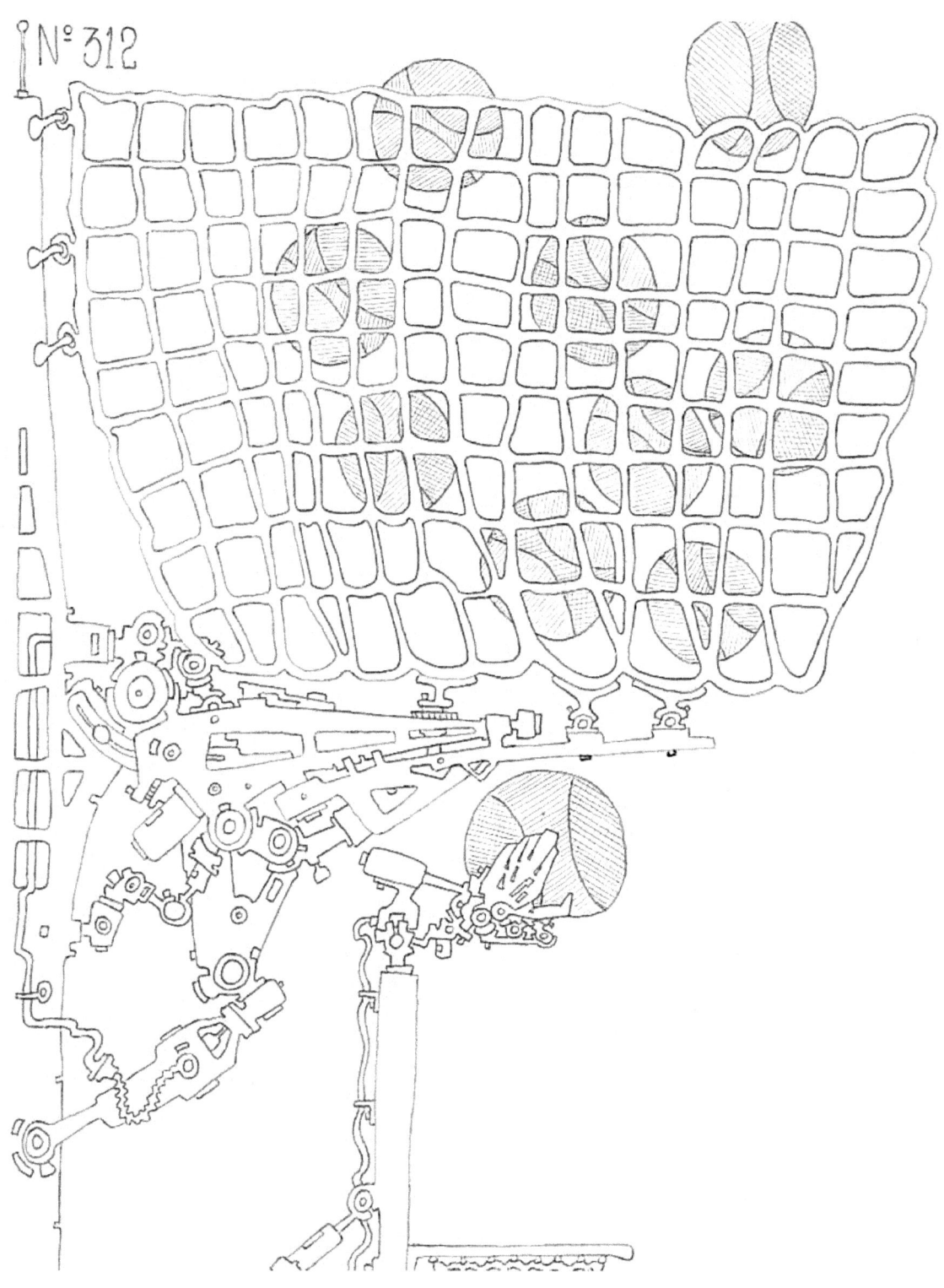

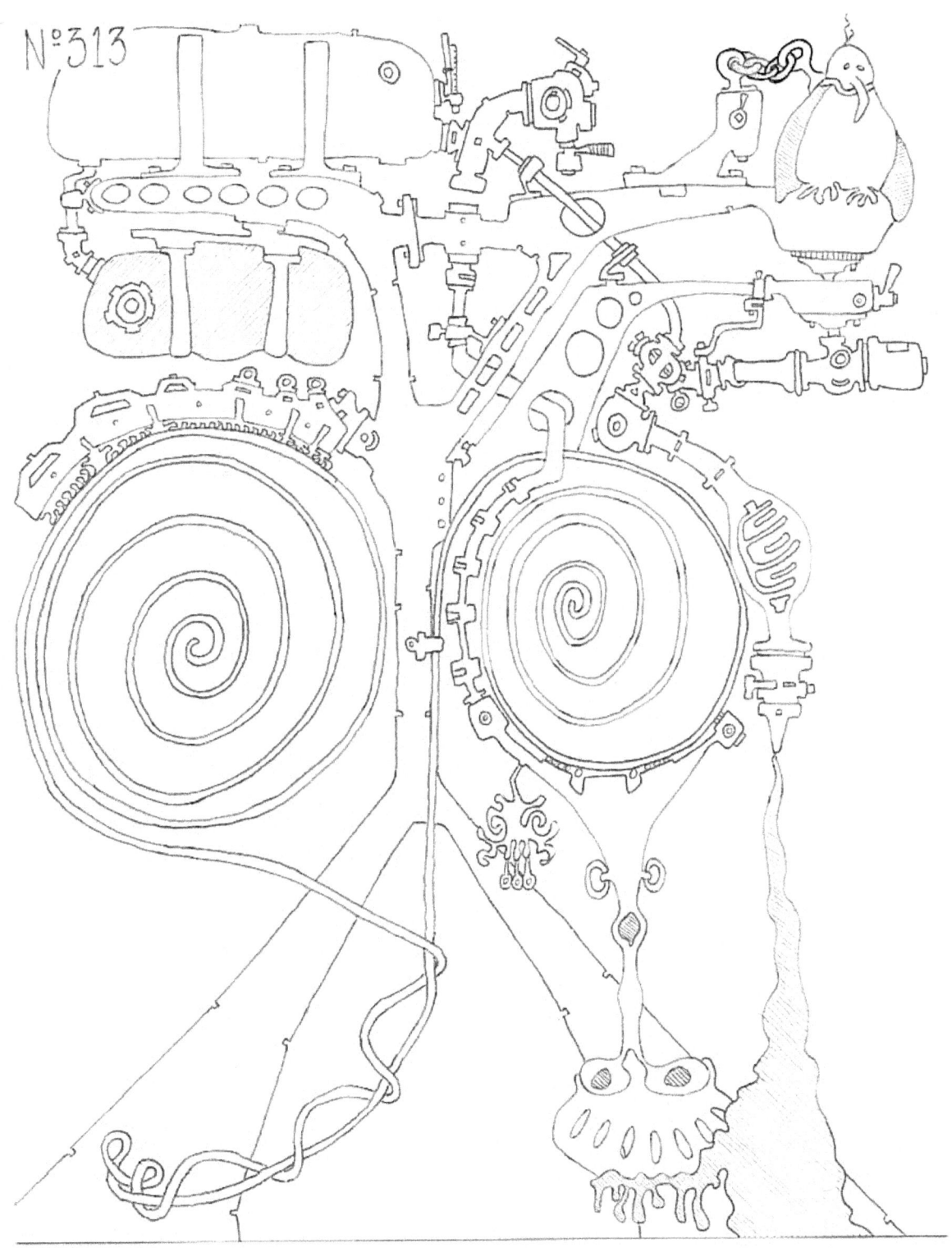

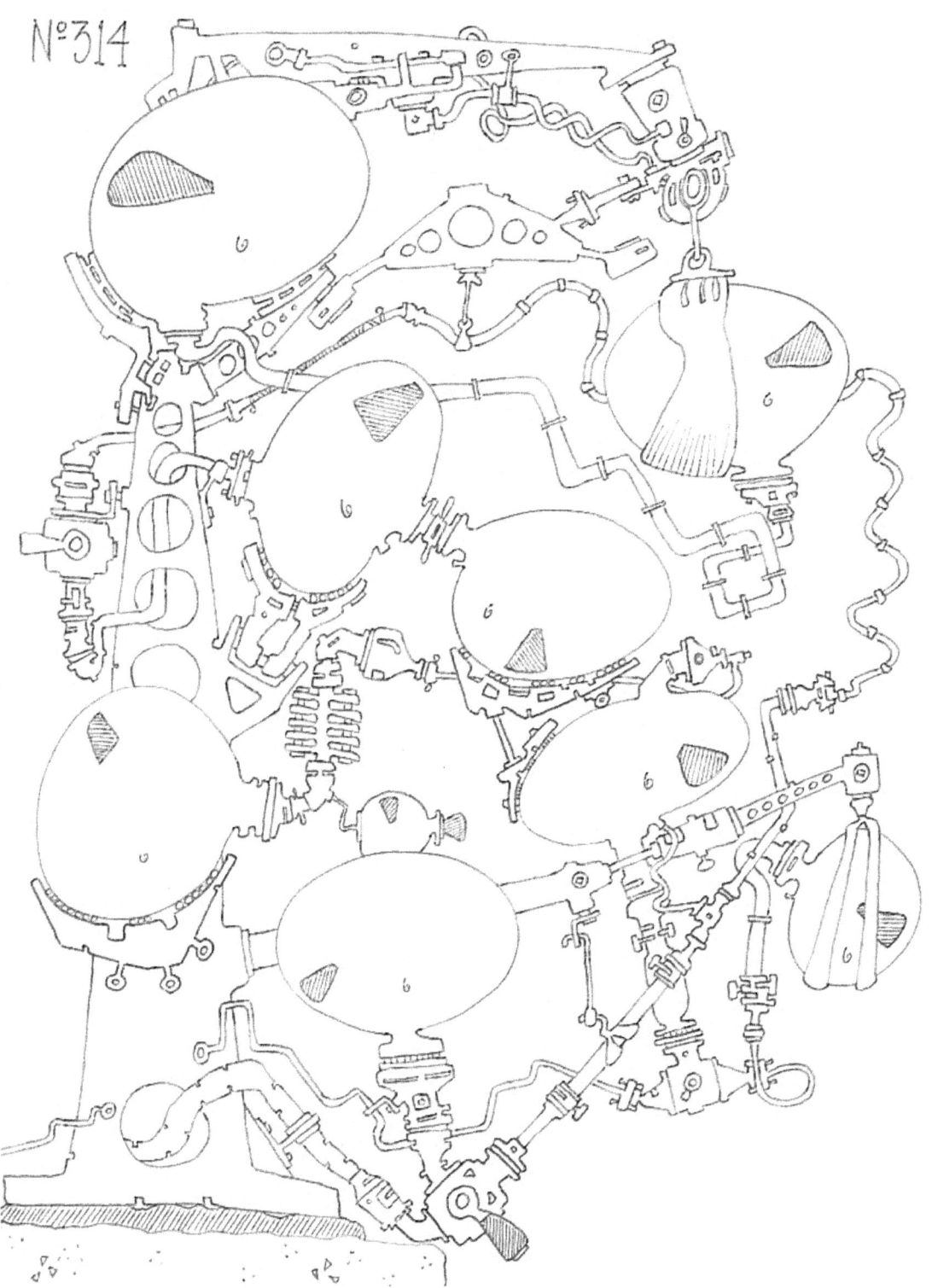

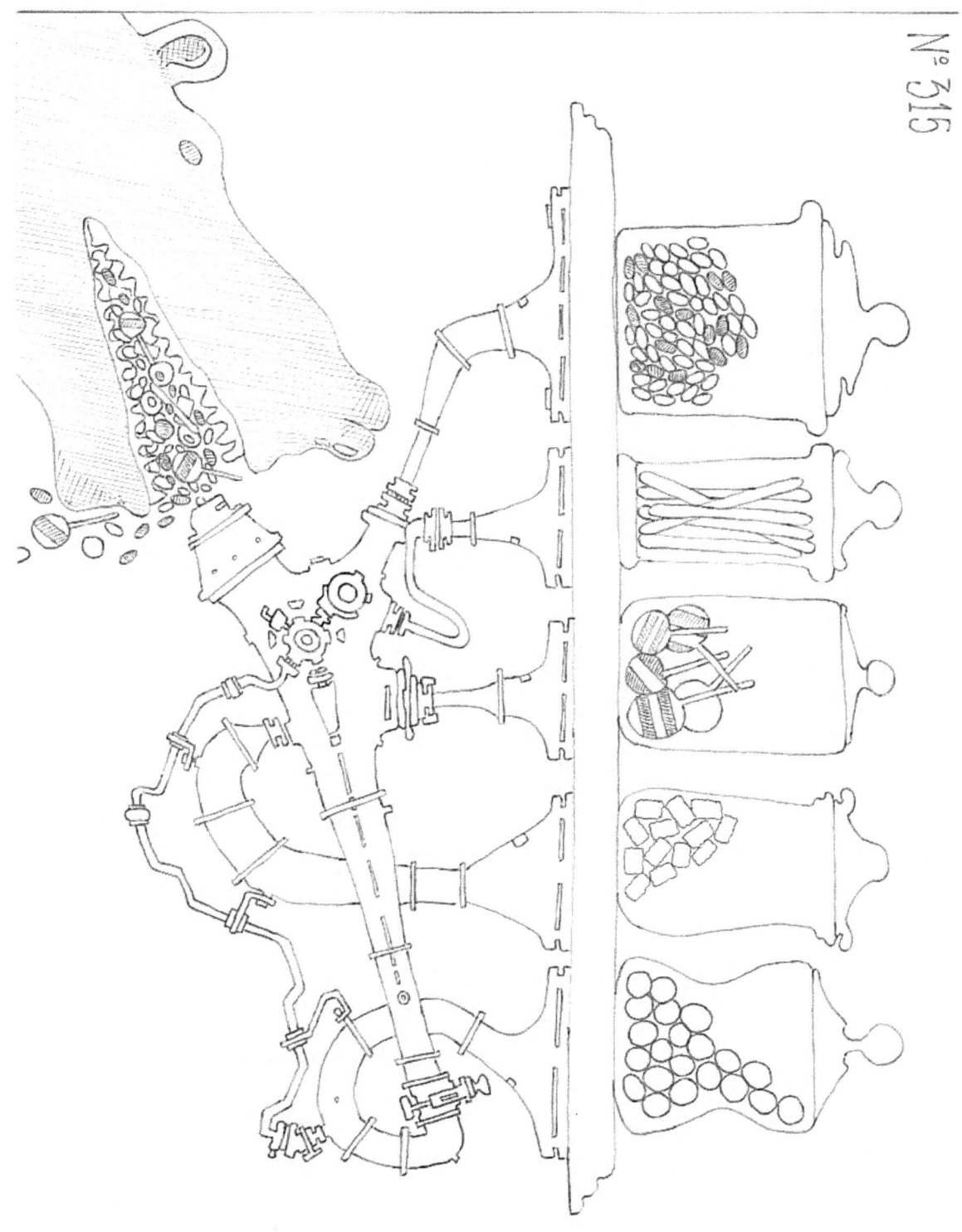

N° 318

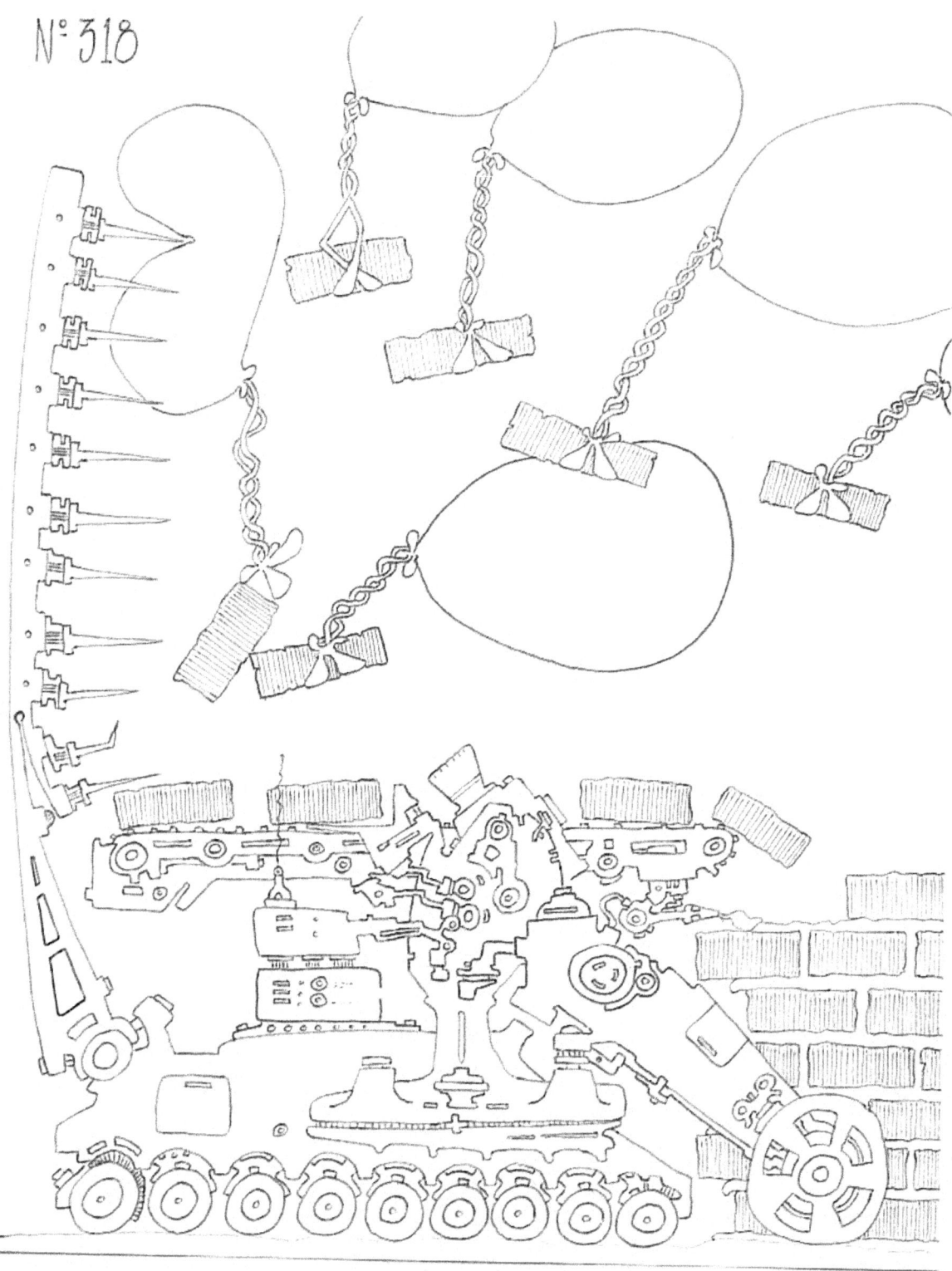

N° 319

N°321

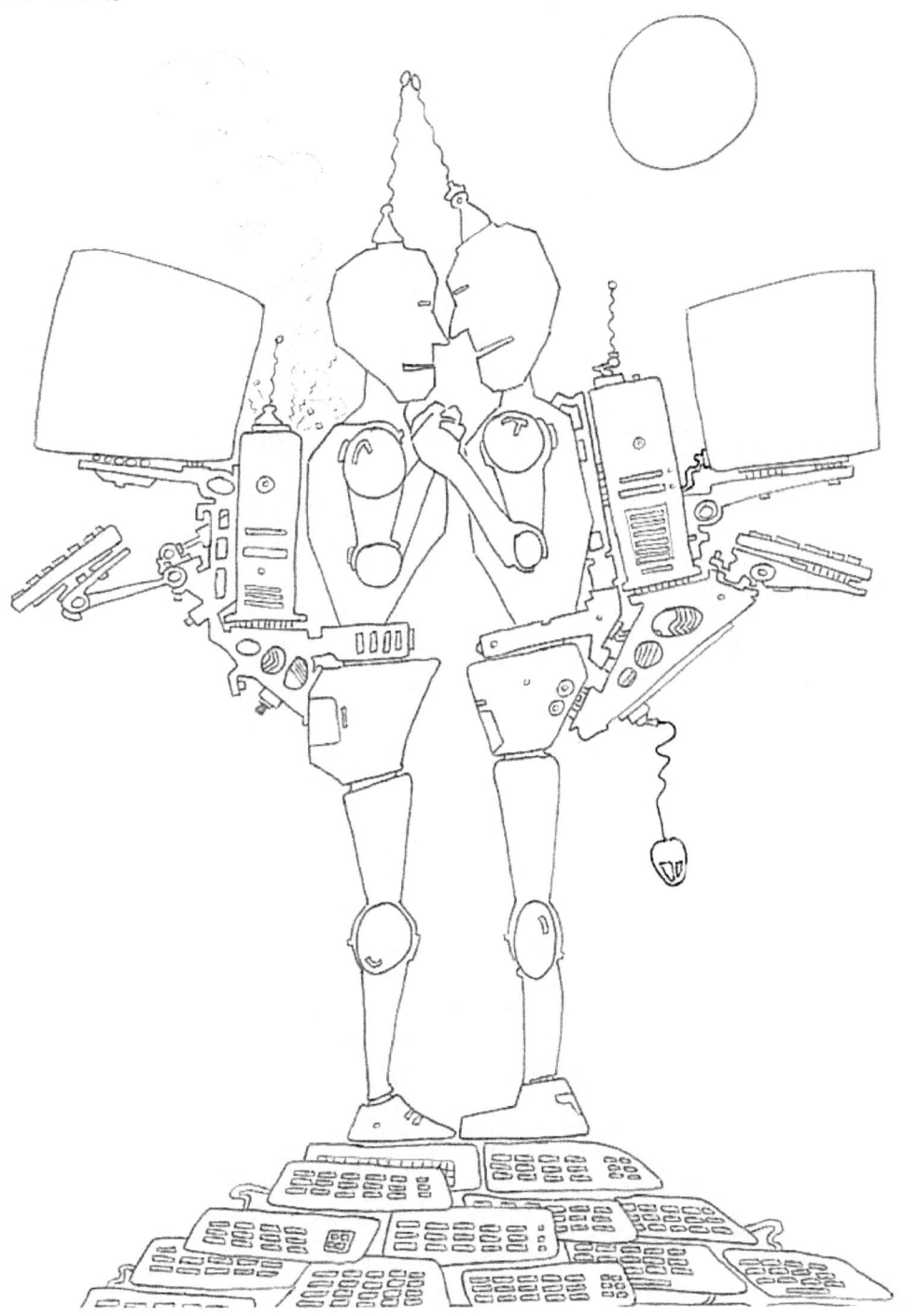

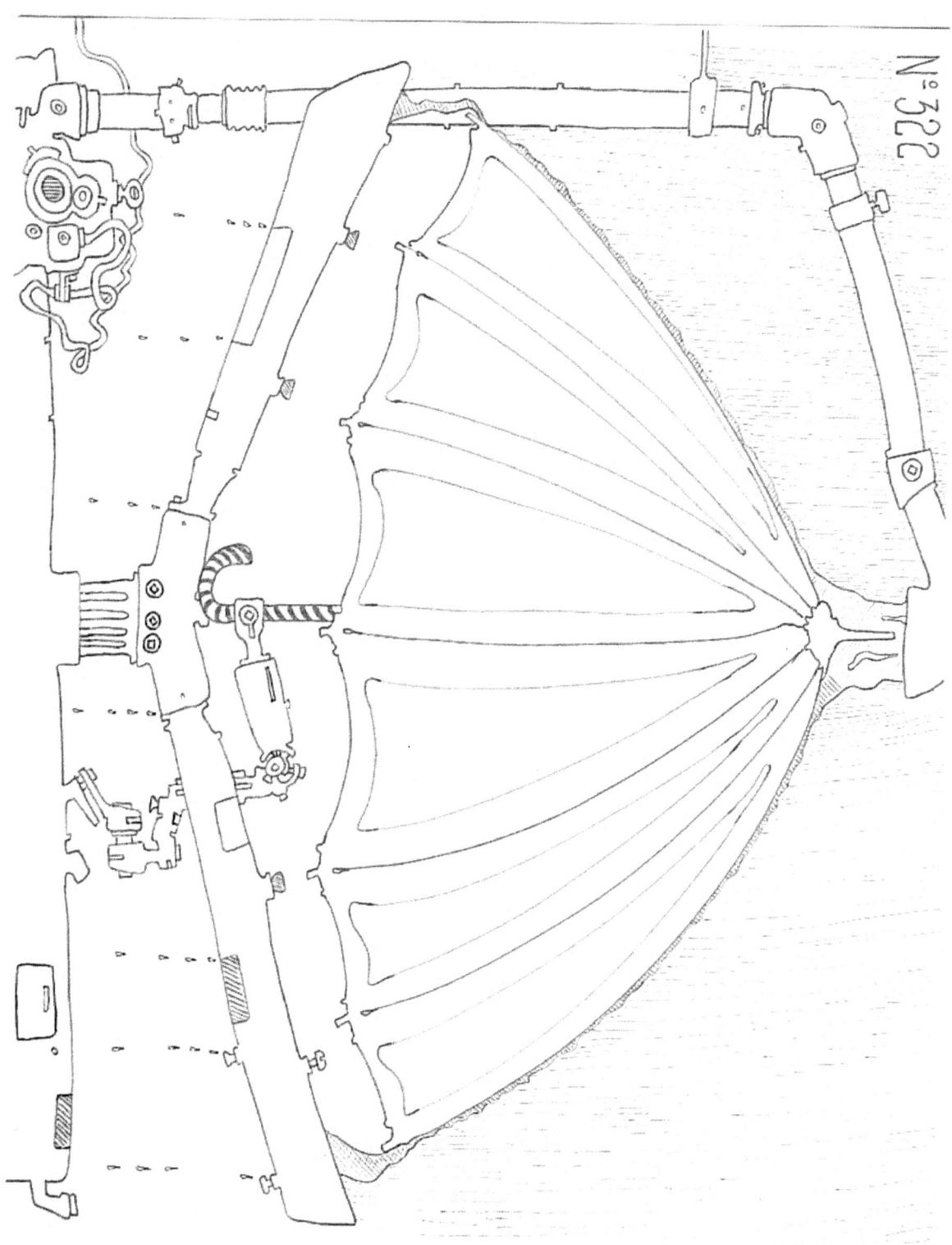

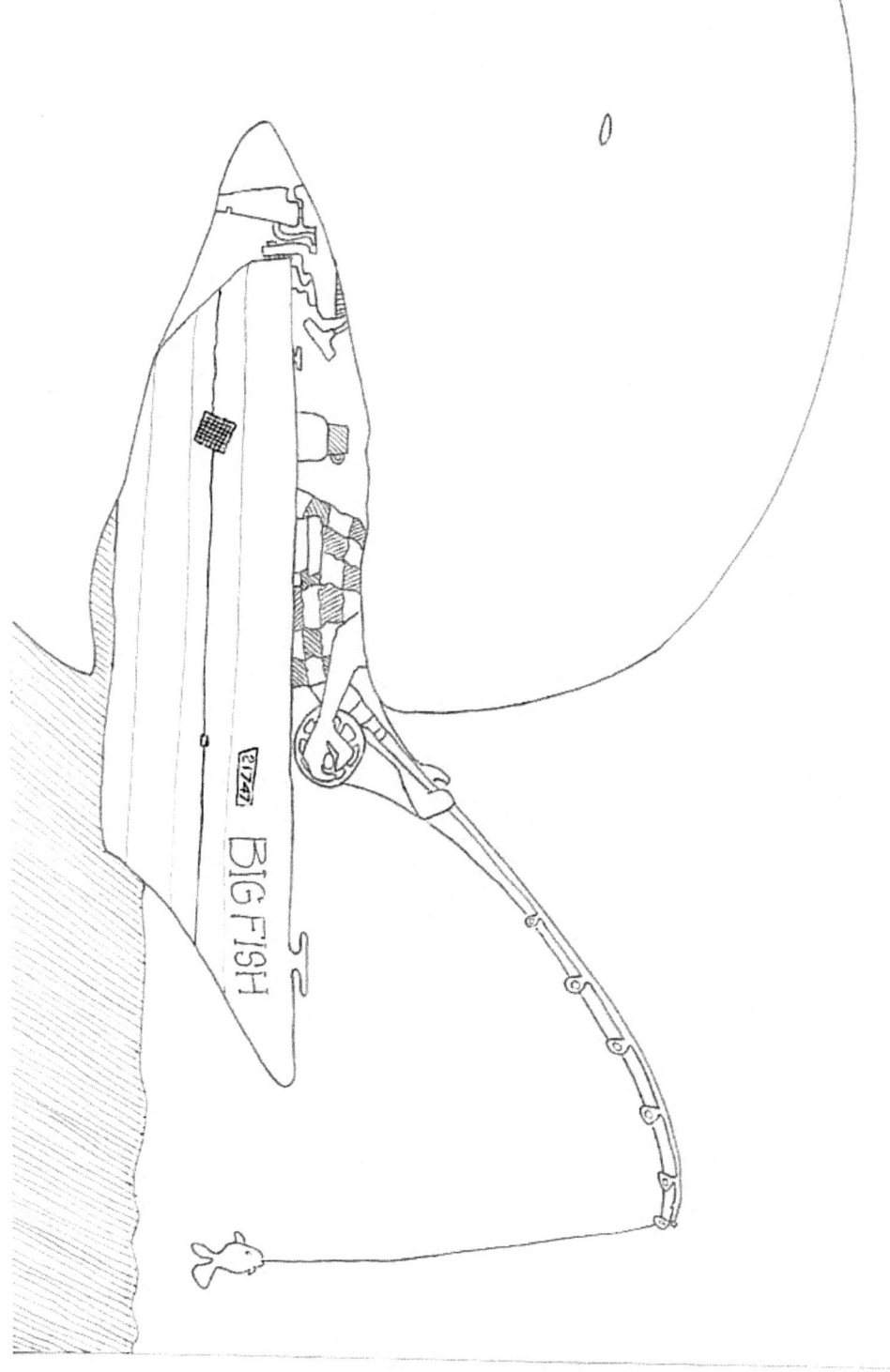

Nº 323

N° 324

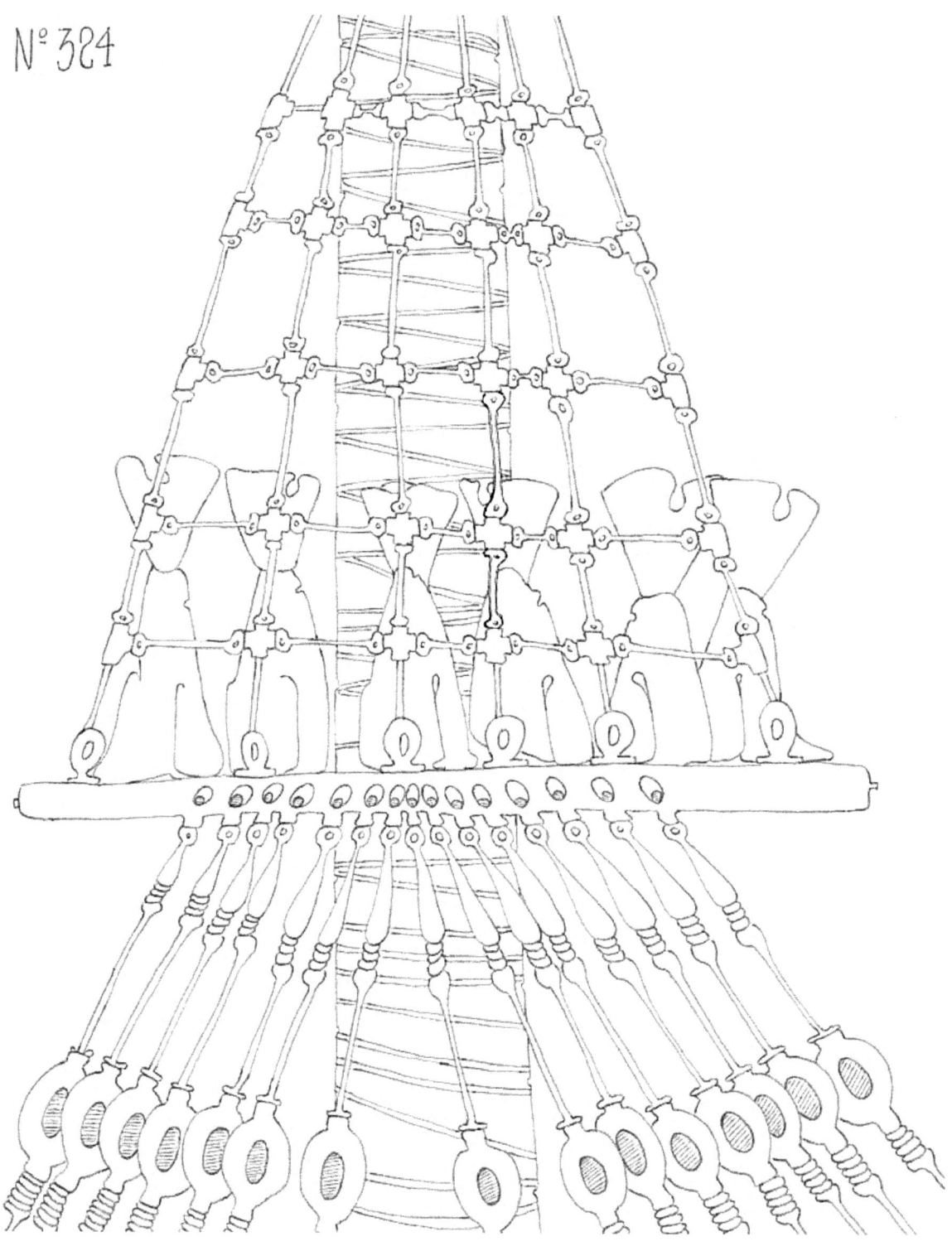

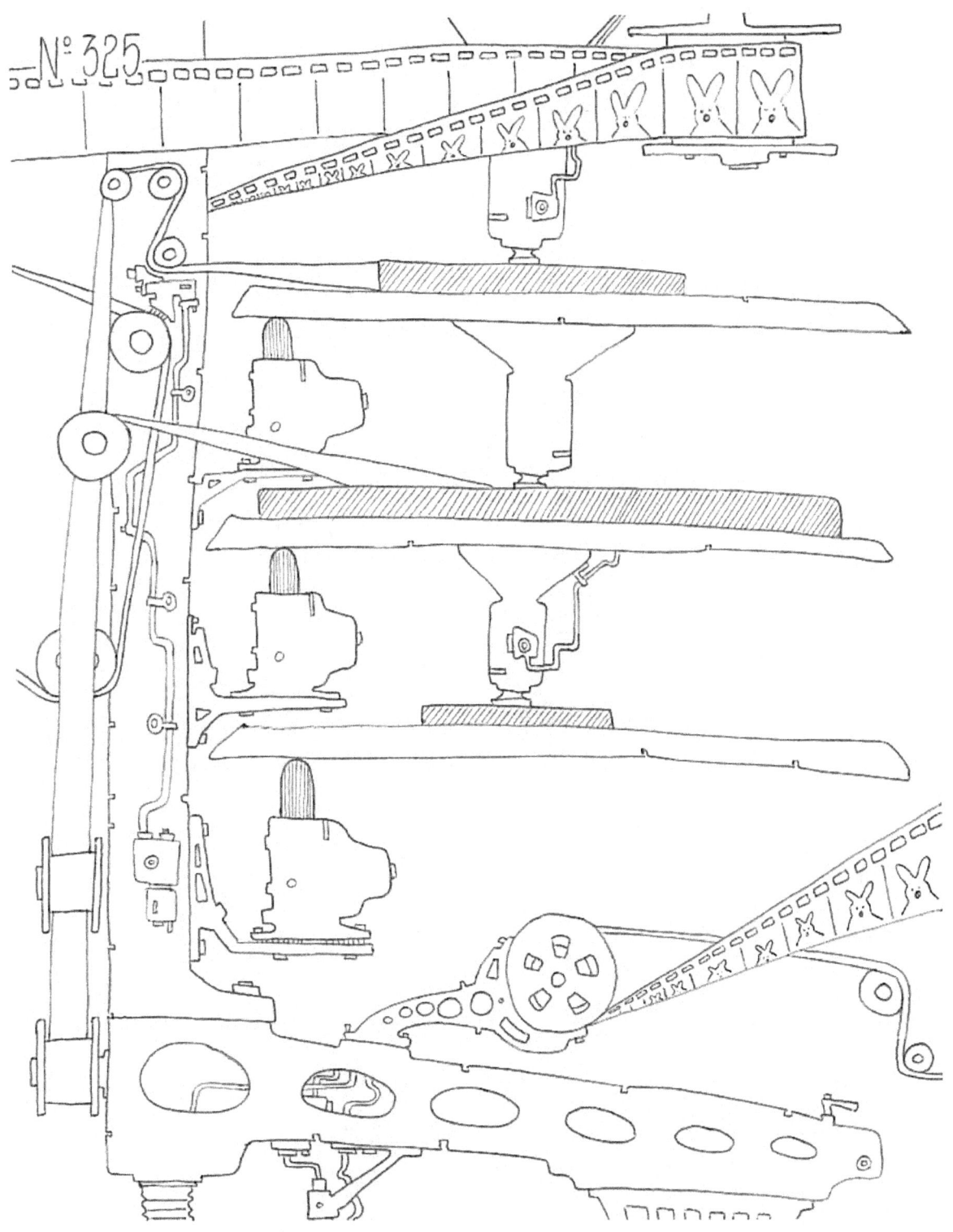

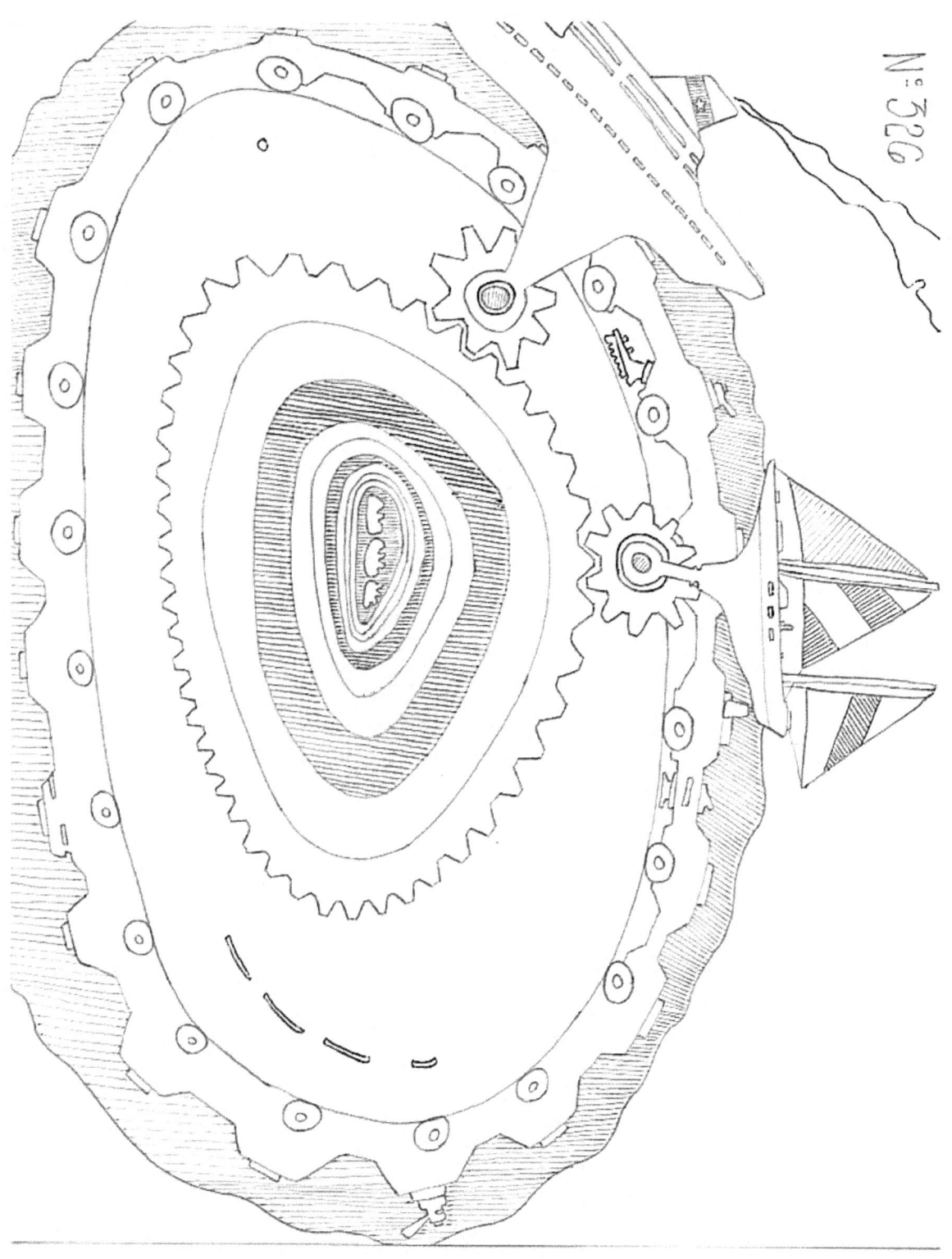

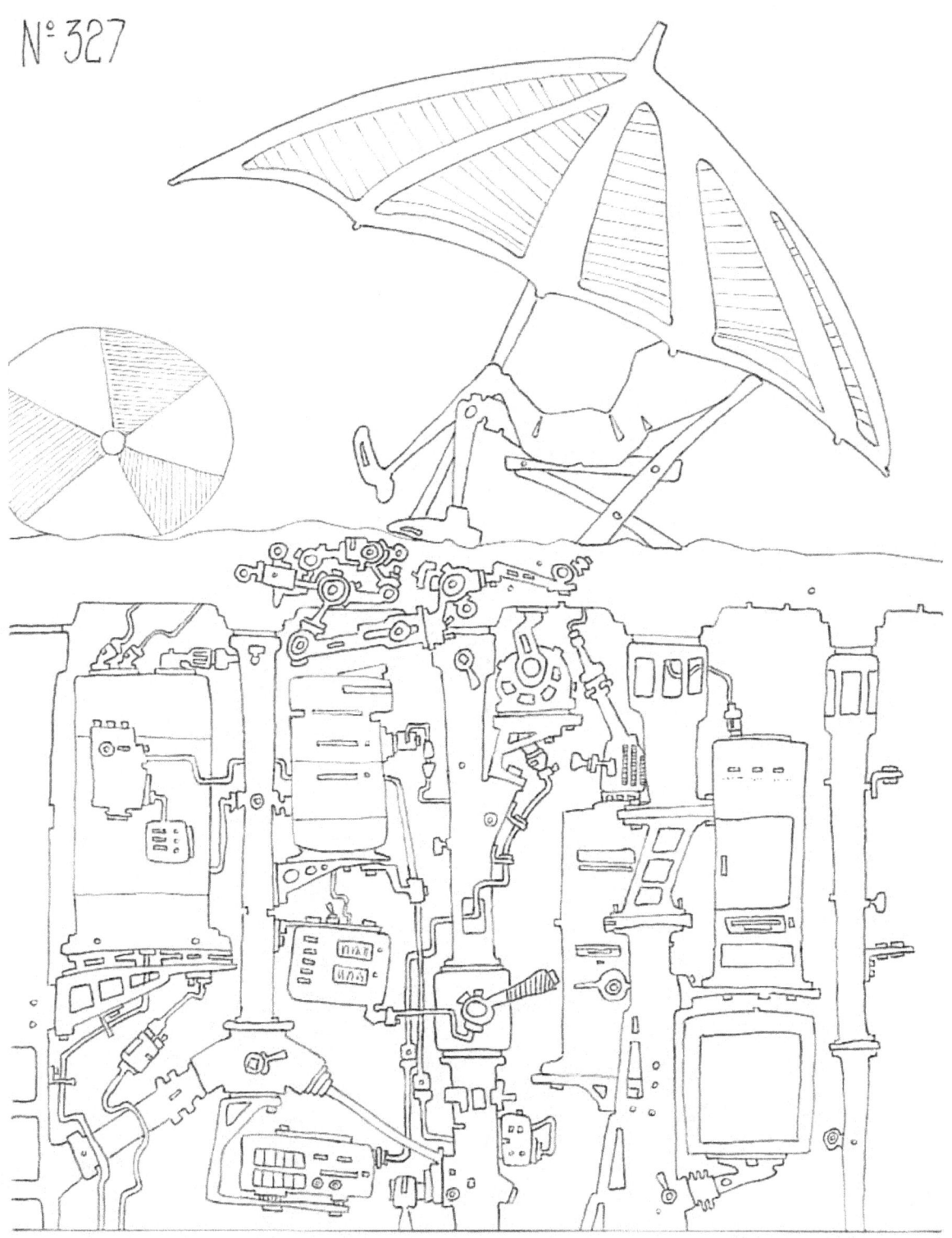

N° 328

N° 329

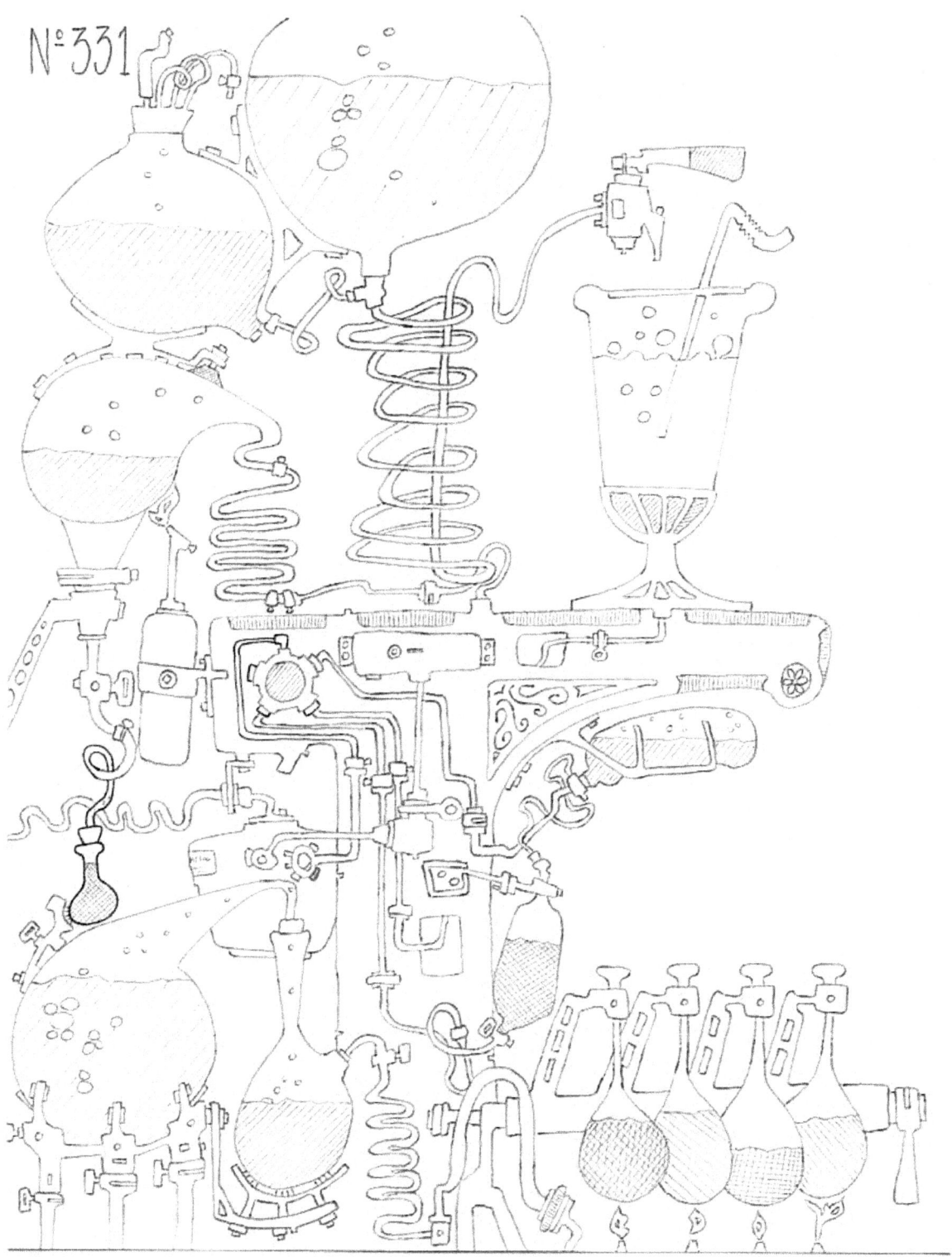

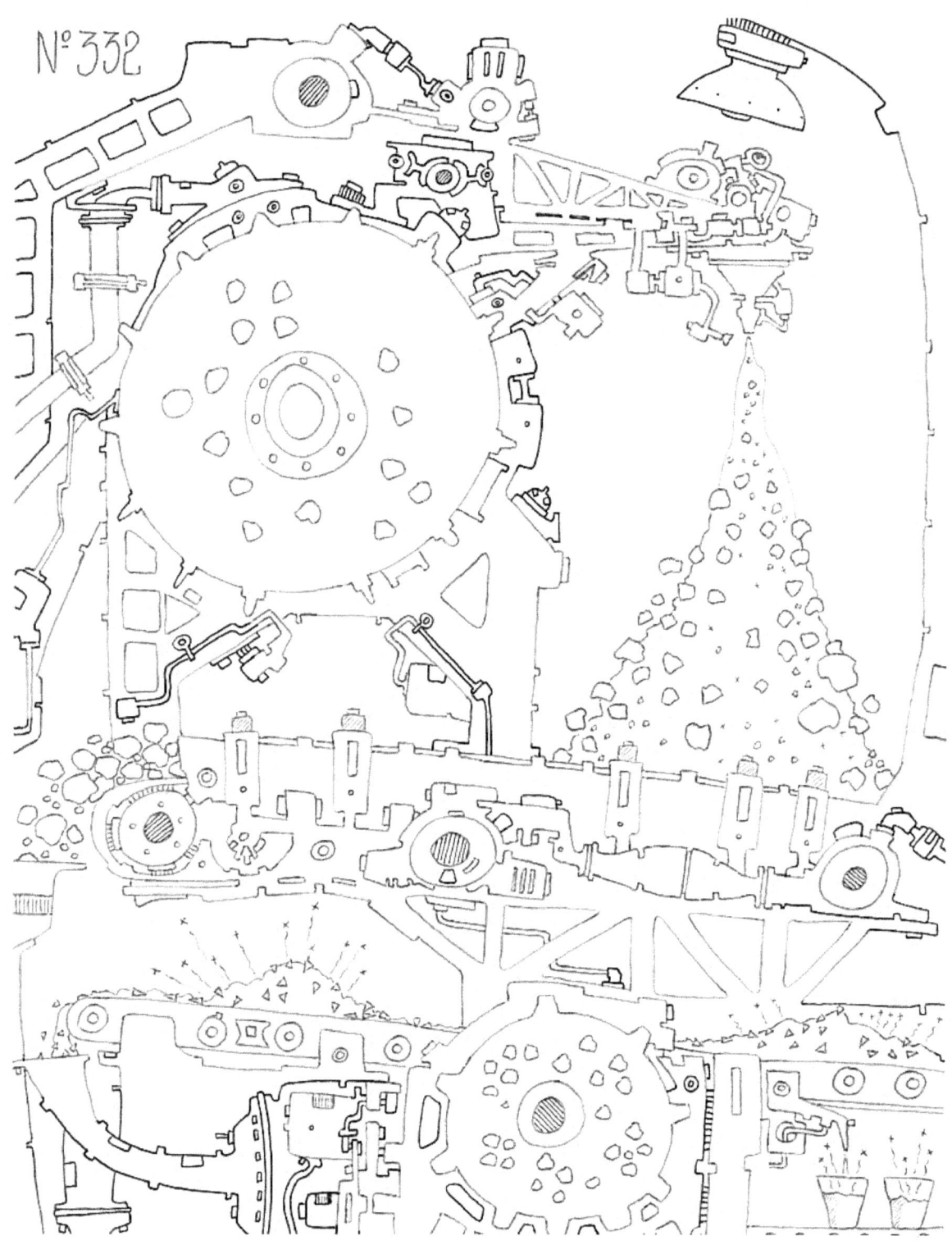

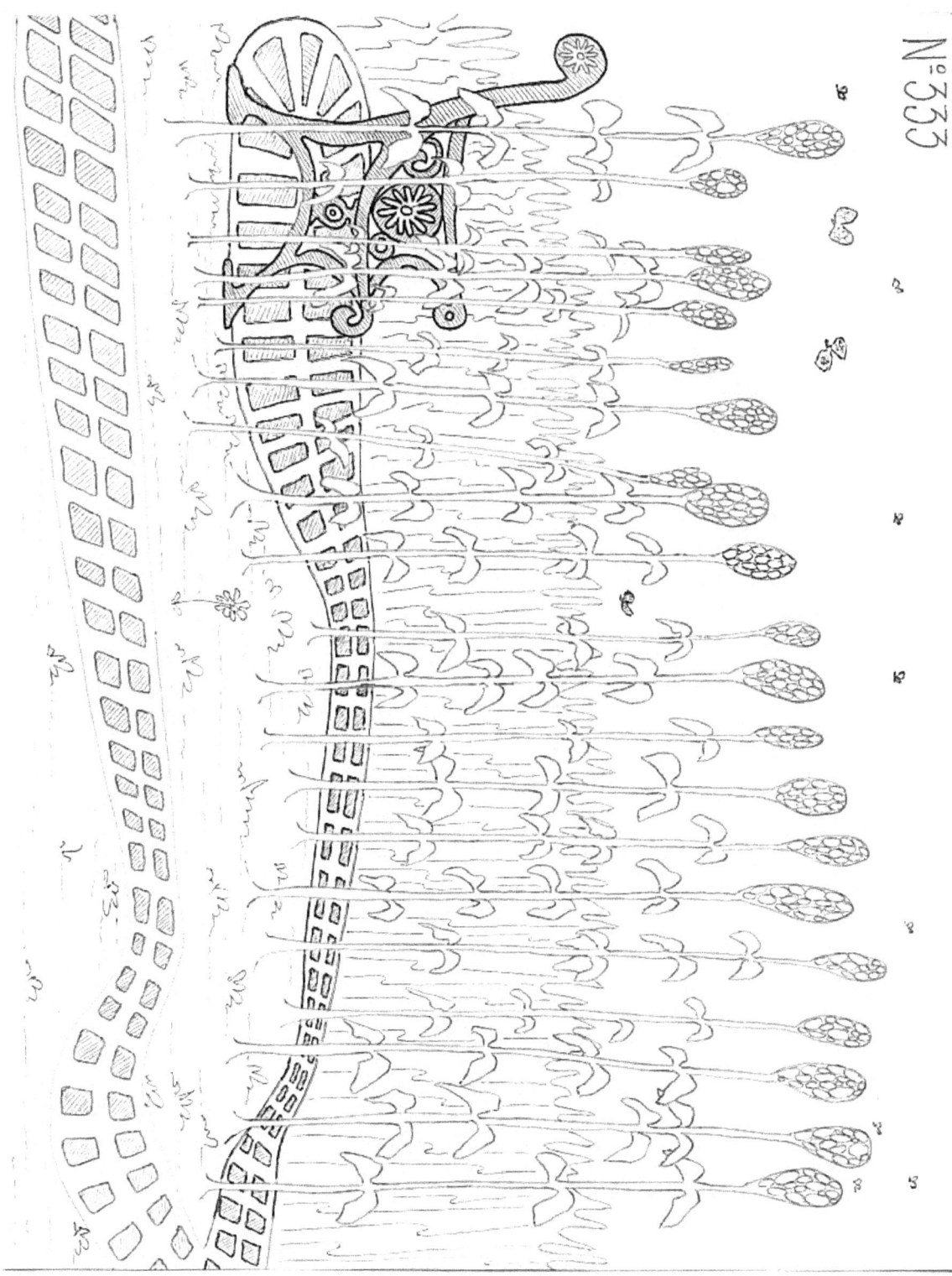

N° 333

N° 334

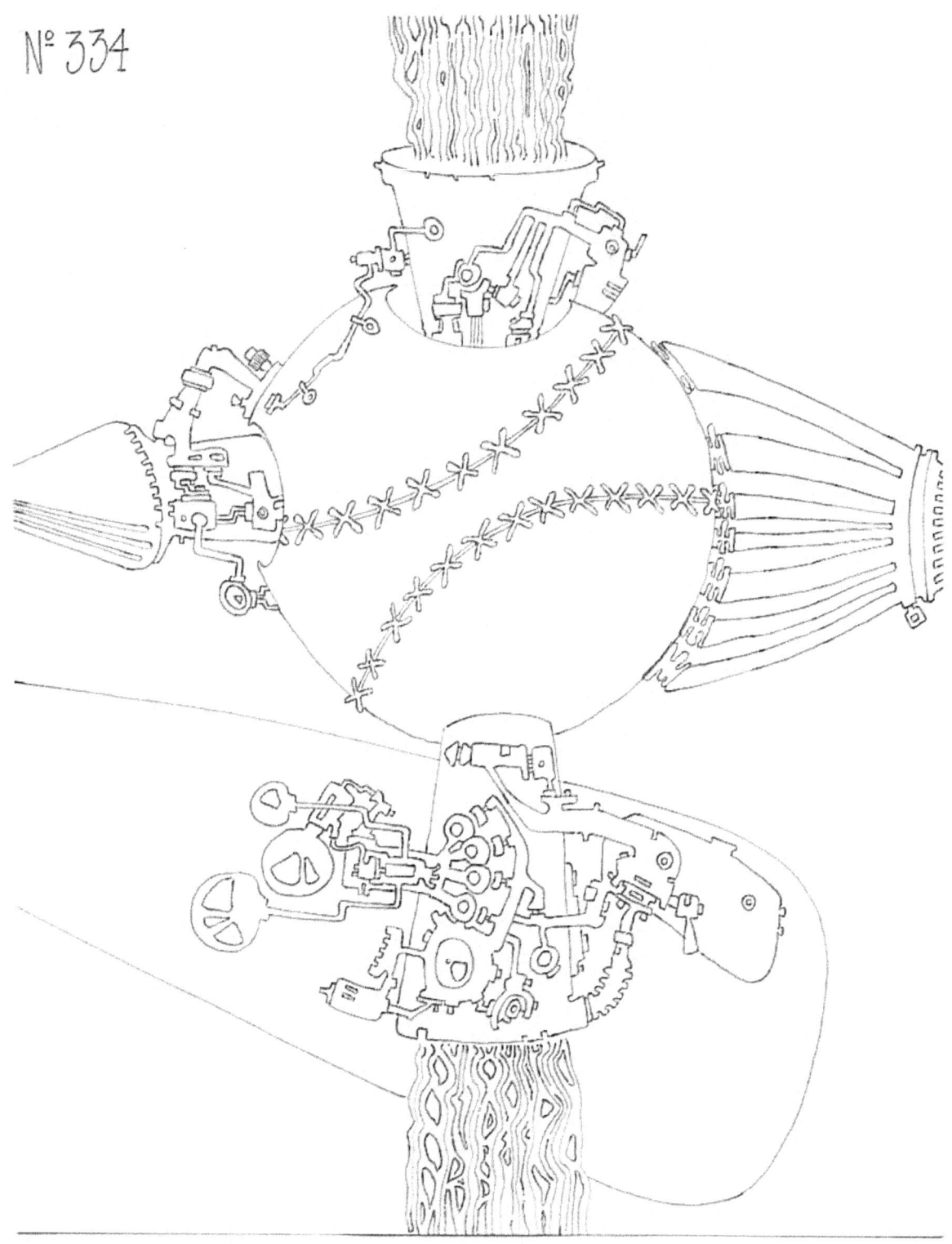

N° 335

N° 336

N° 337

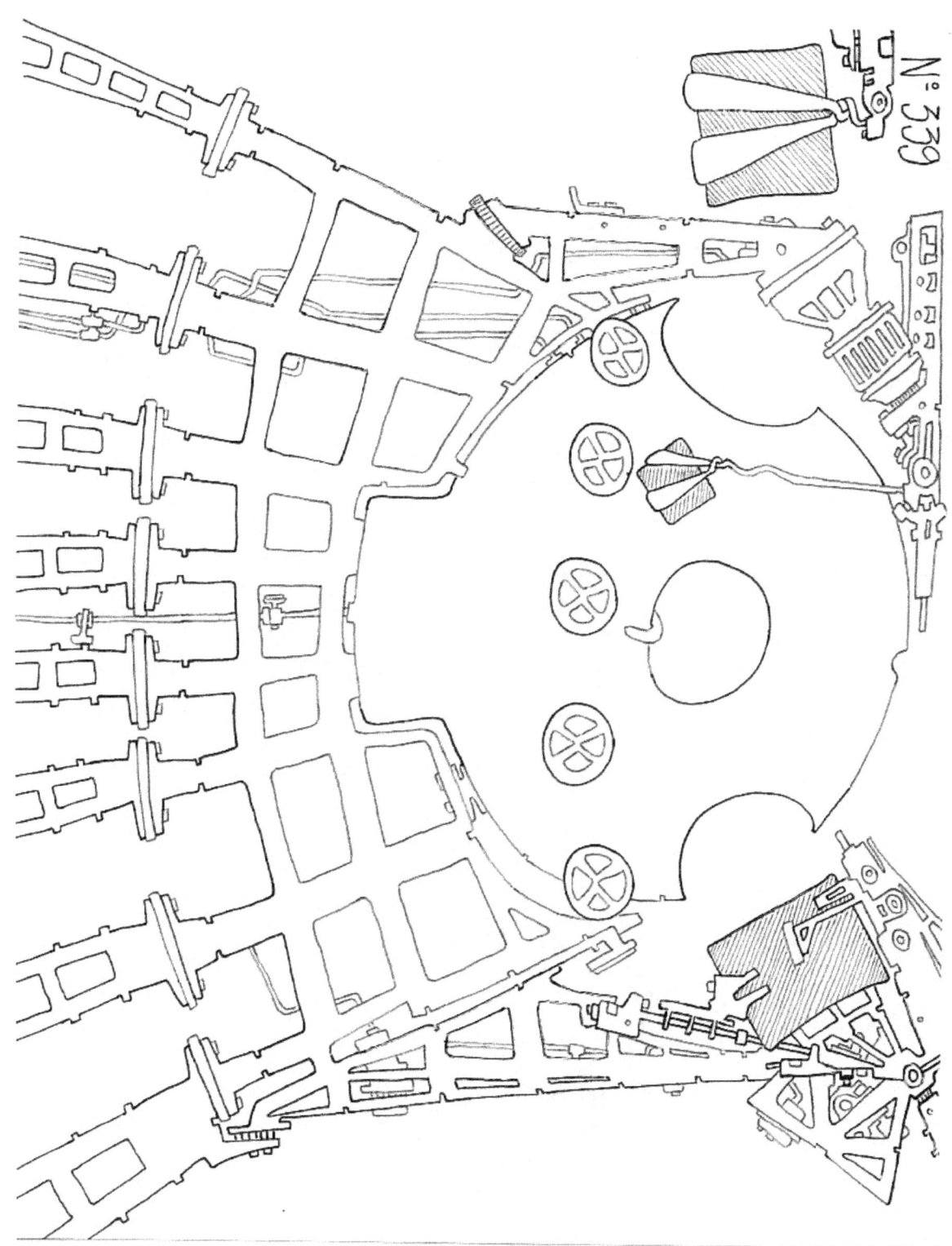

N° 340

Nº 341

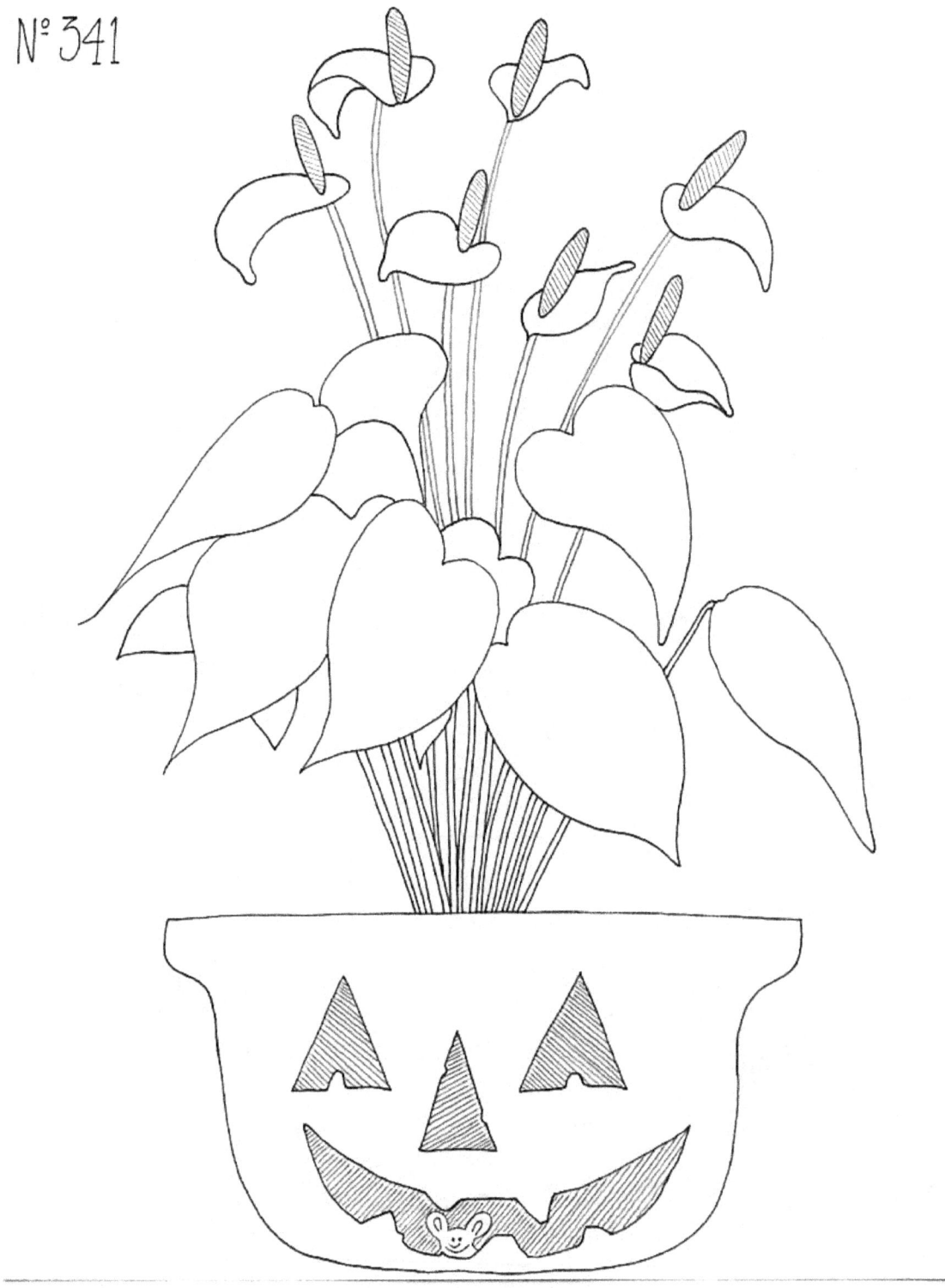

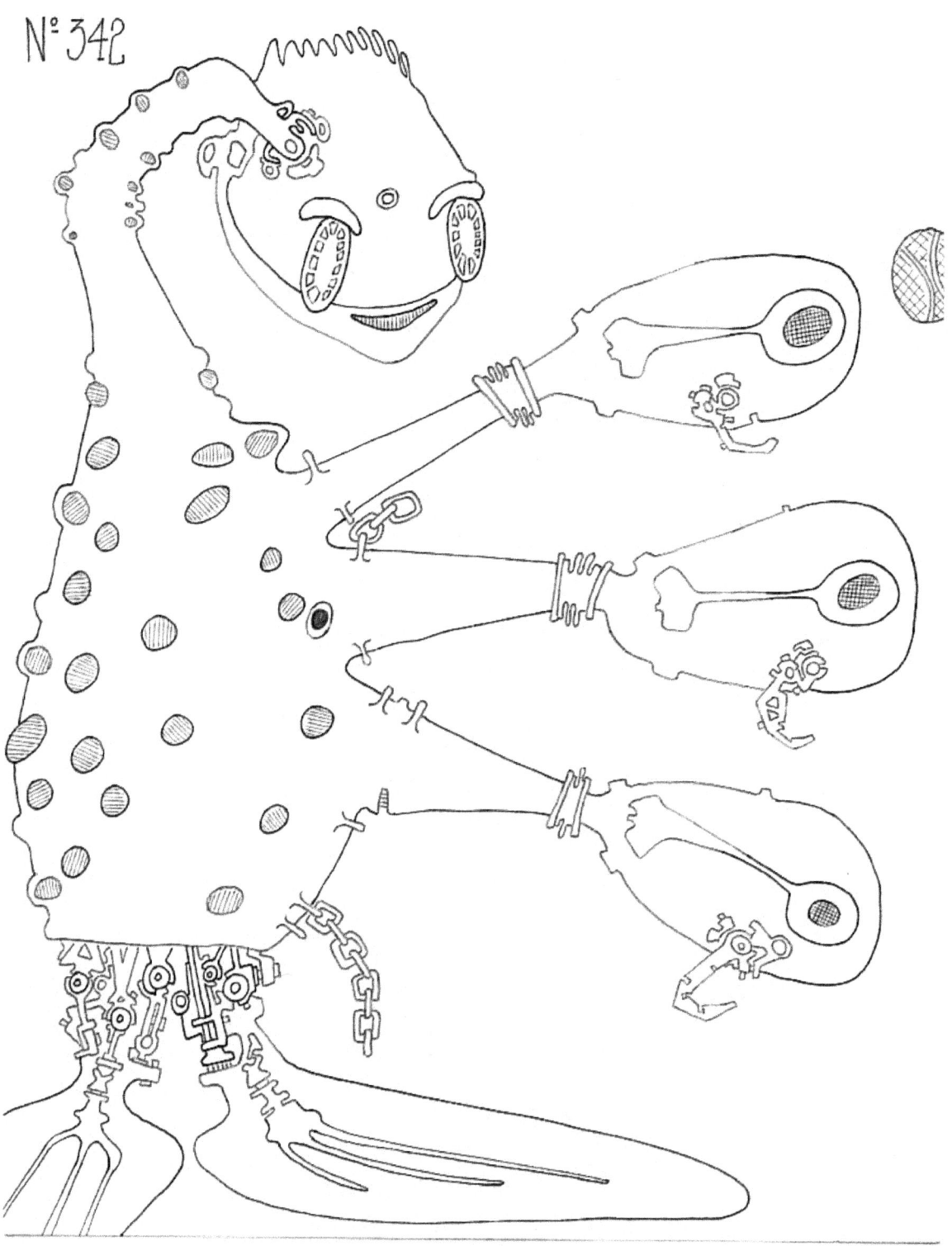

Nº 343

N° 344

N° 345

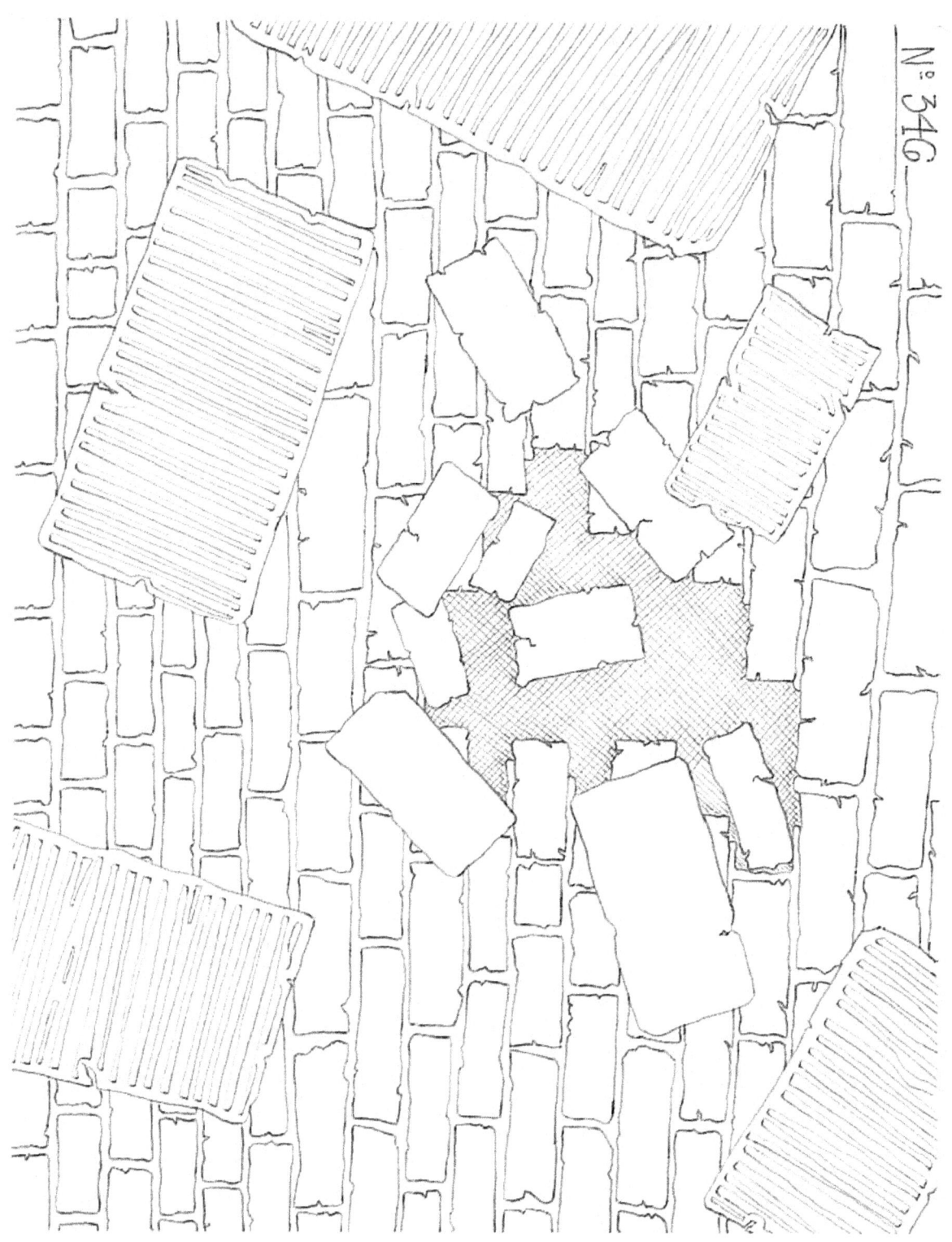

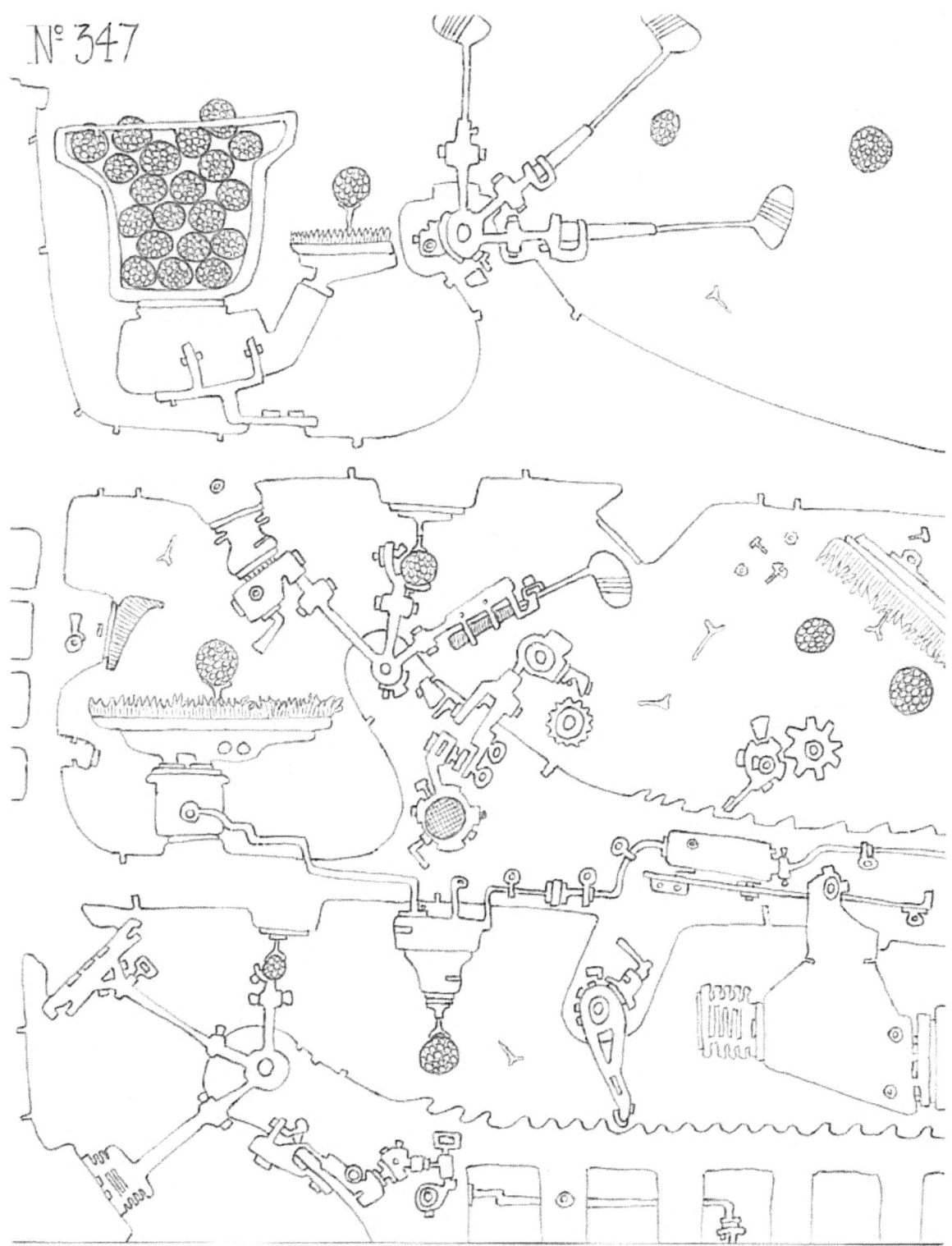
N° 347

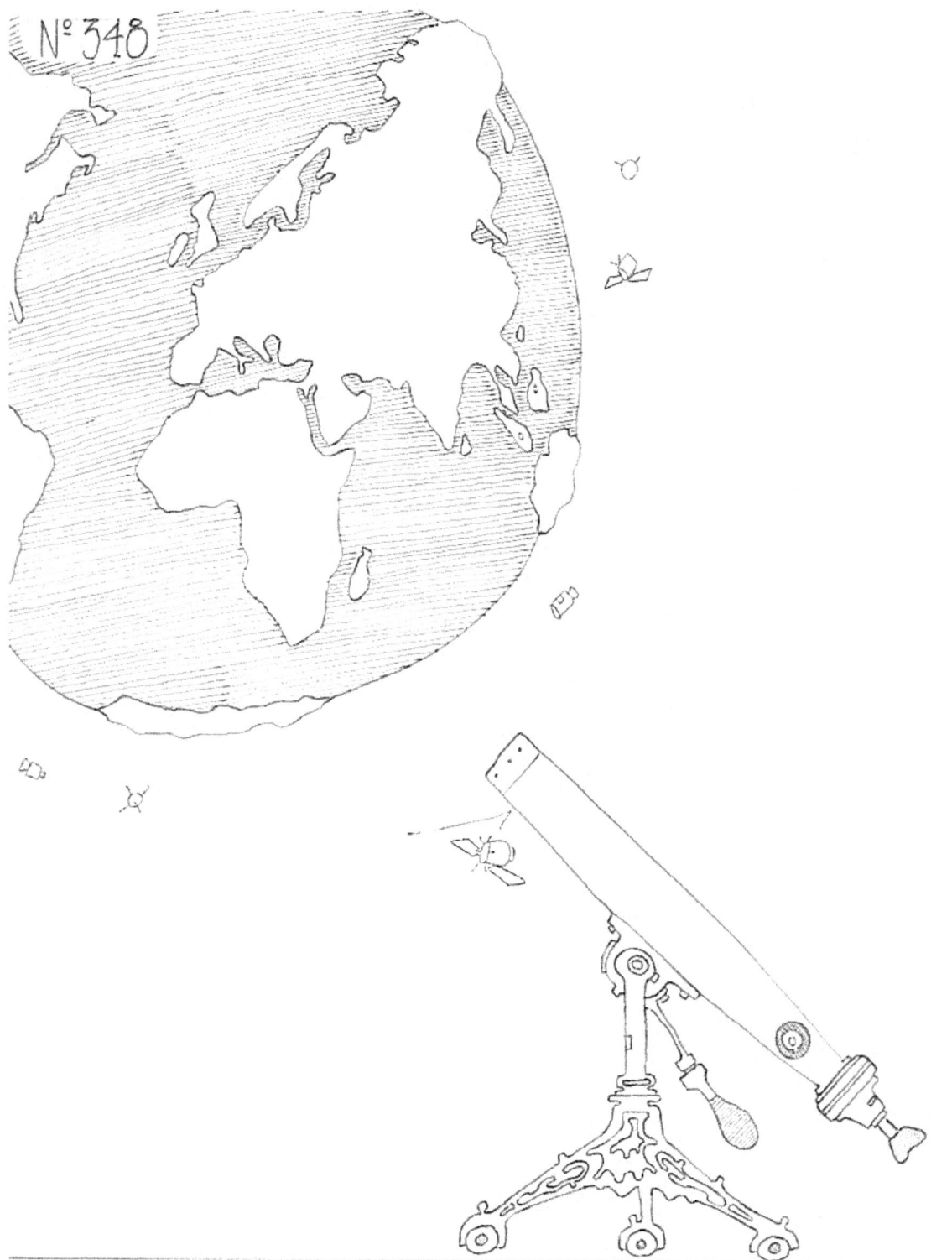

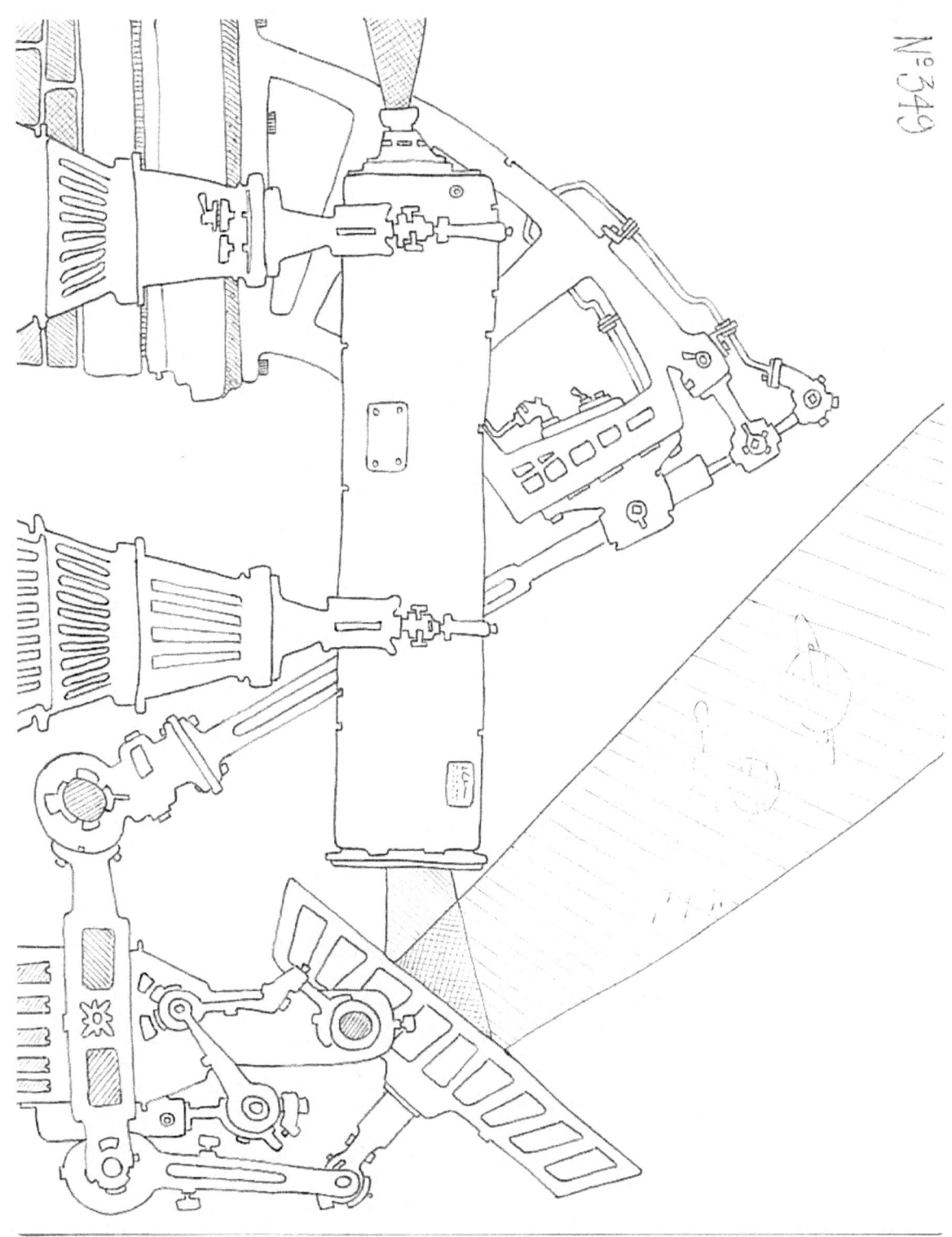

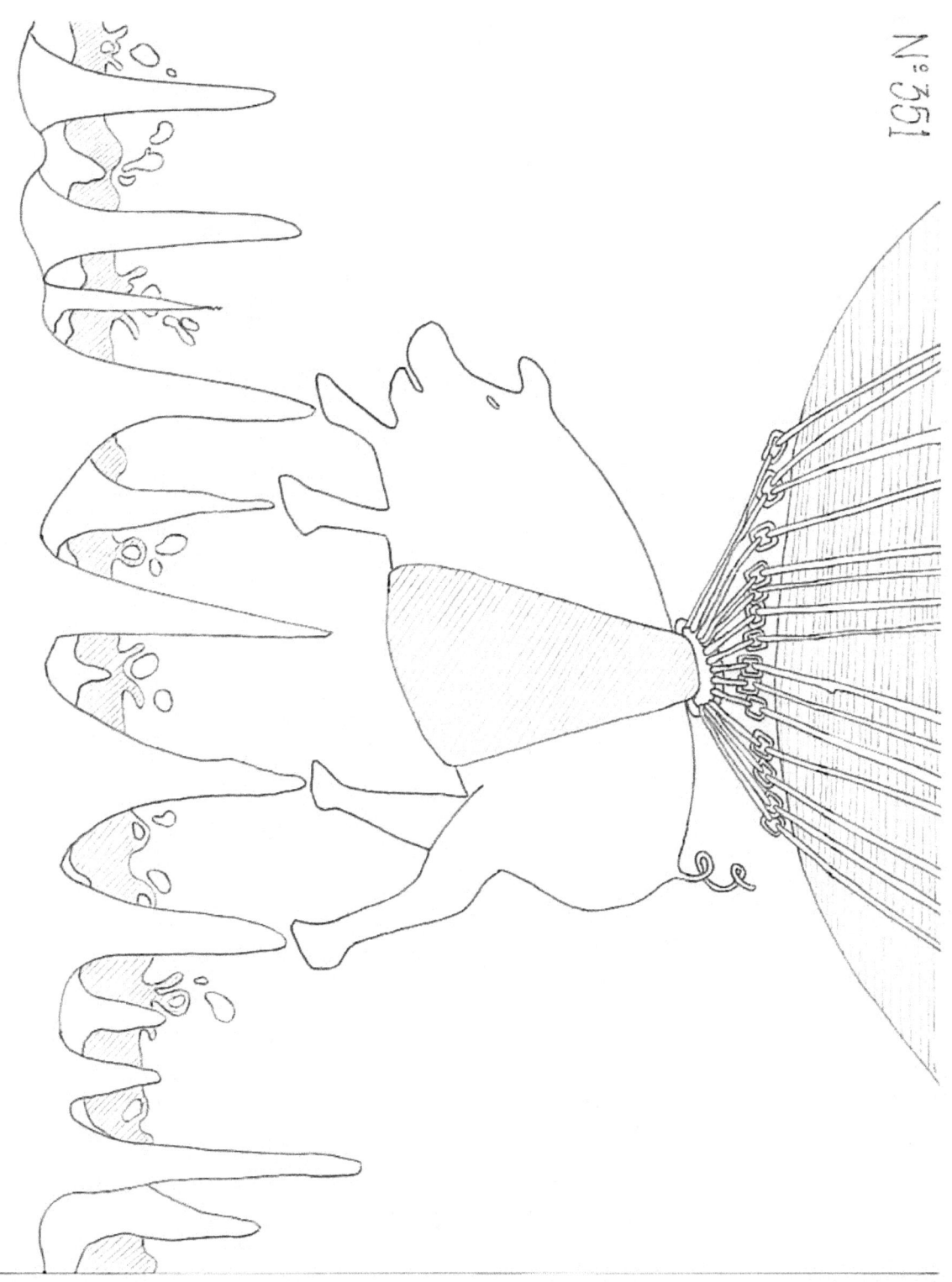

Nº 351

N° 352

N° 352

N° 354
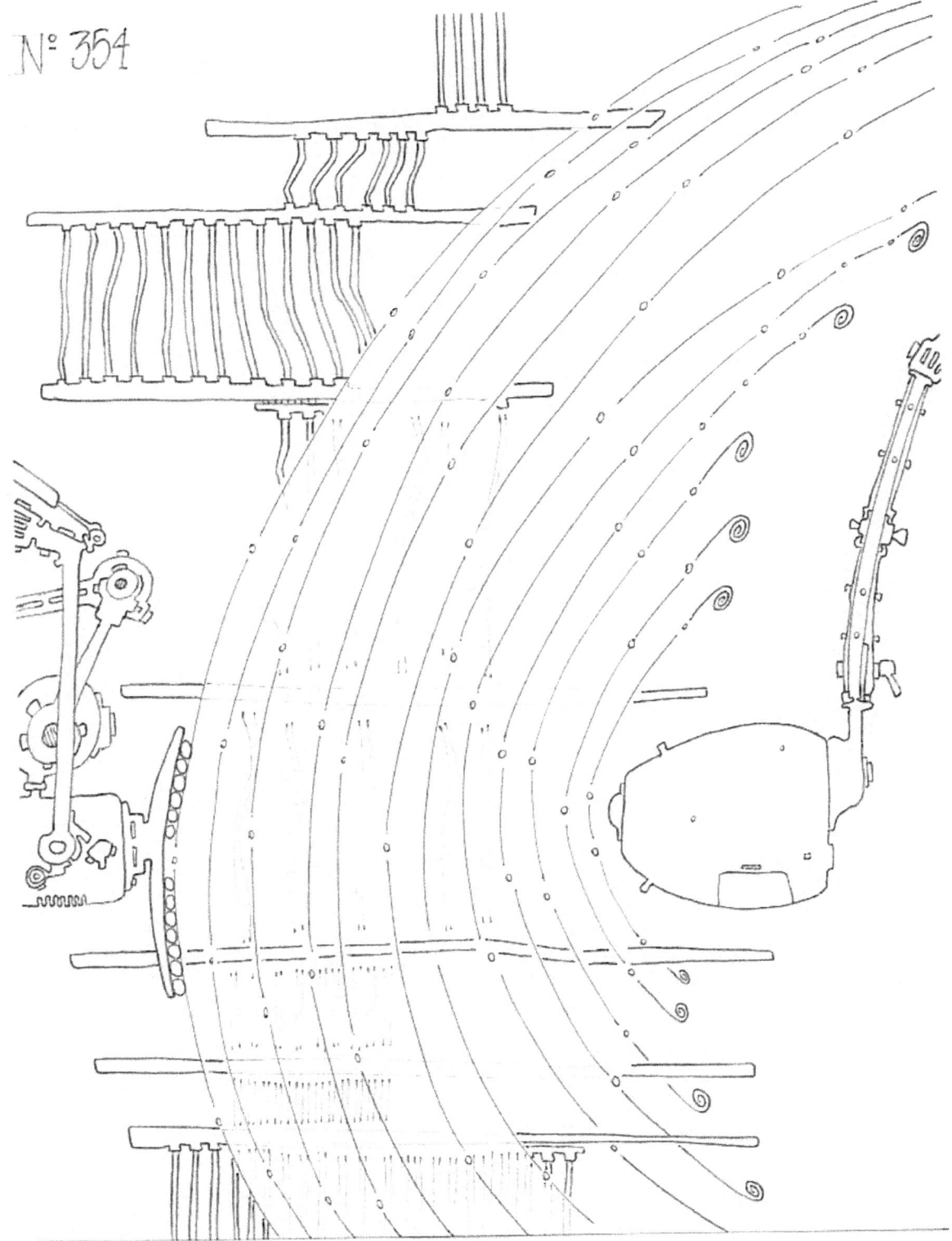

N° 356

N° 358

N° 359

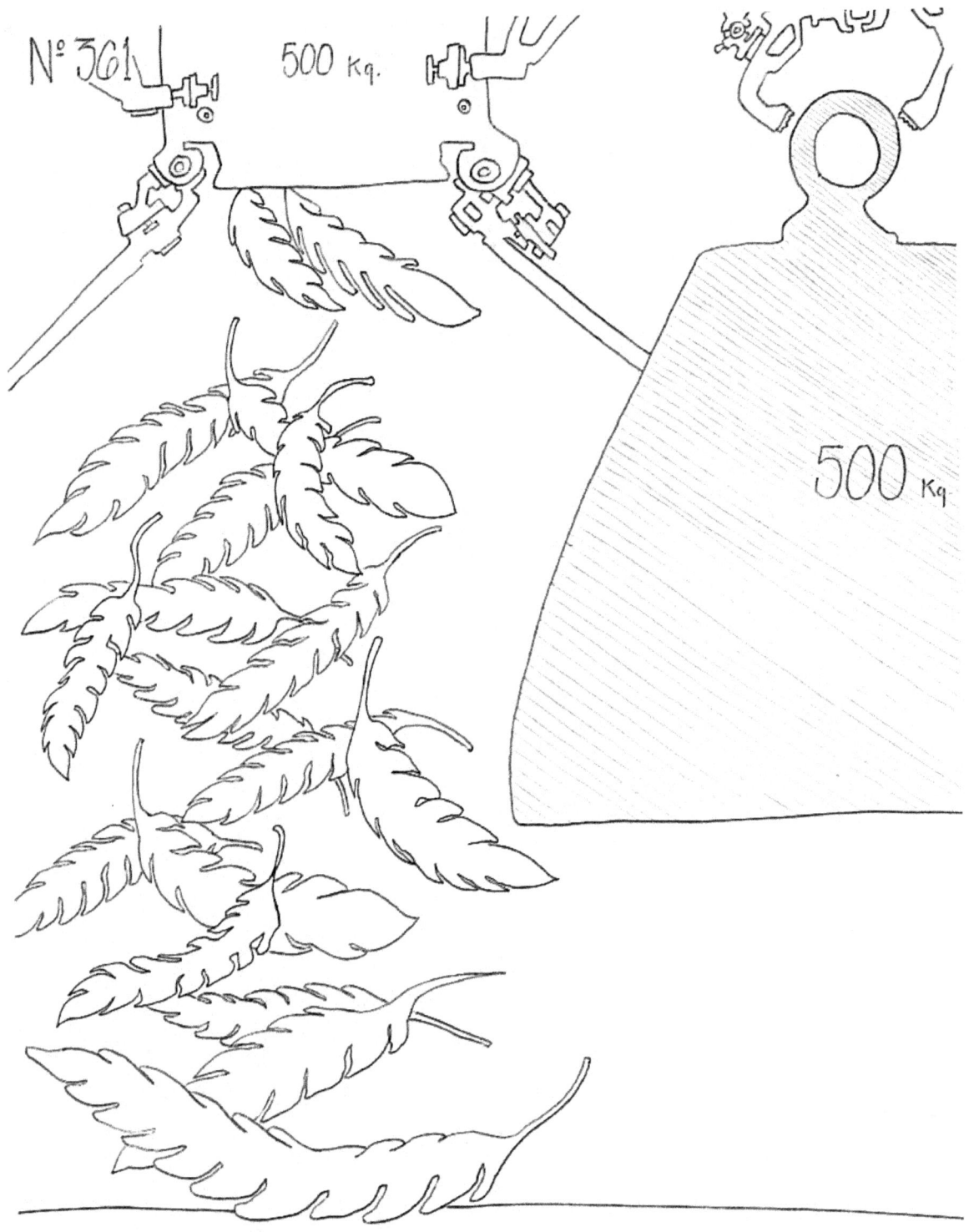

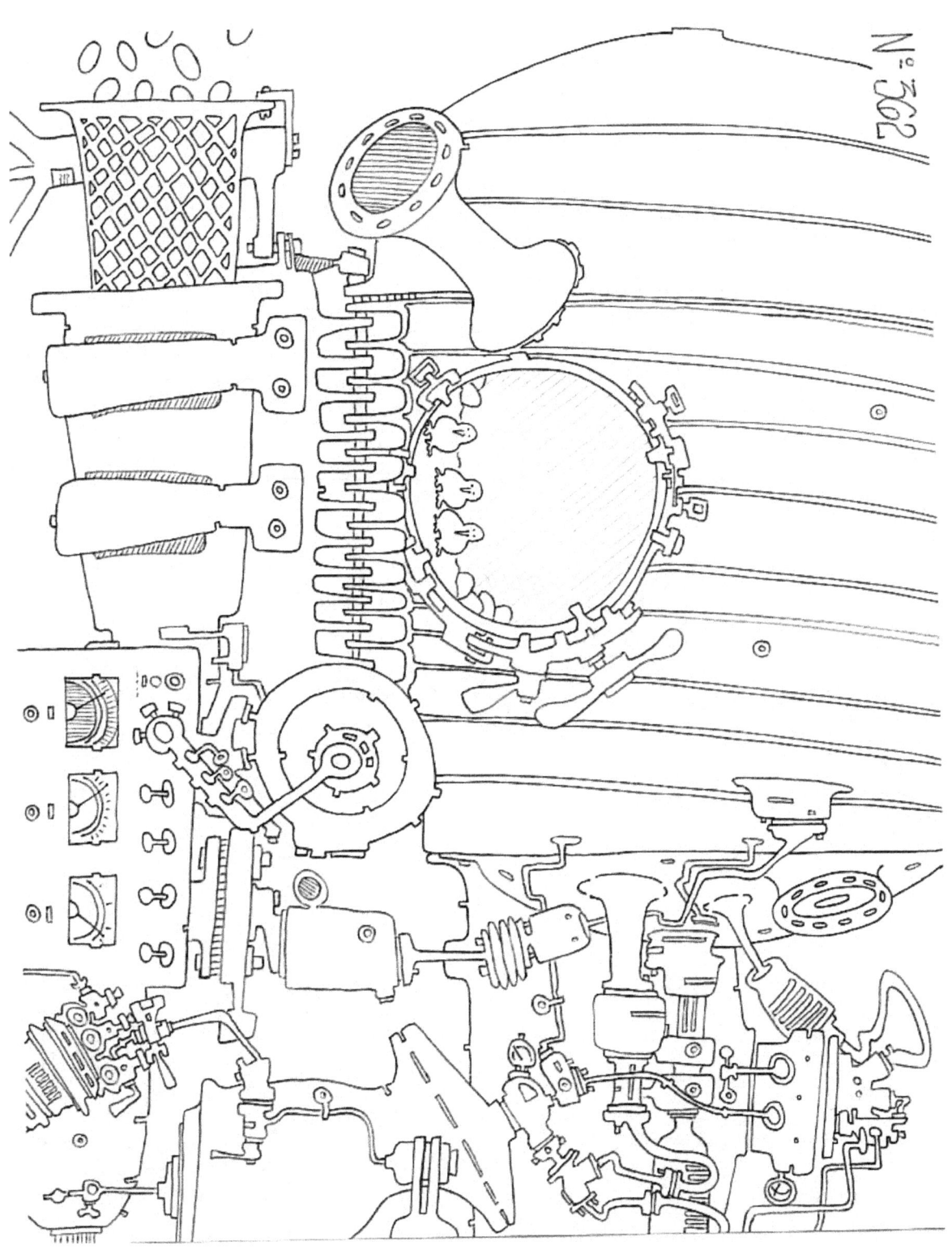

N° 363

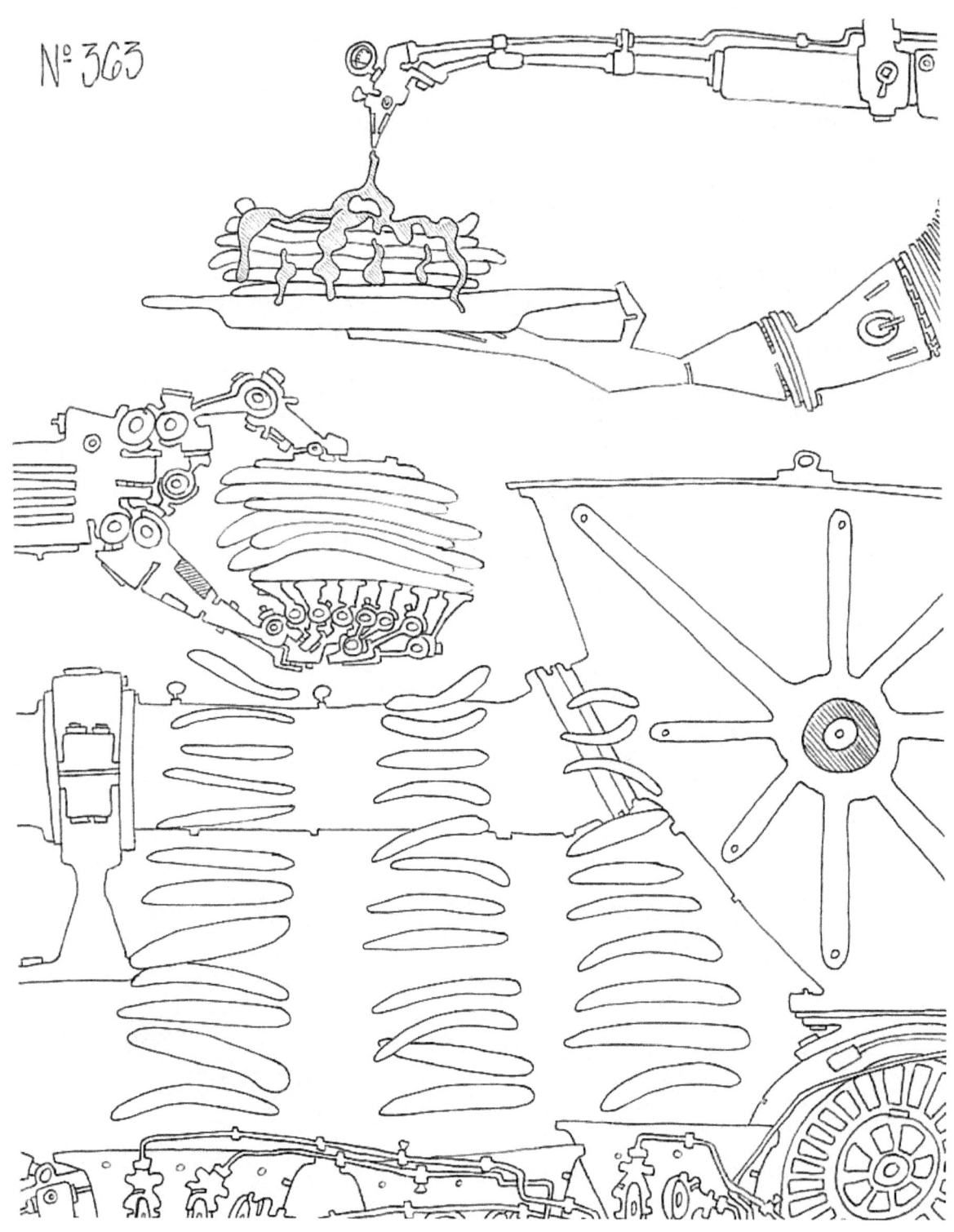

N° 364

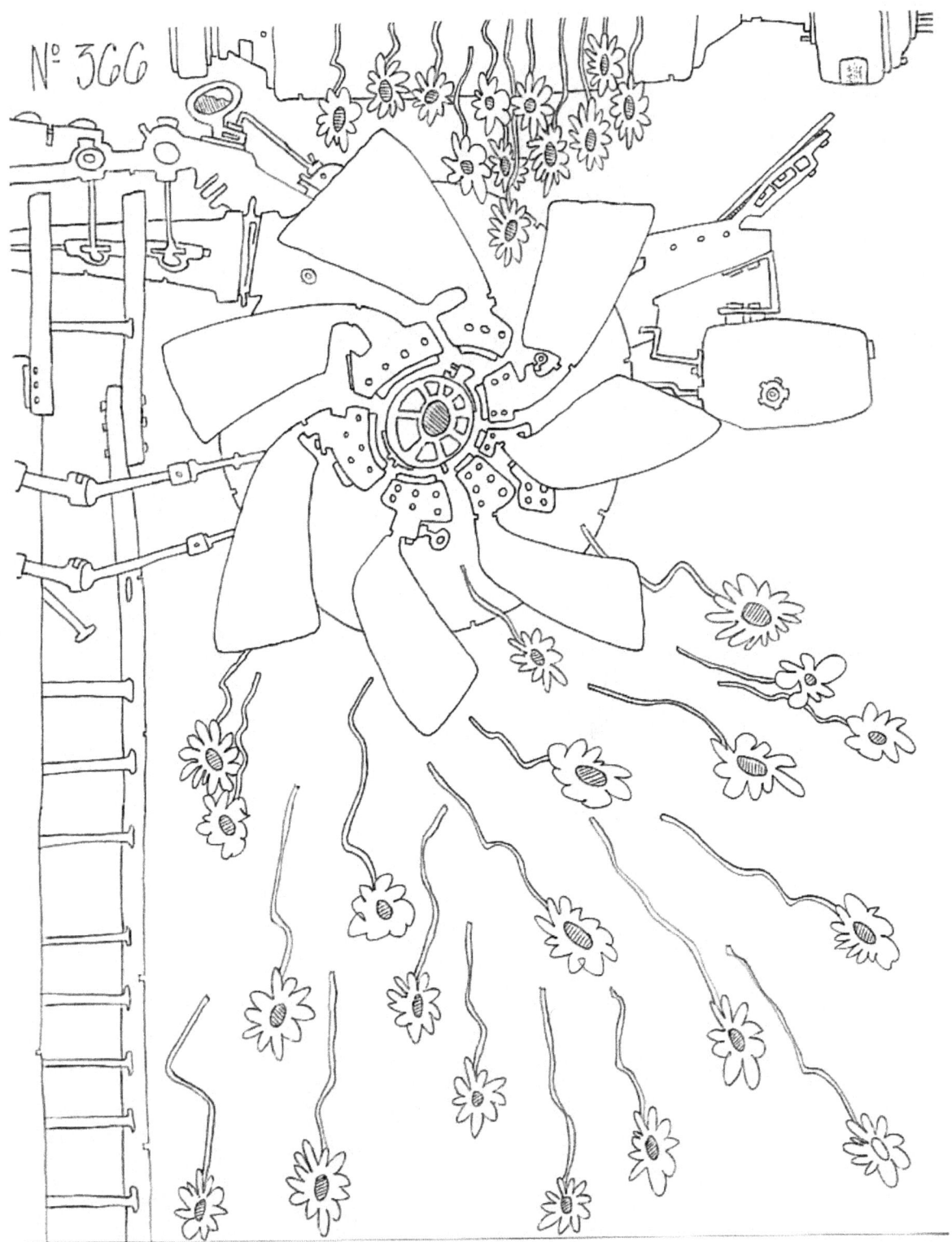

Nº 368

N° 370

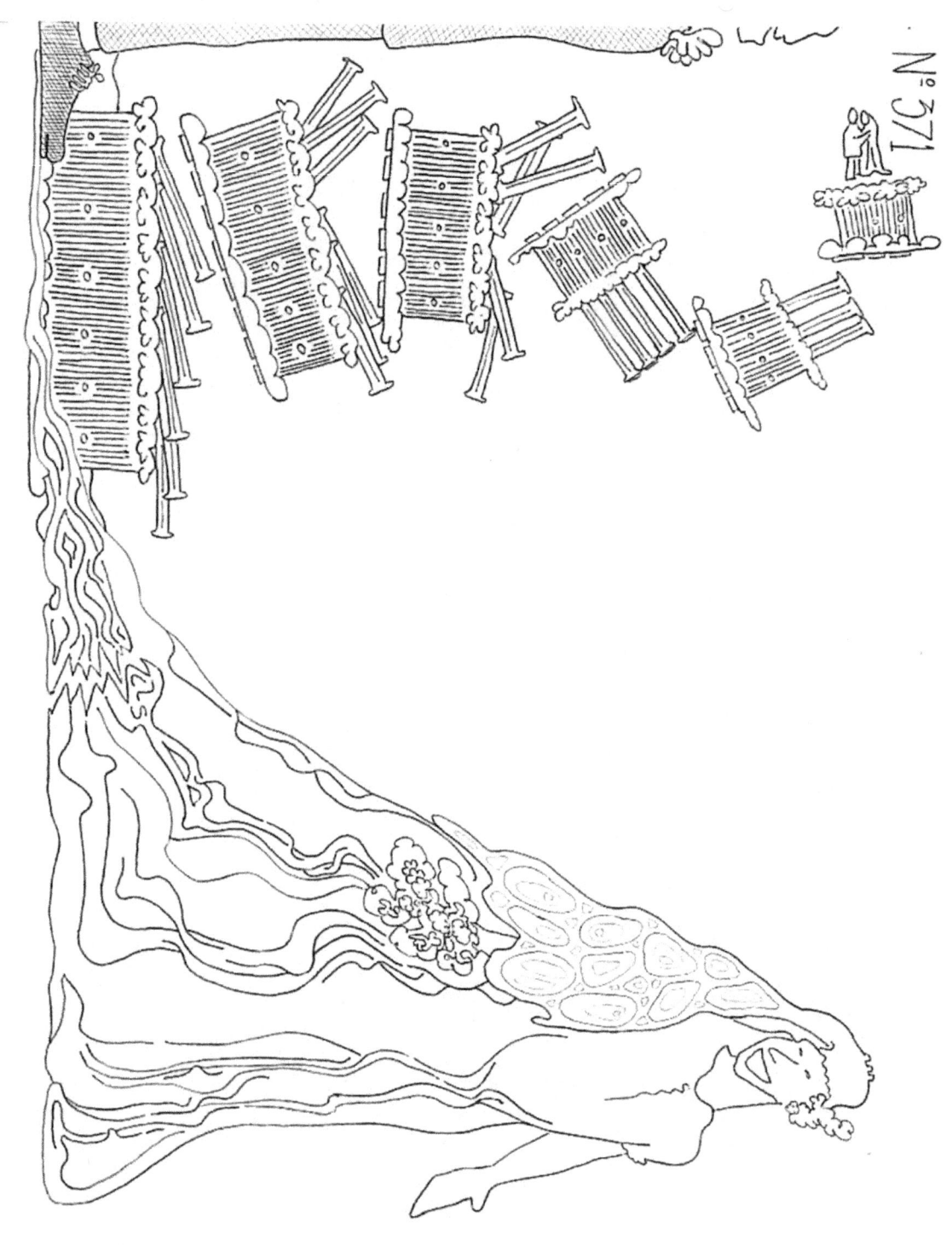

N° 372

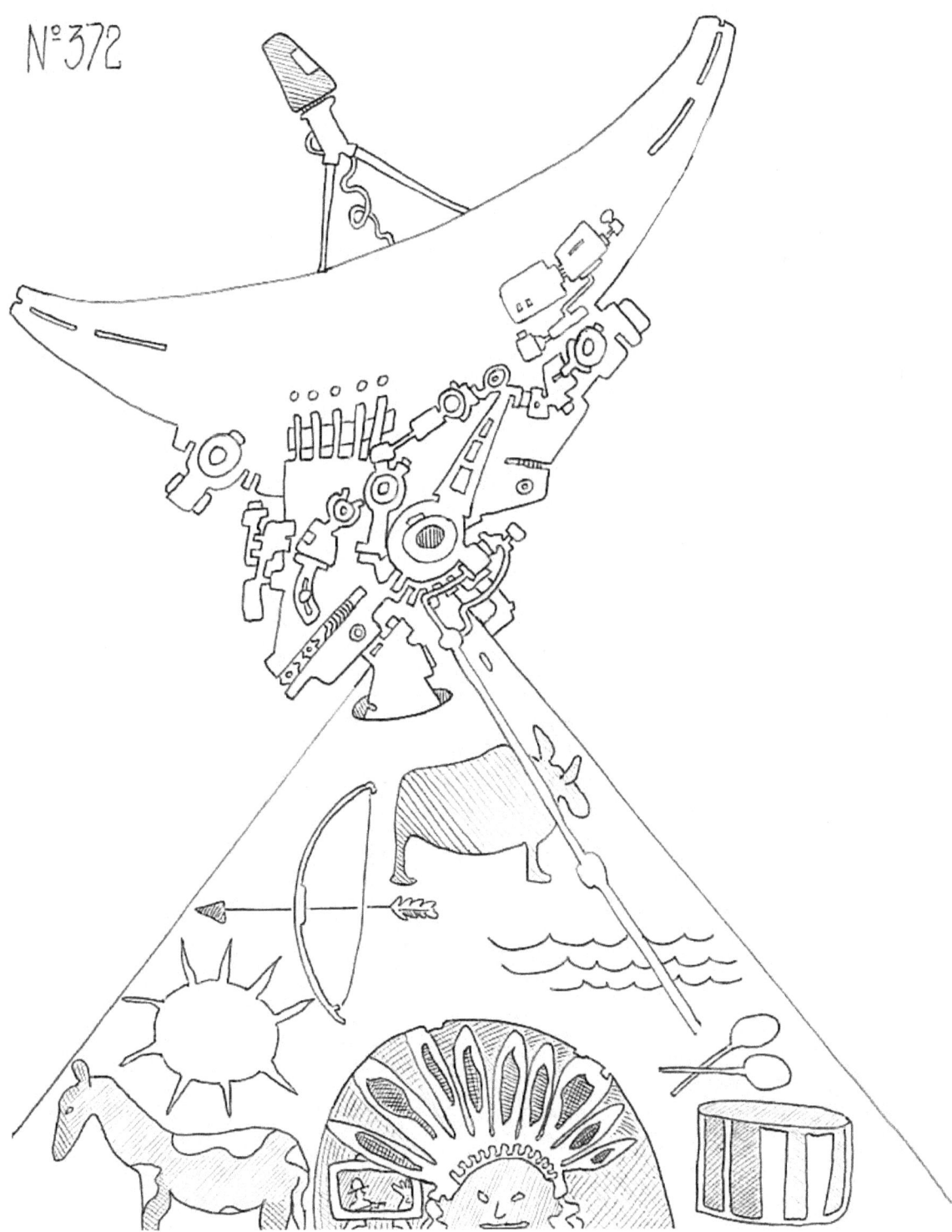

№ 373

N° 374

N° 375

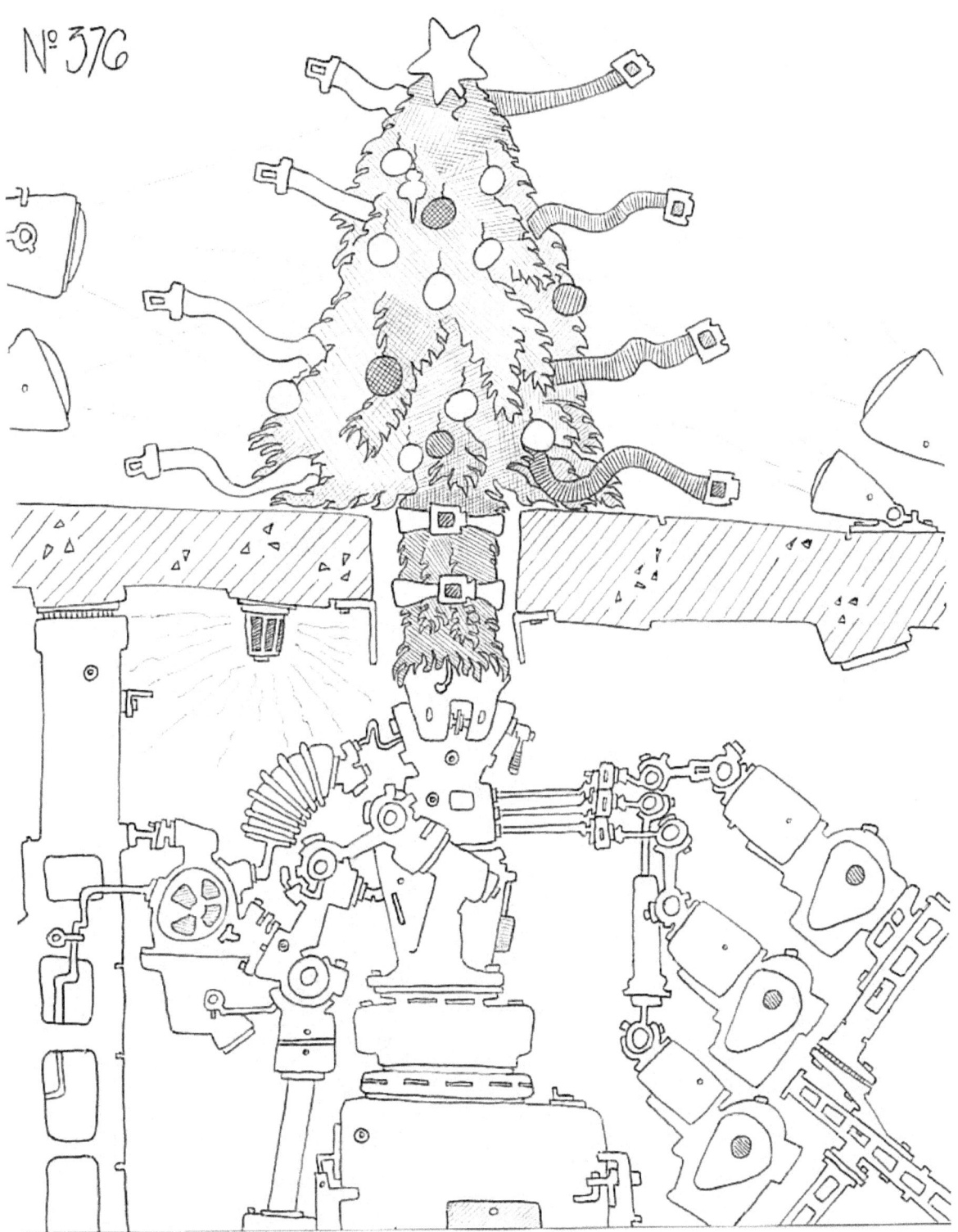

N° 377

N° 378

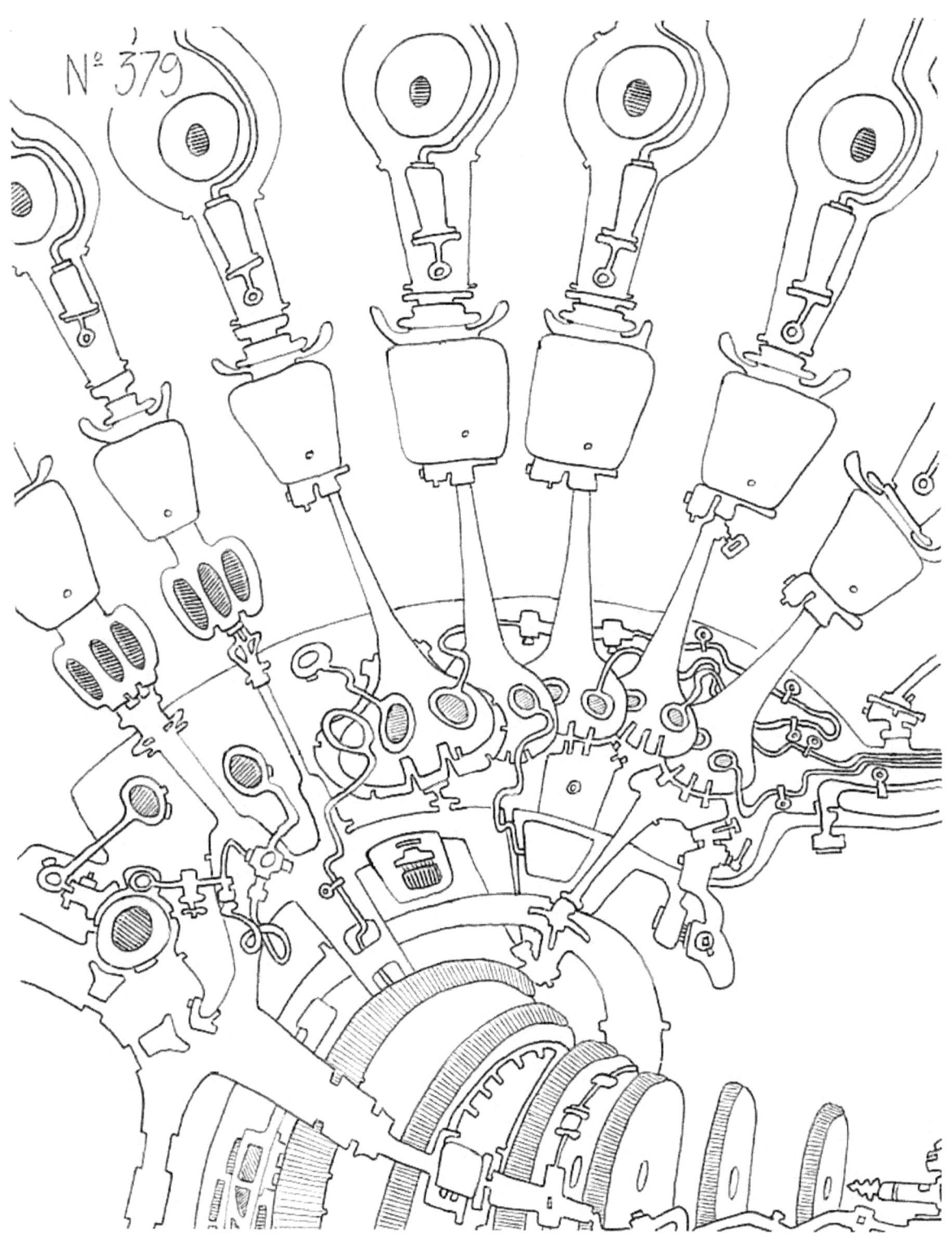

N° 384

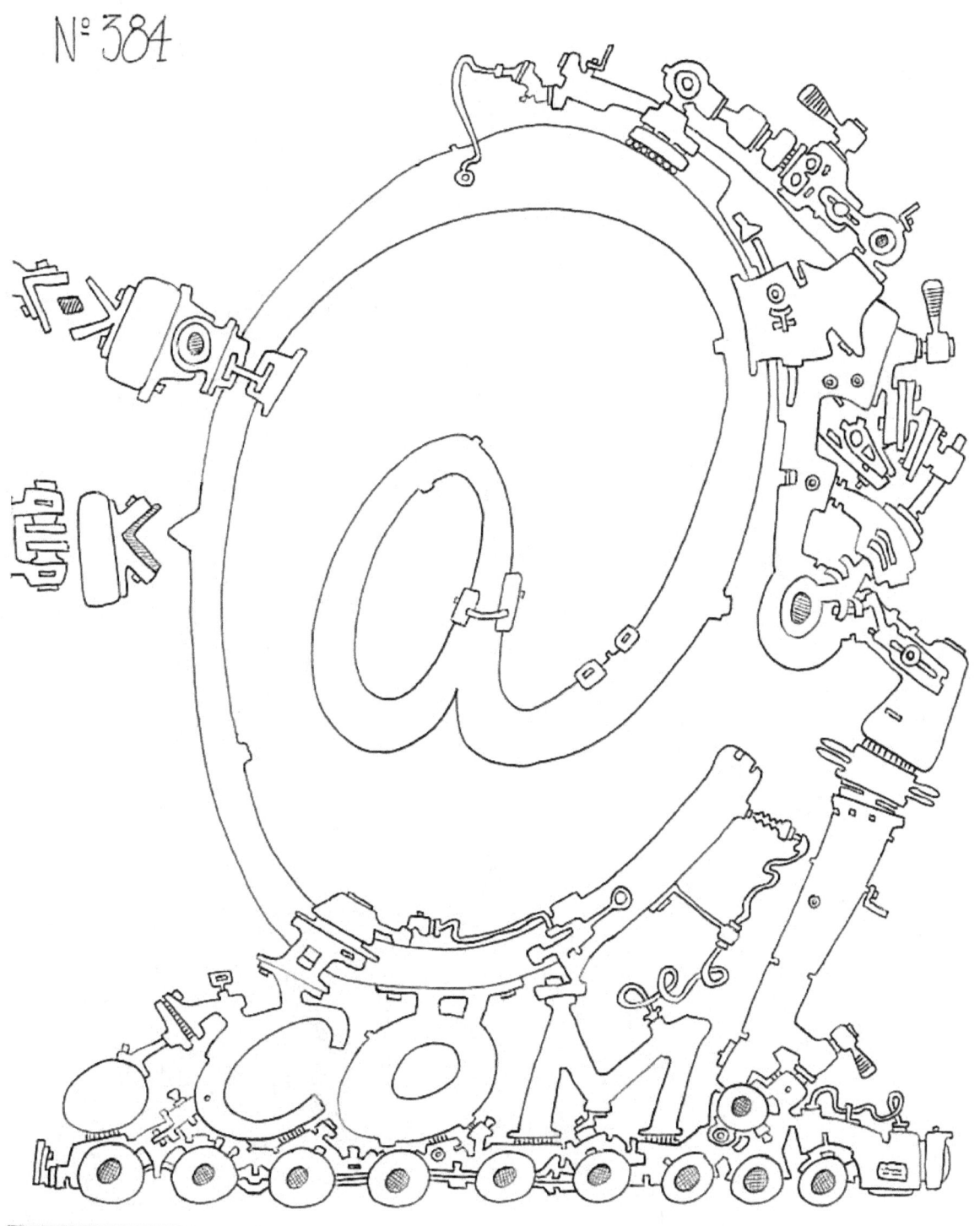

N° 386

N°388

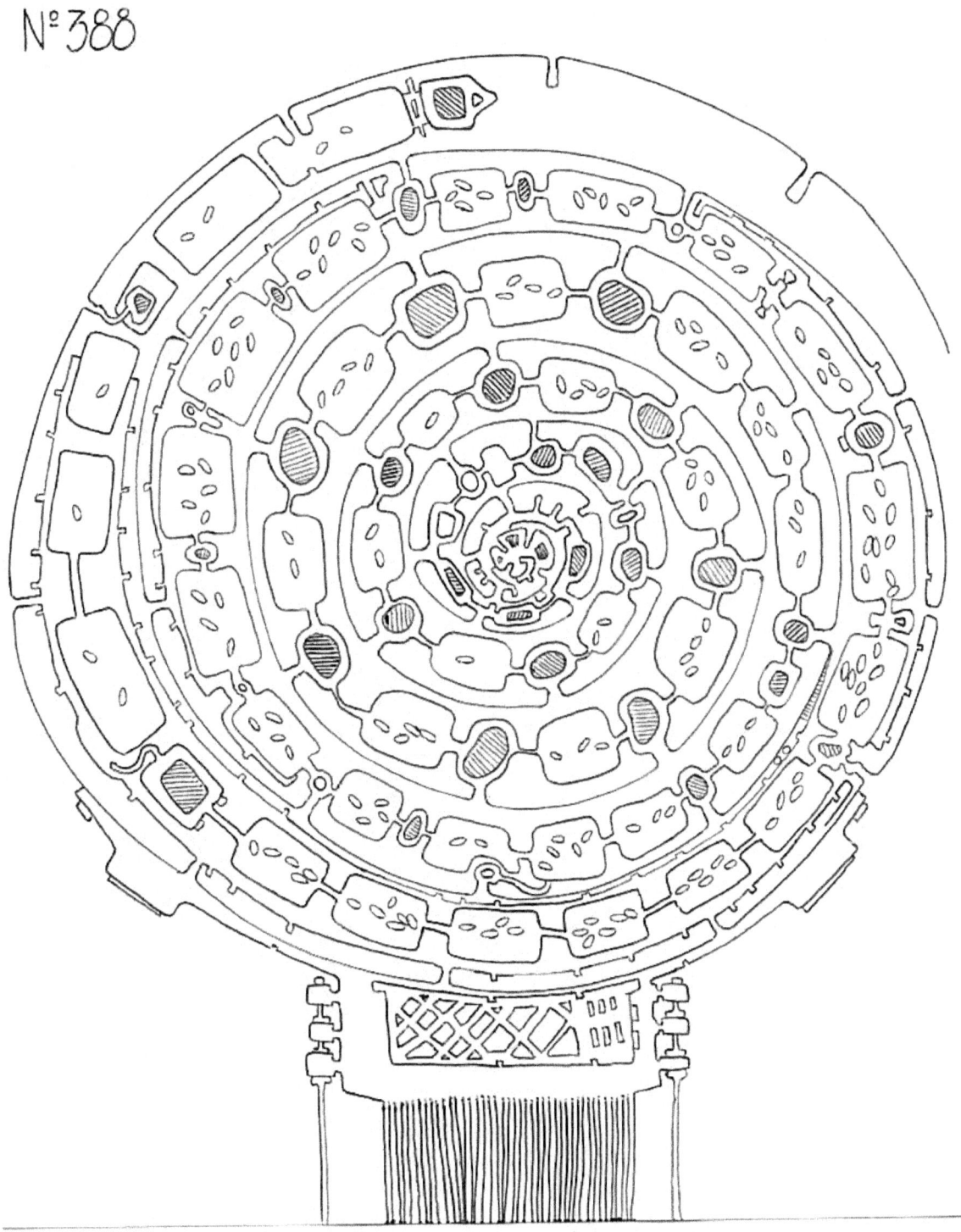

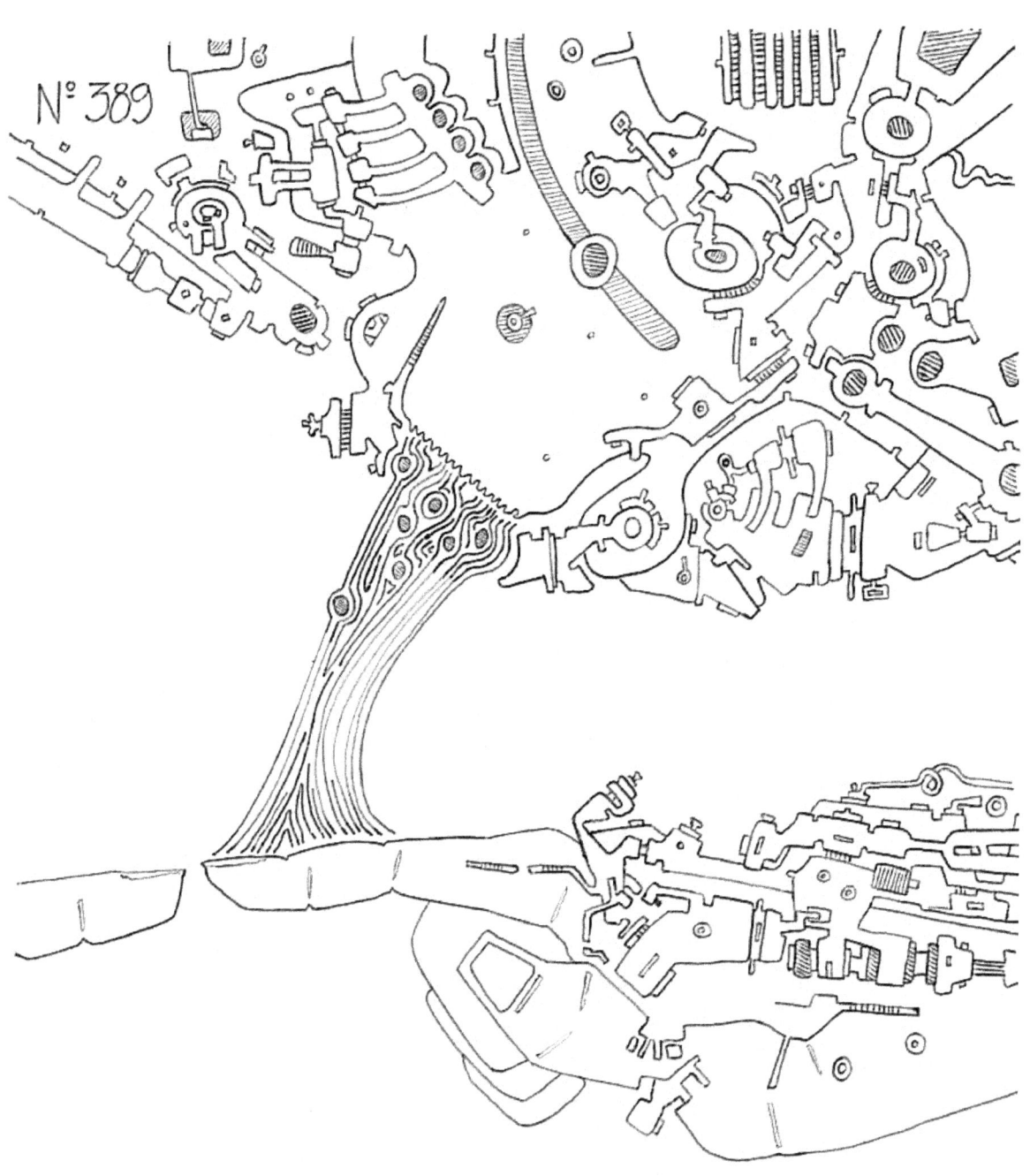

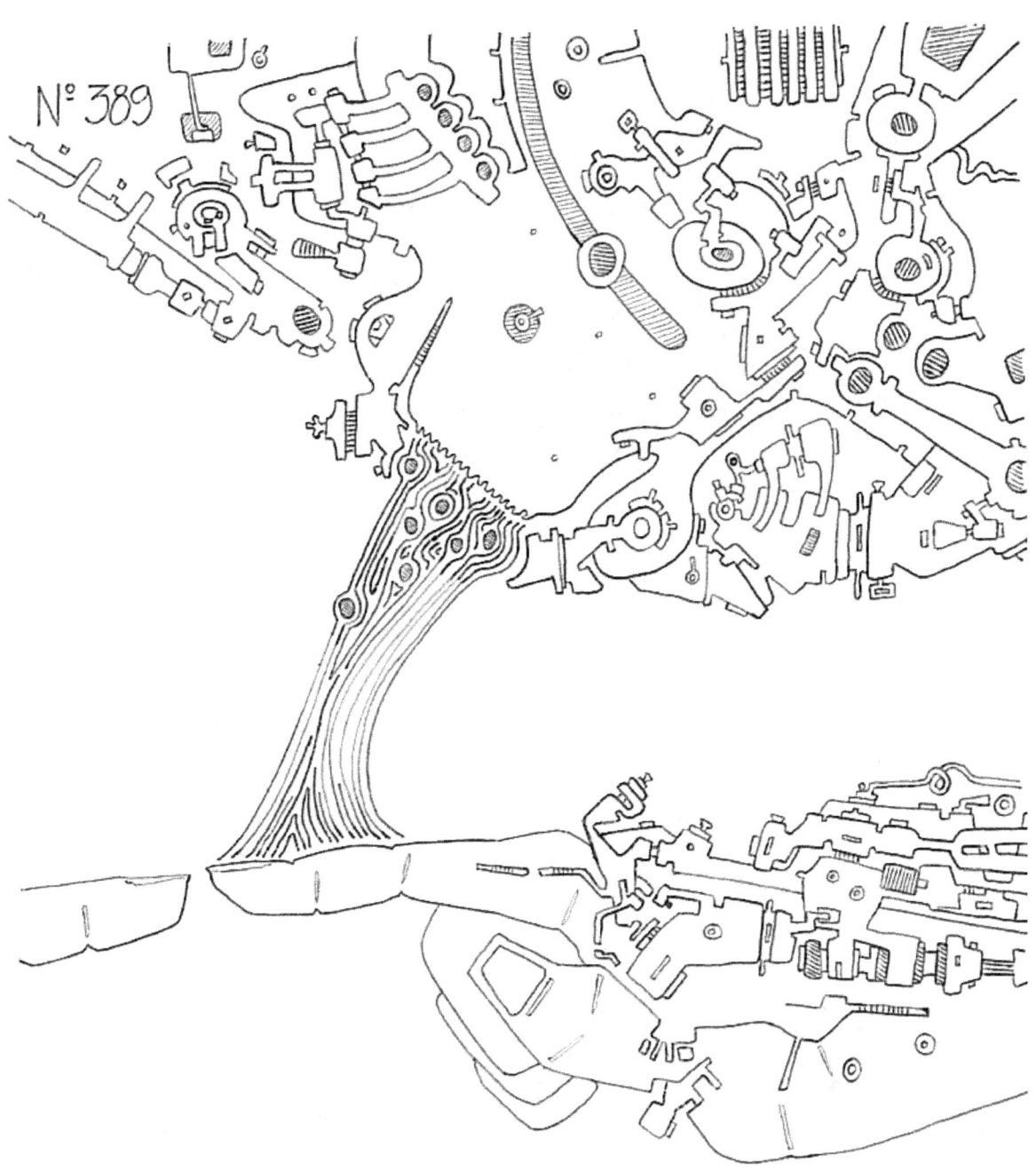

N° 390

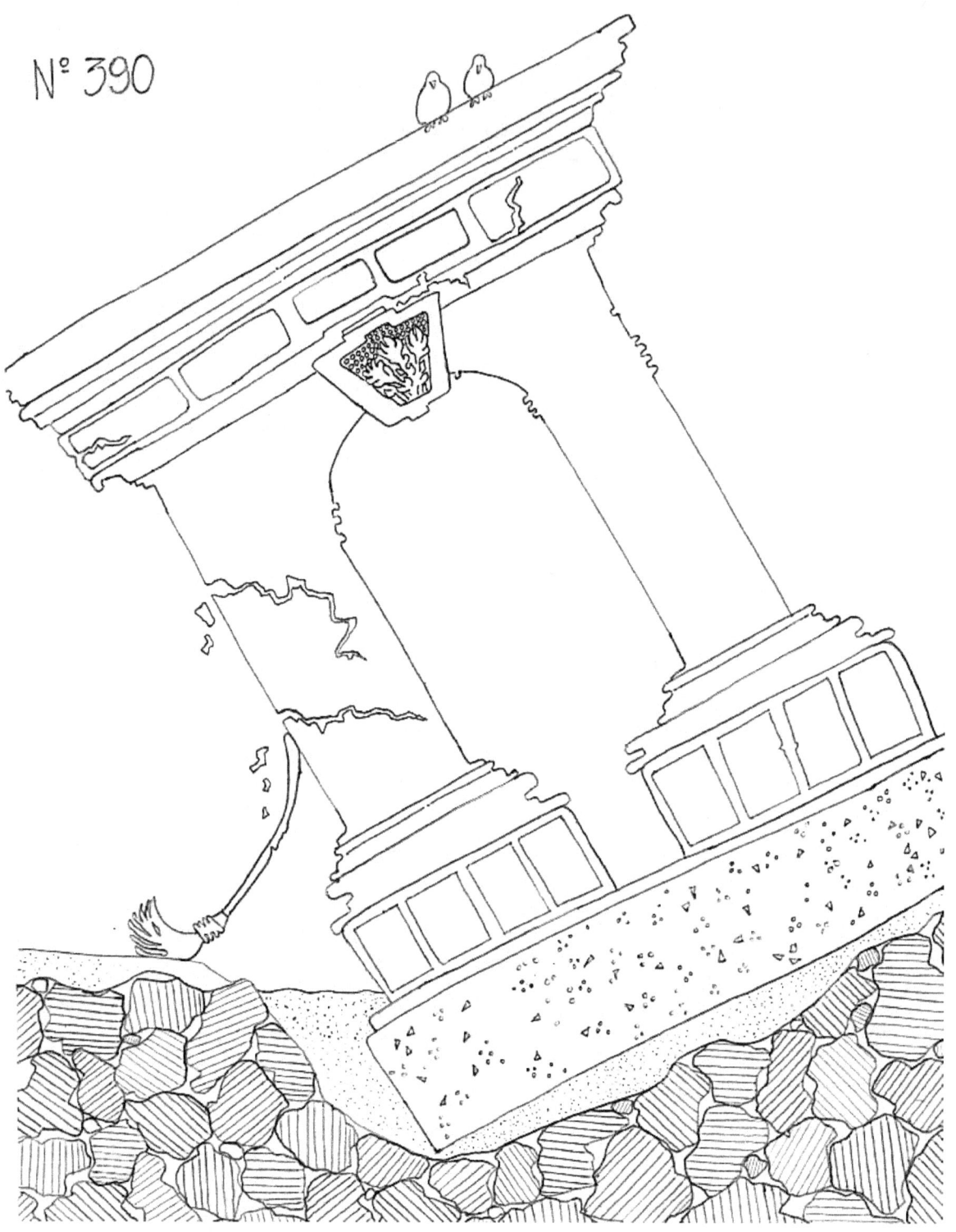

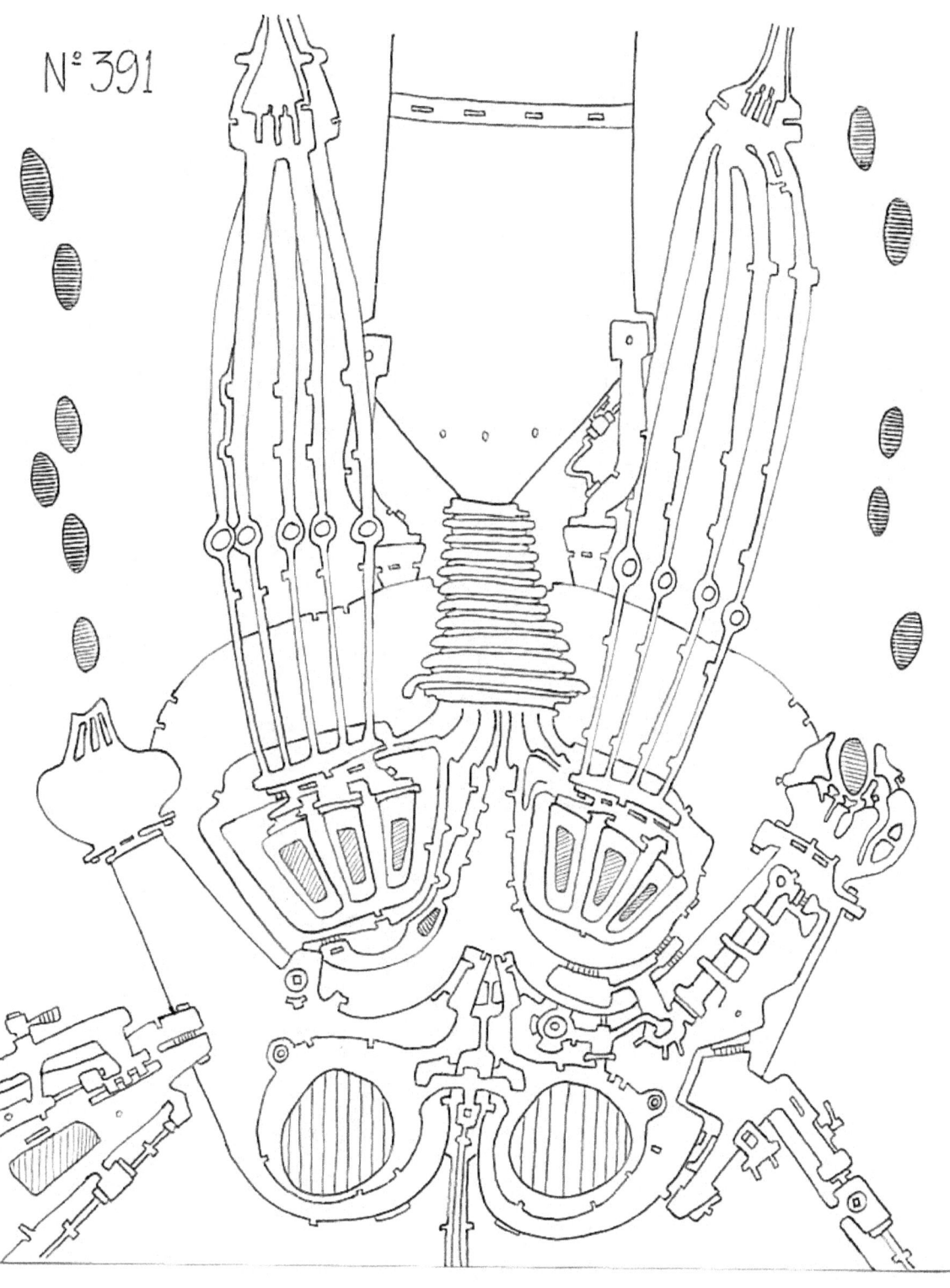

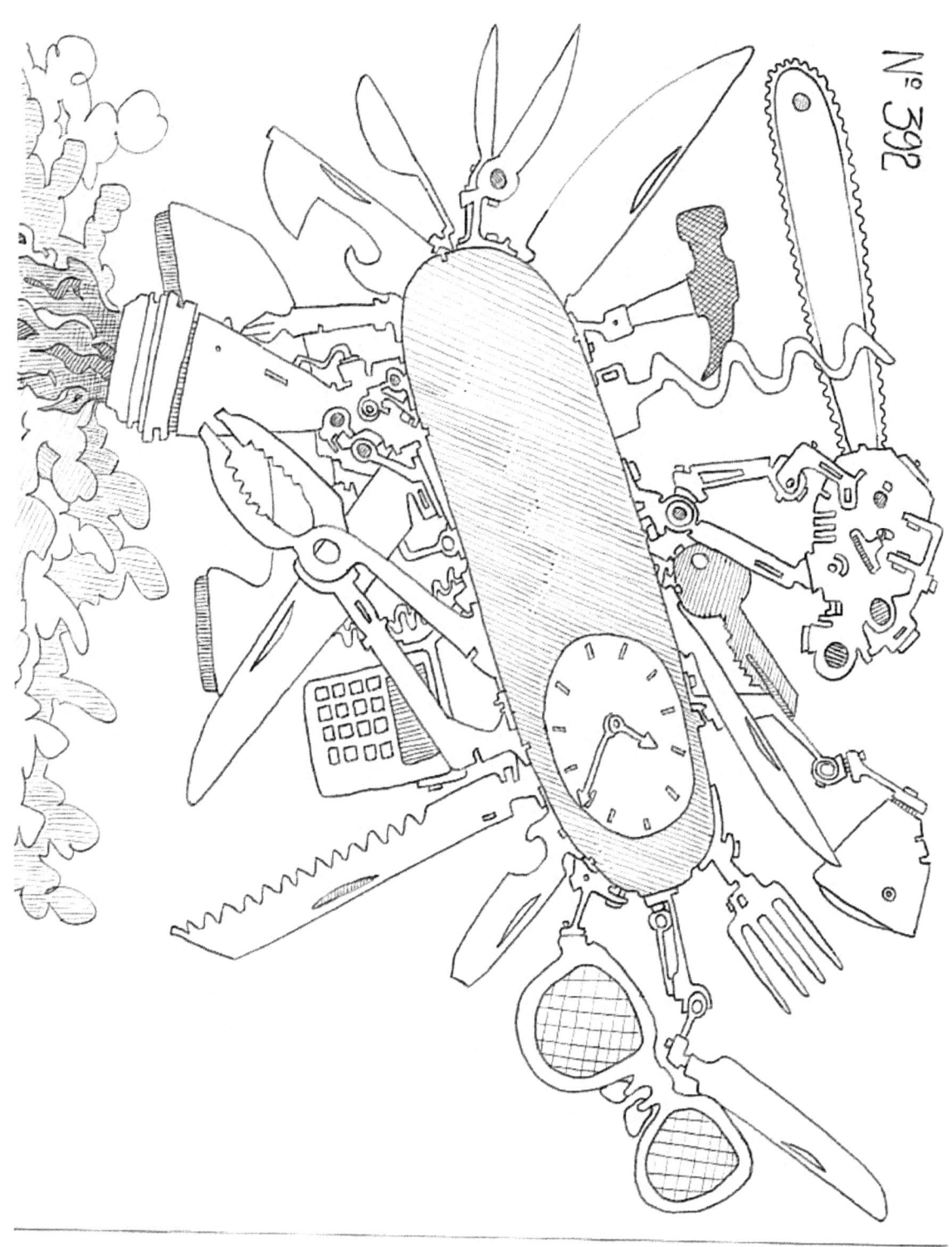

N° 394

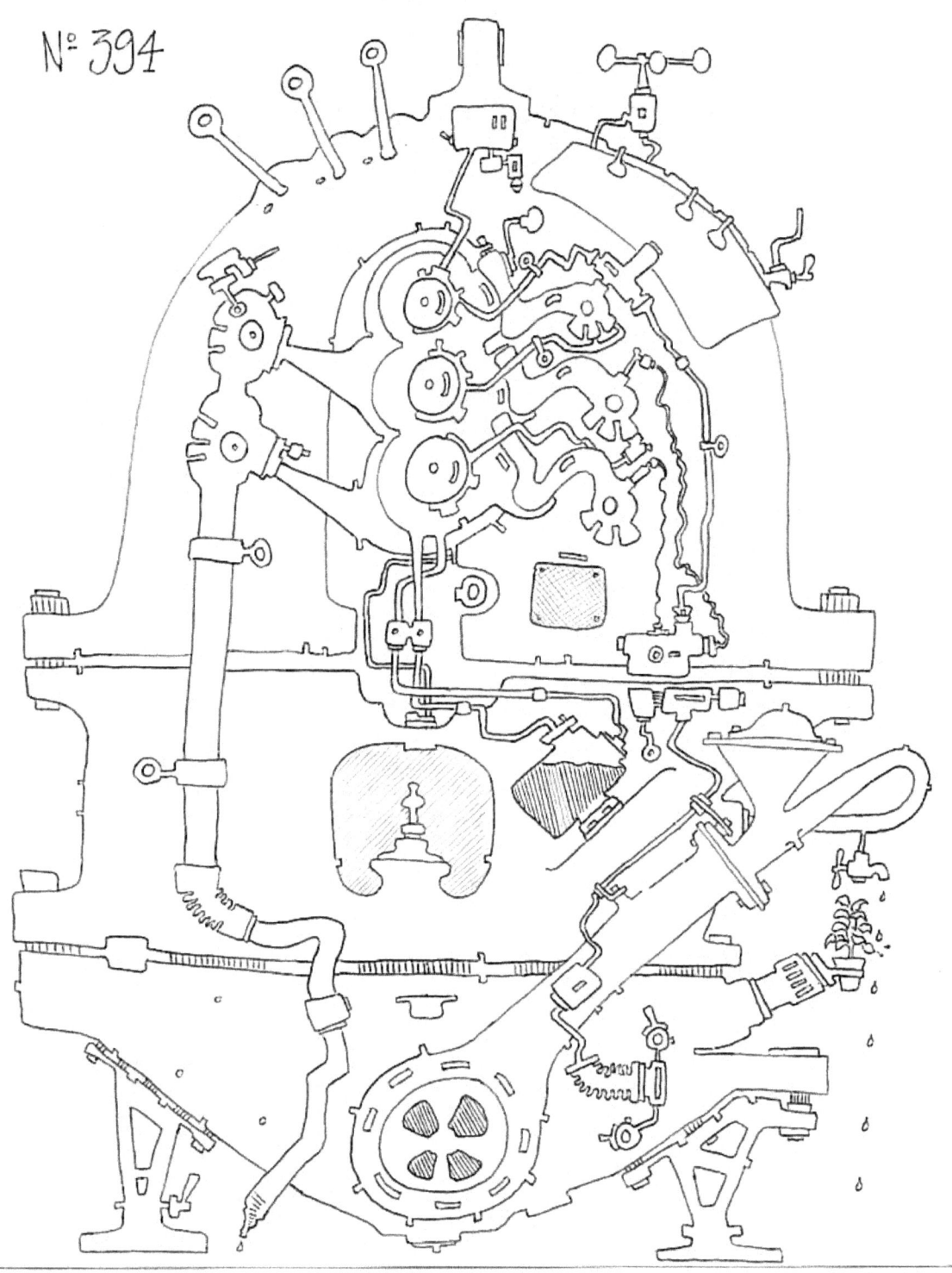

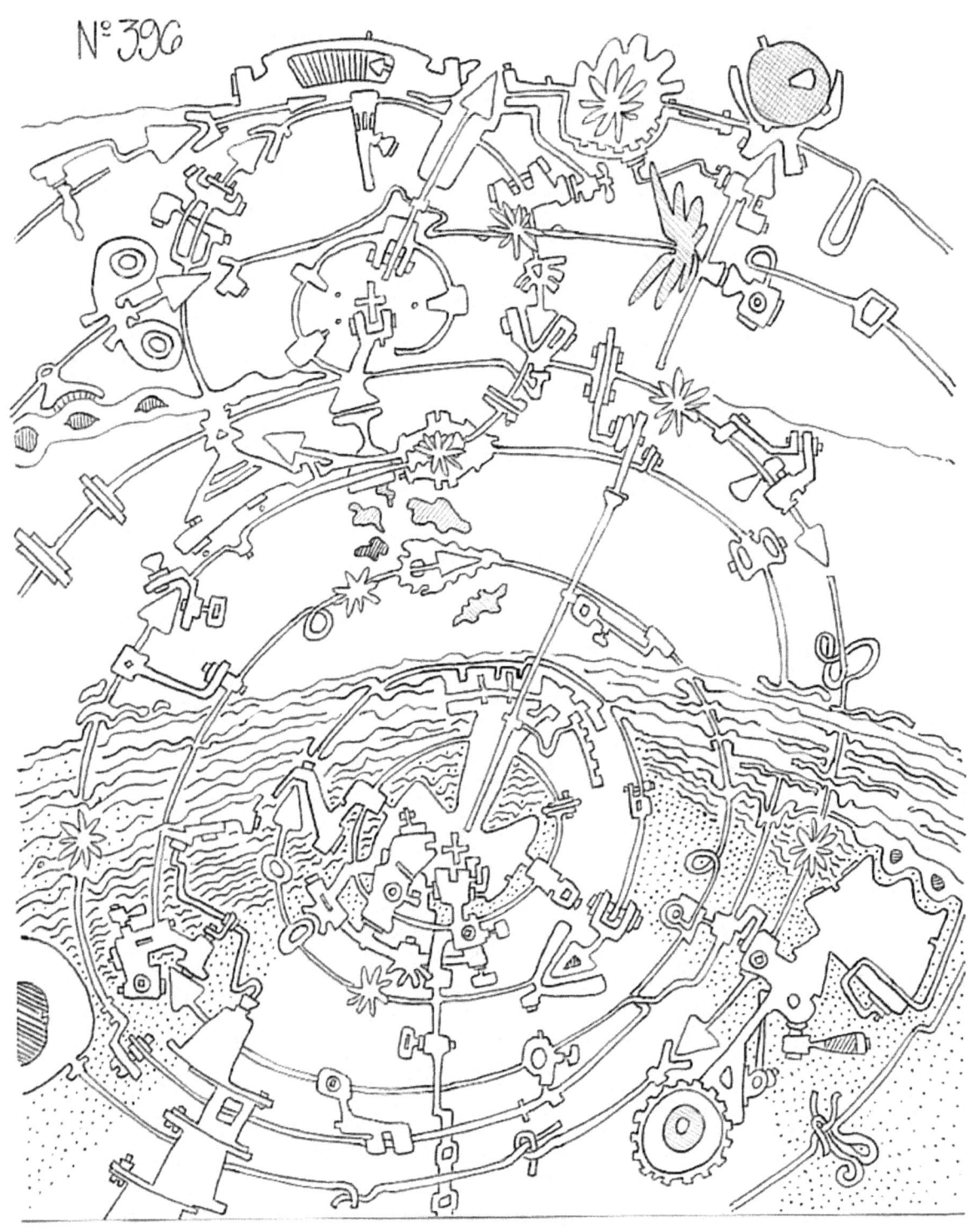

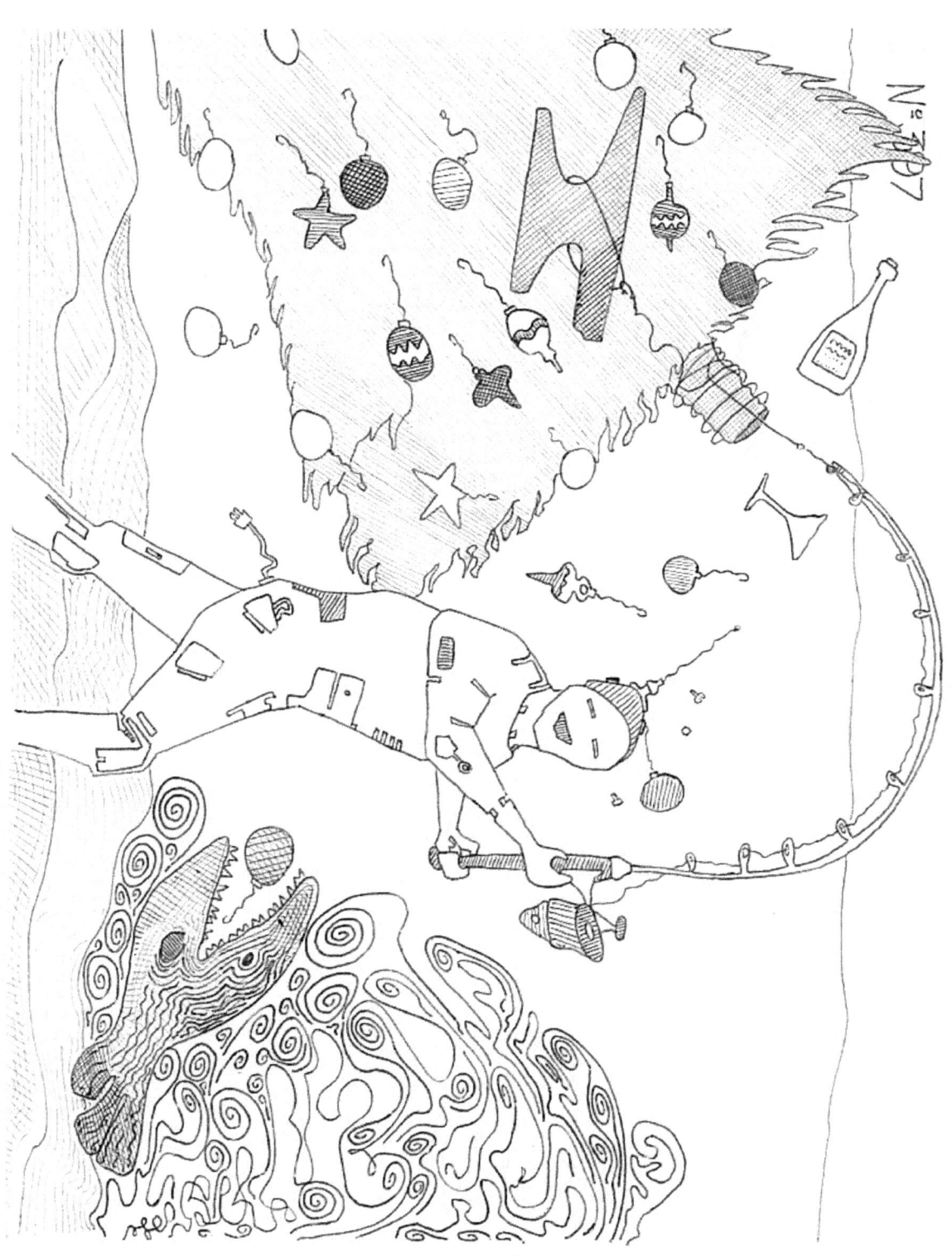

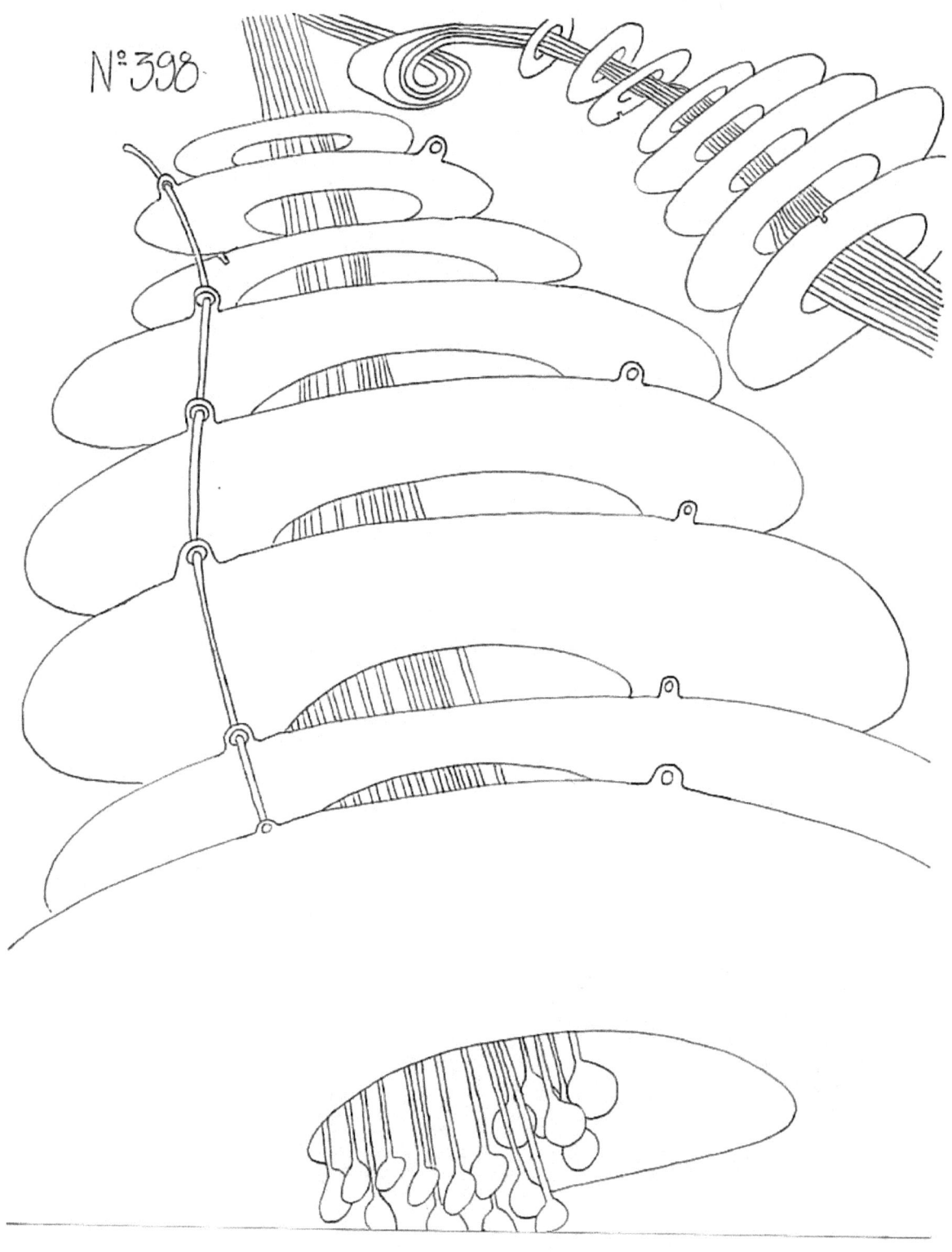

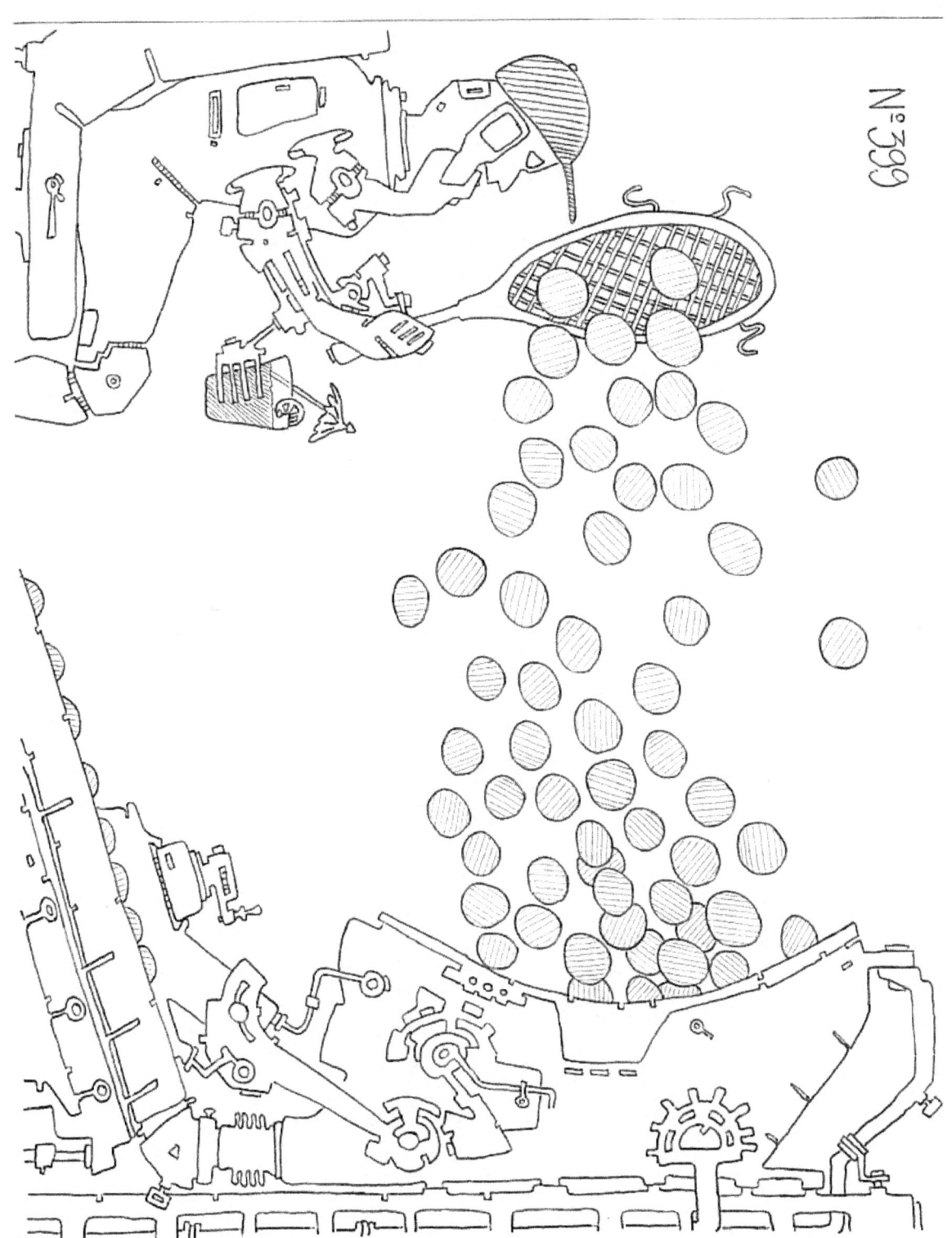

N° 400

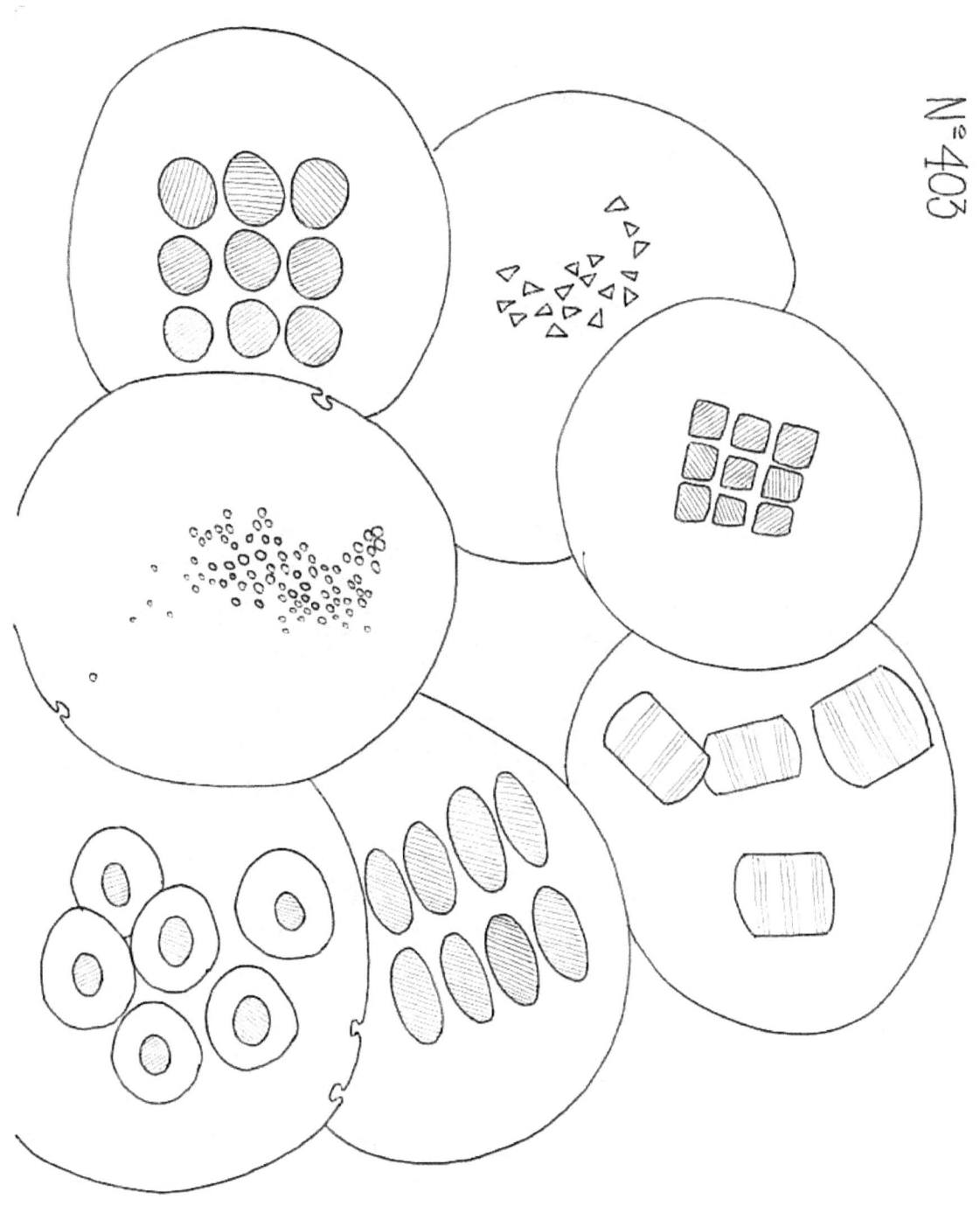

Nº 403

N° 404

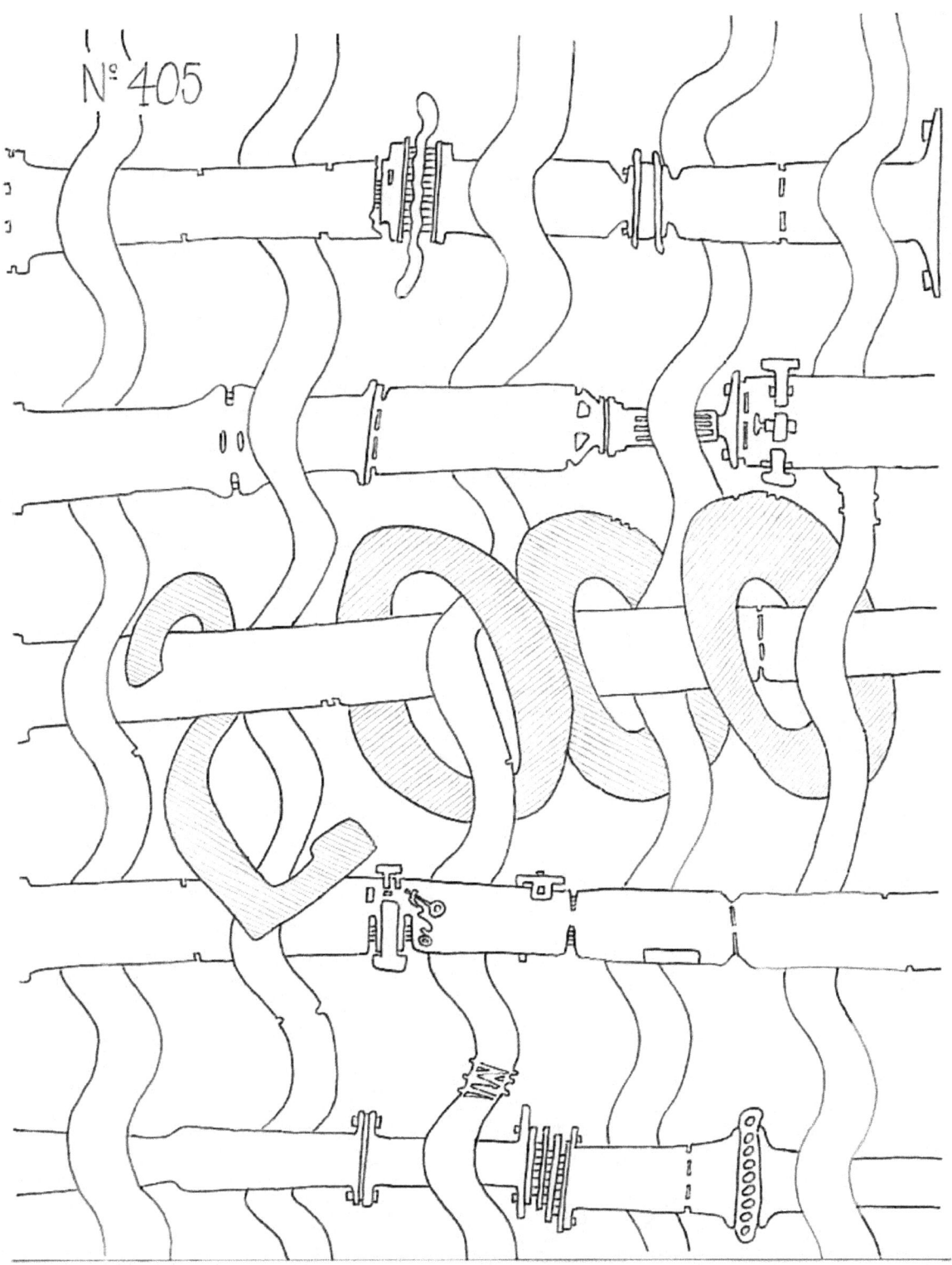

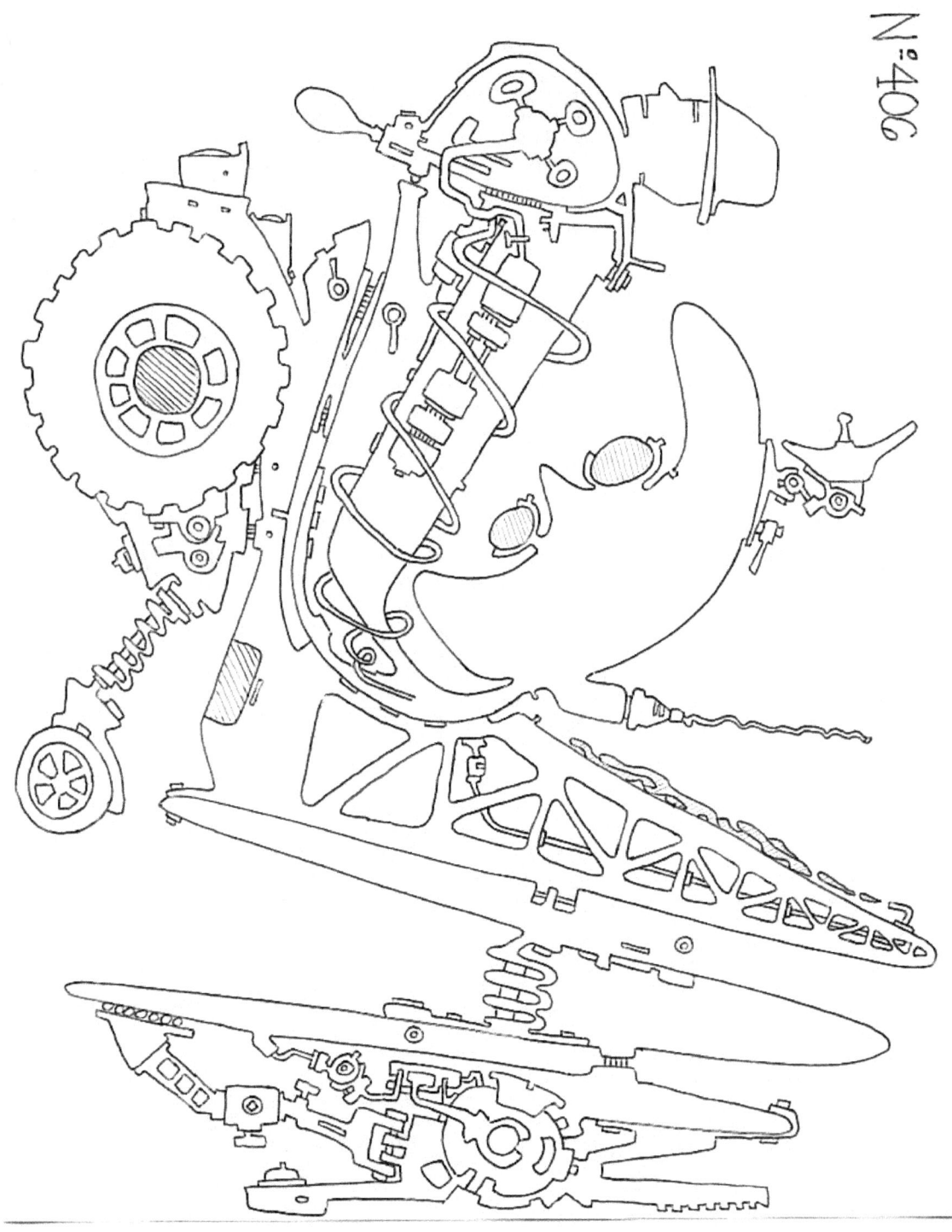

Nº 407

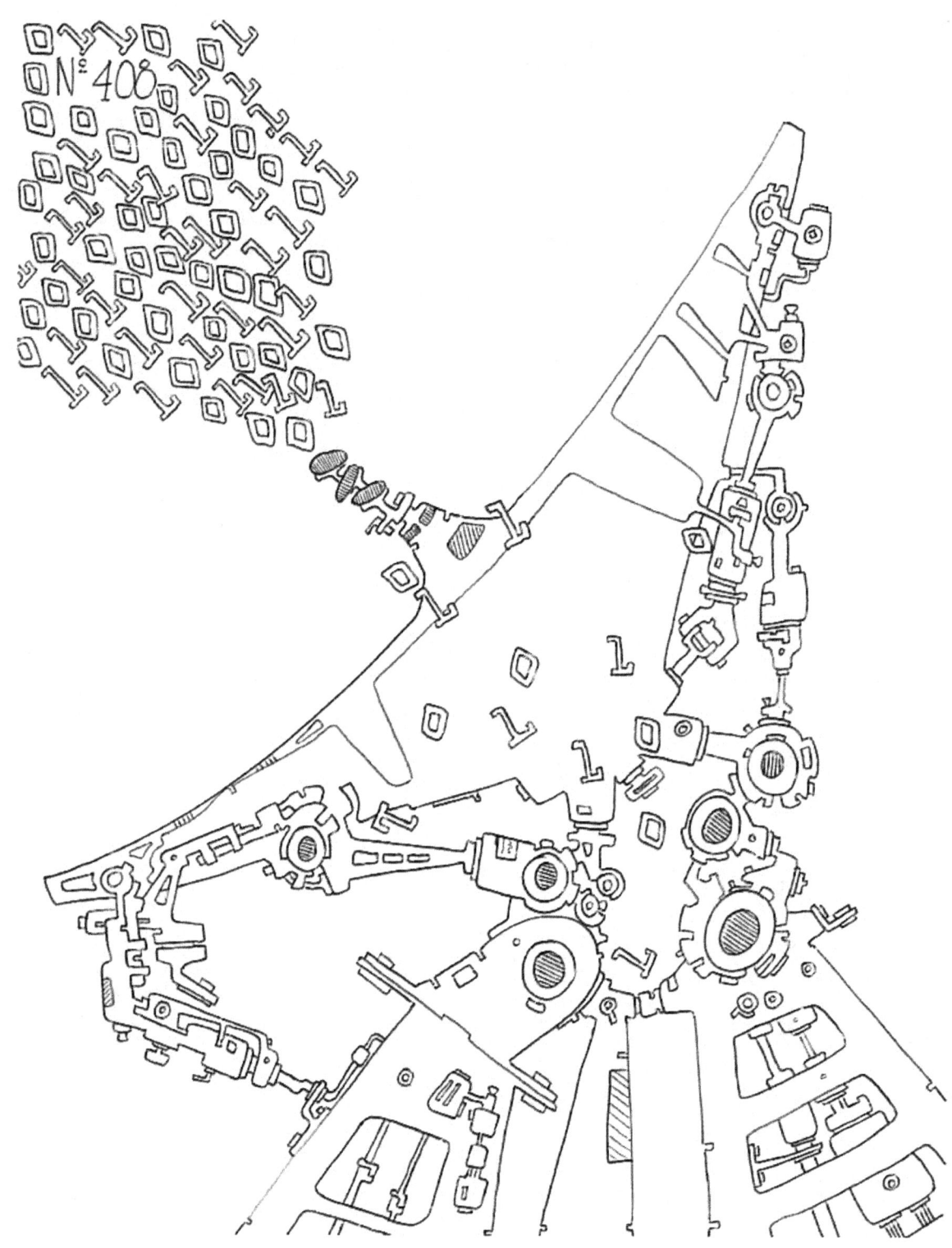

N° 409

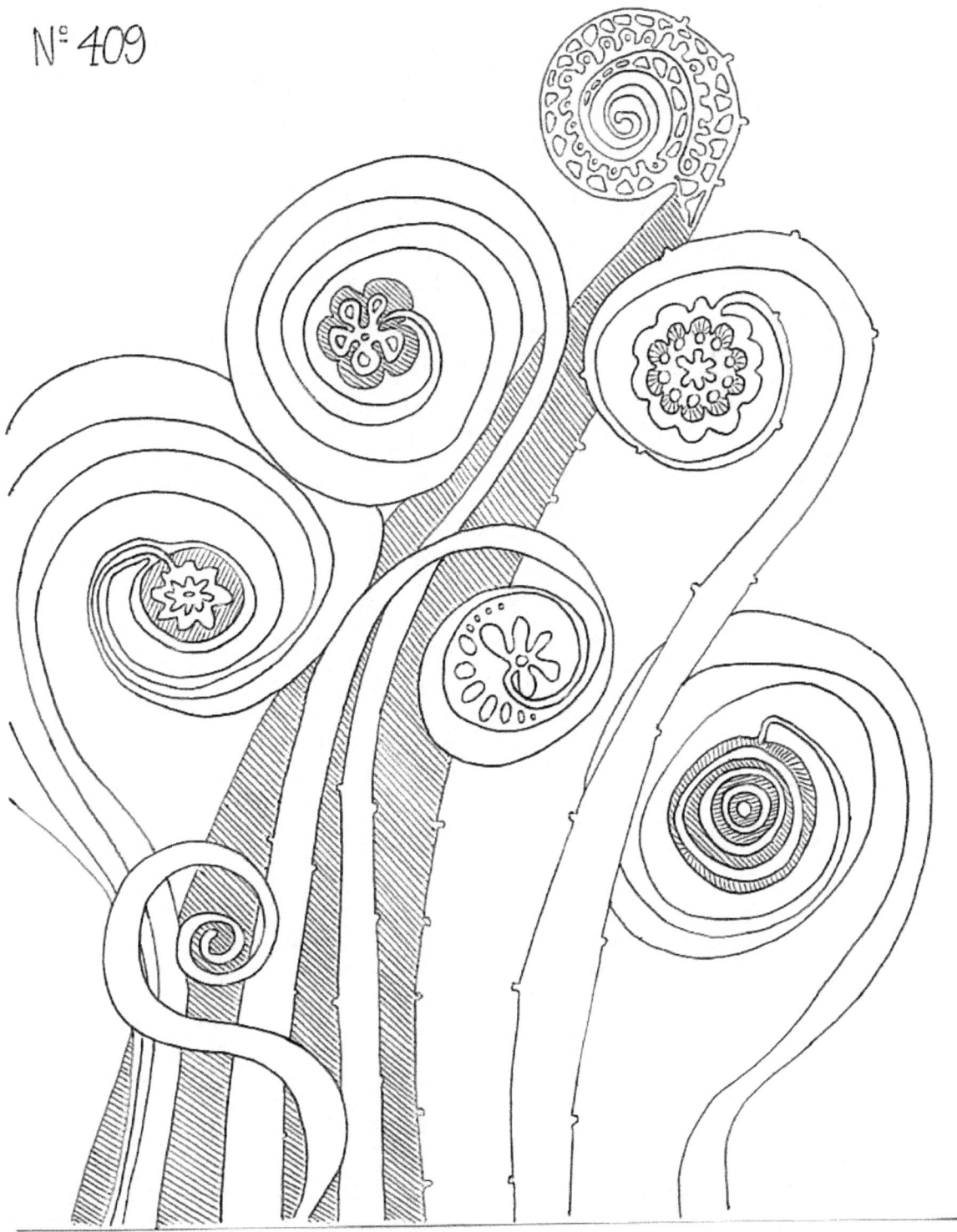

Nº 410

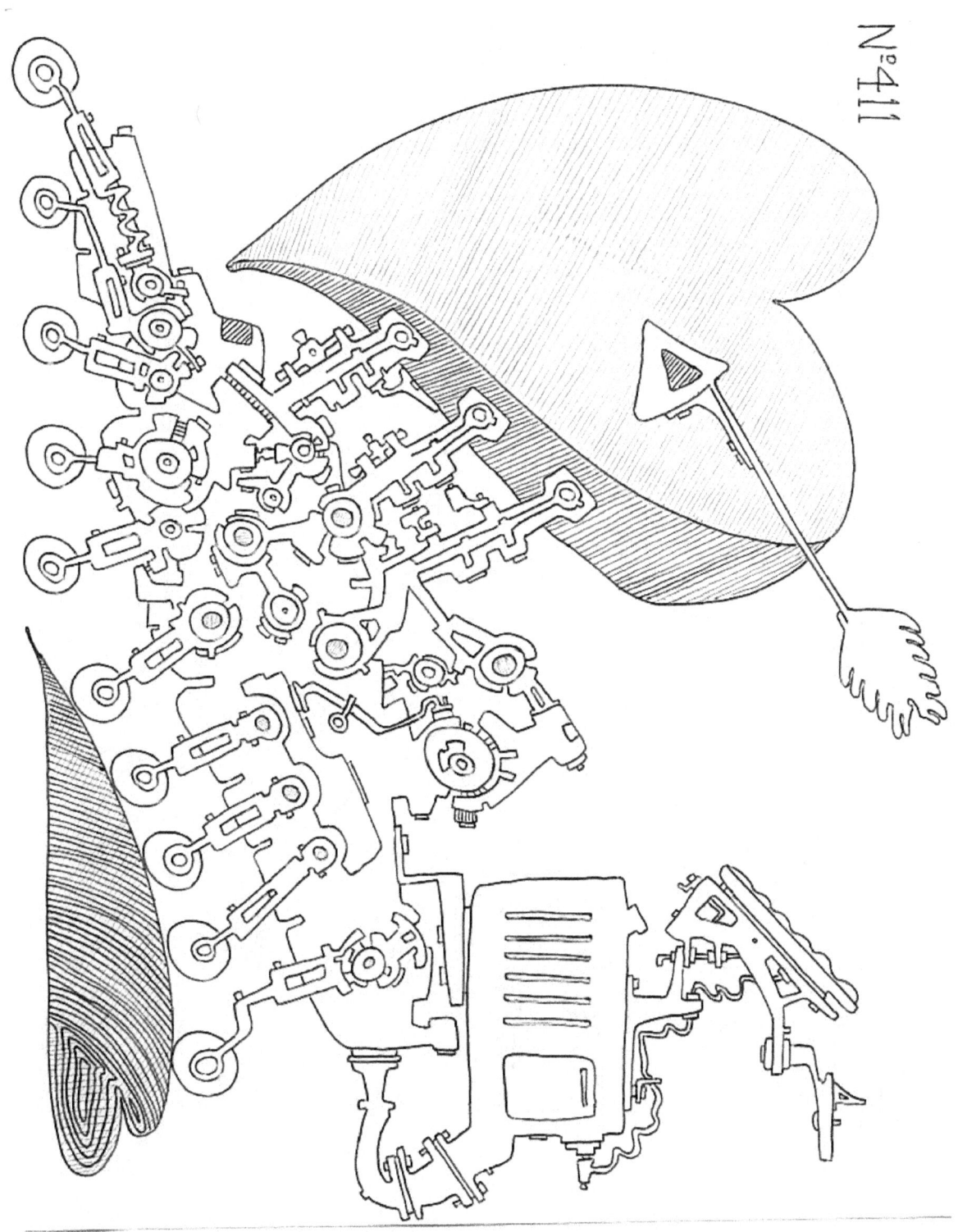

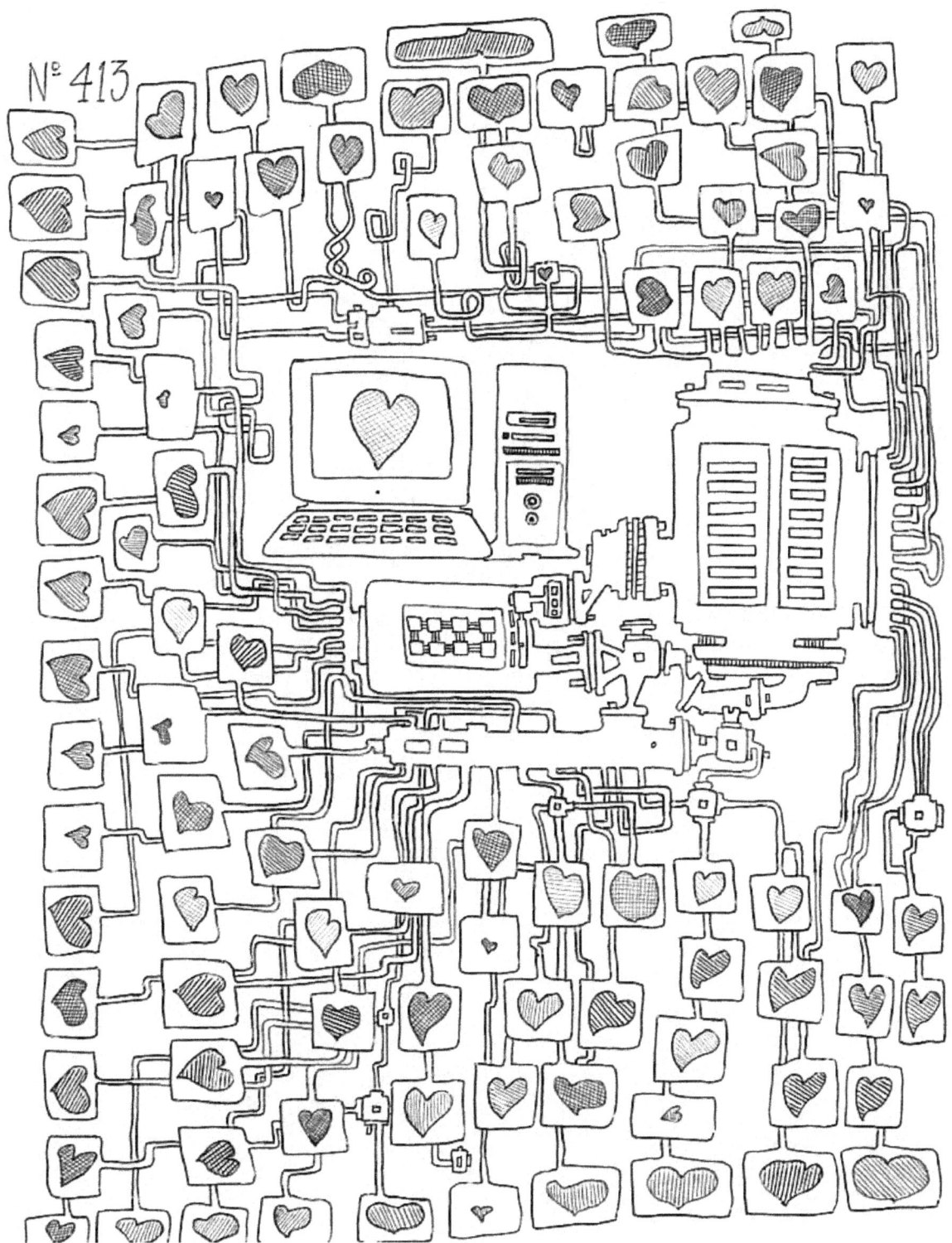

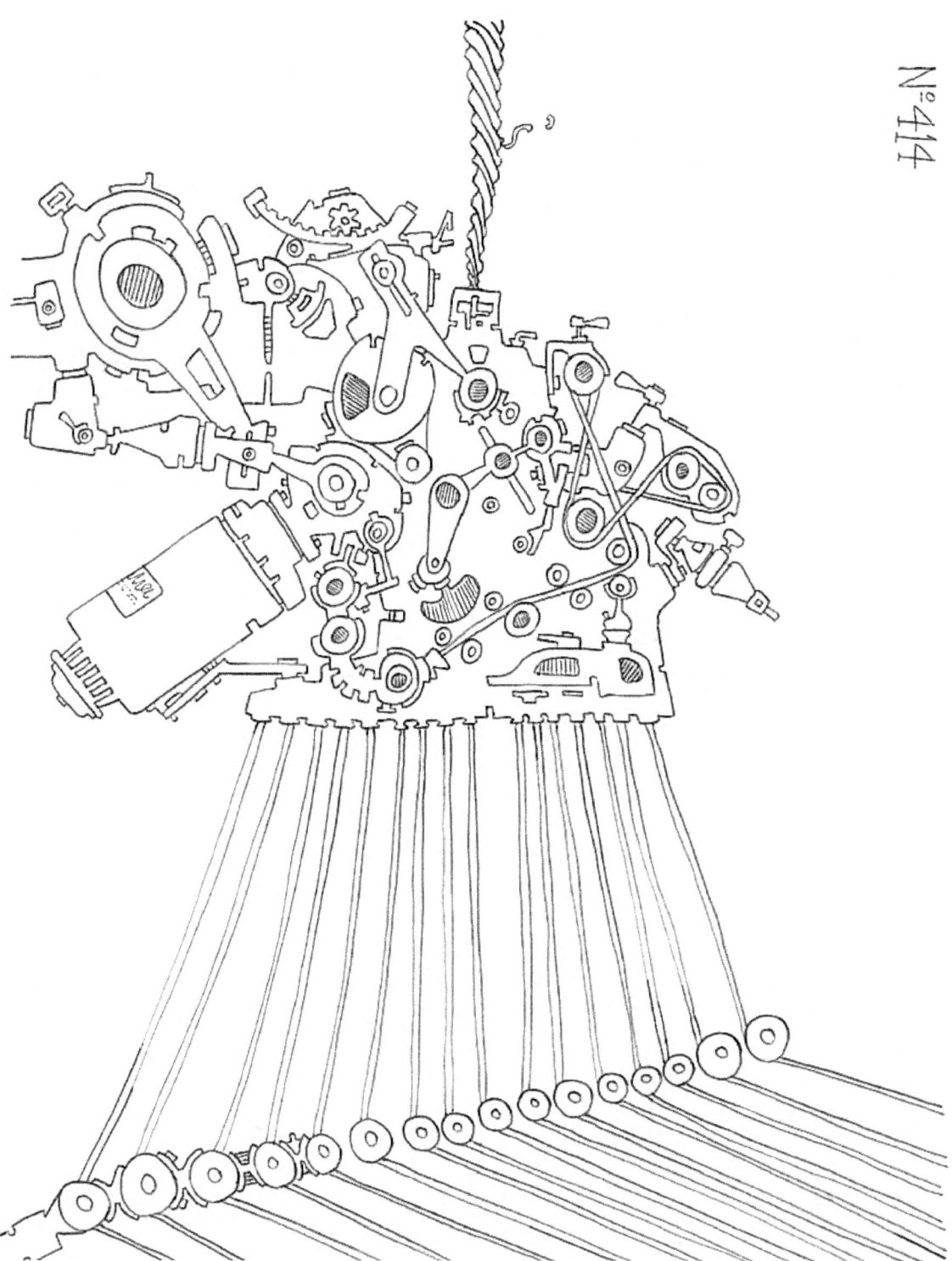

Nº 414

N°415

N° 416

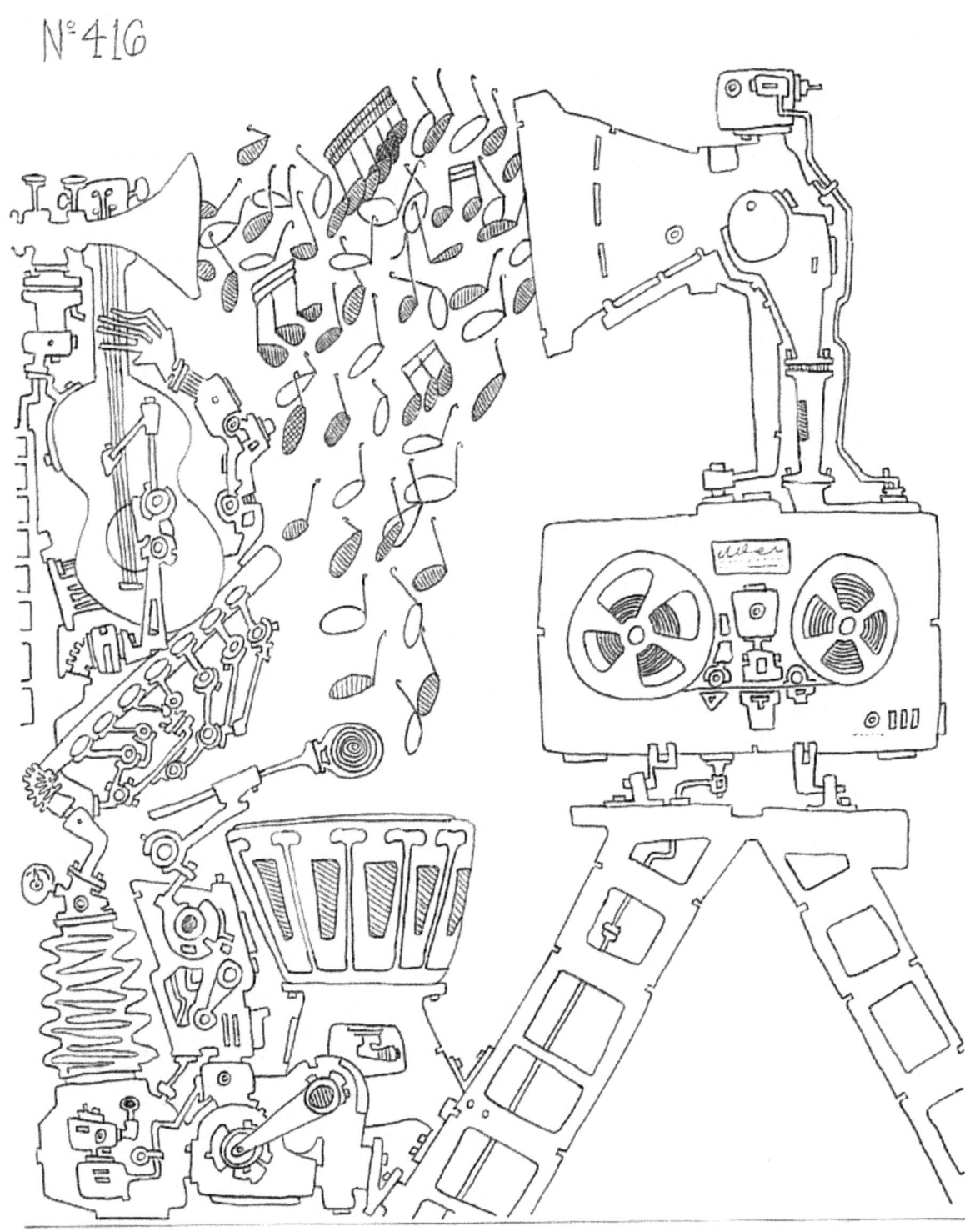

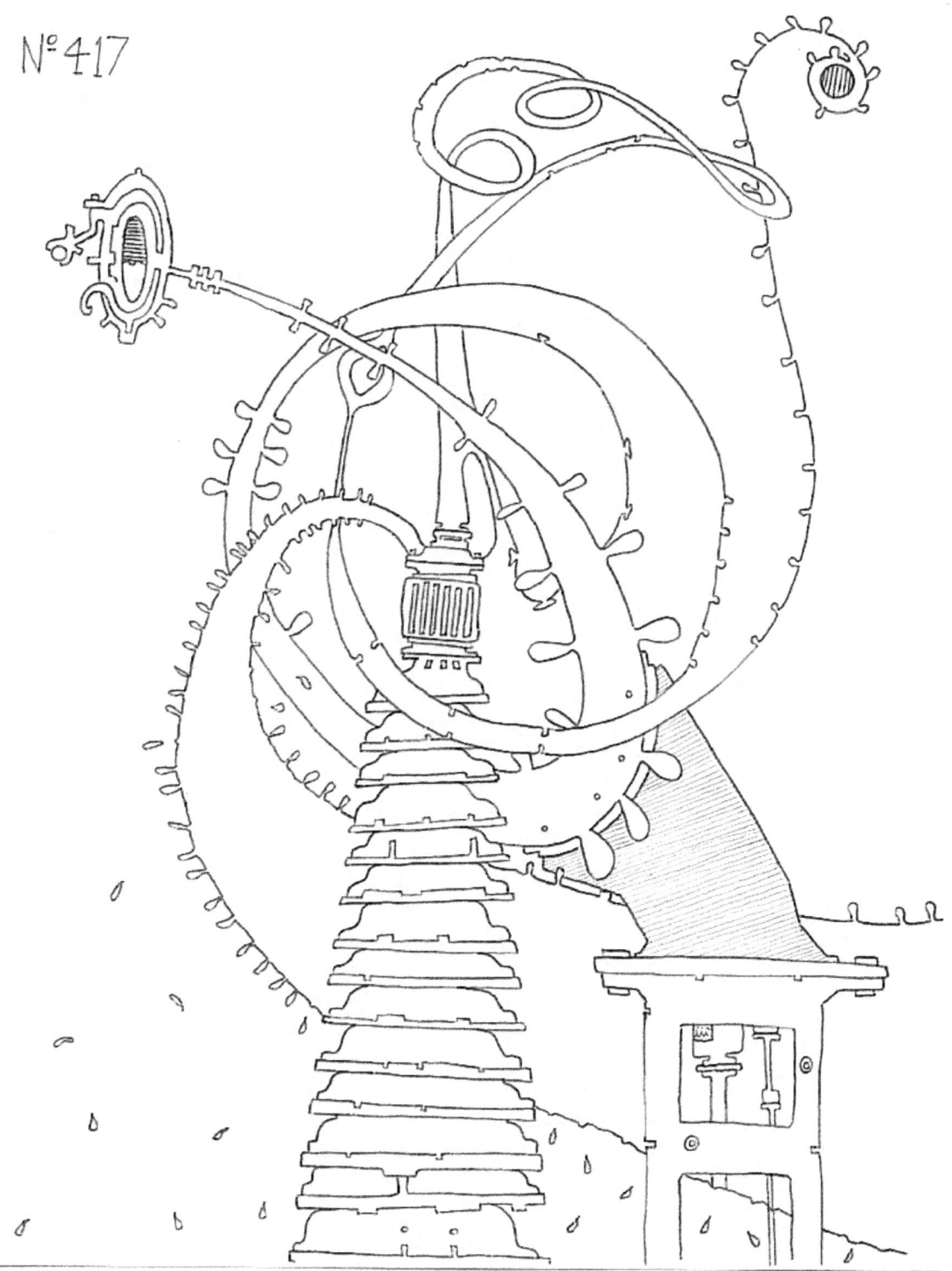

Nº 417

N° 418
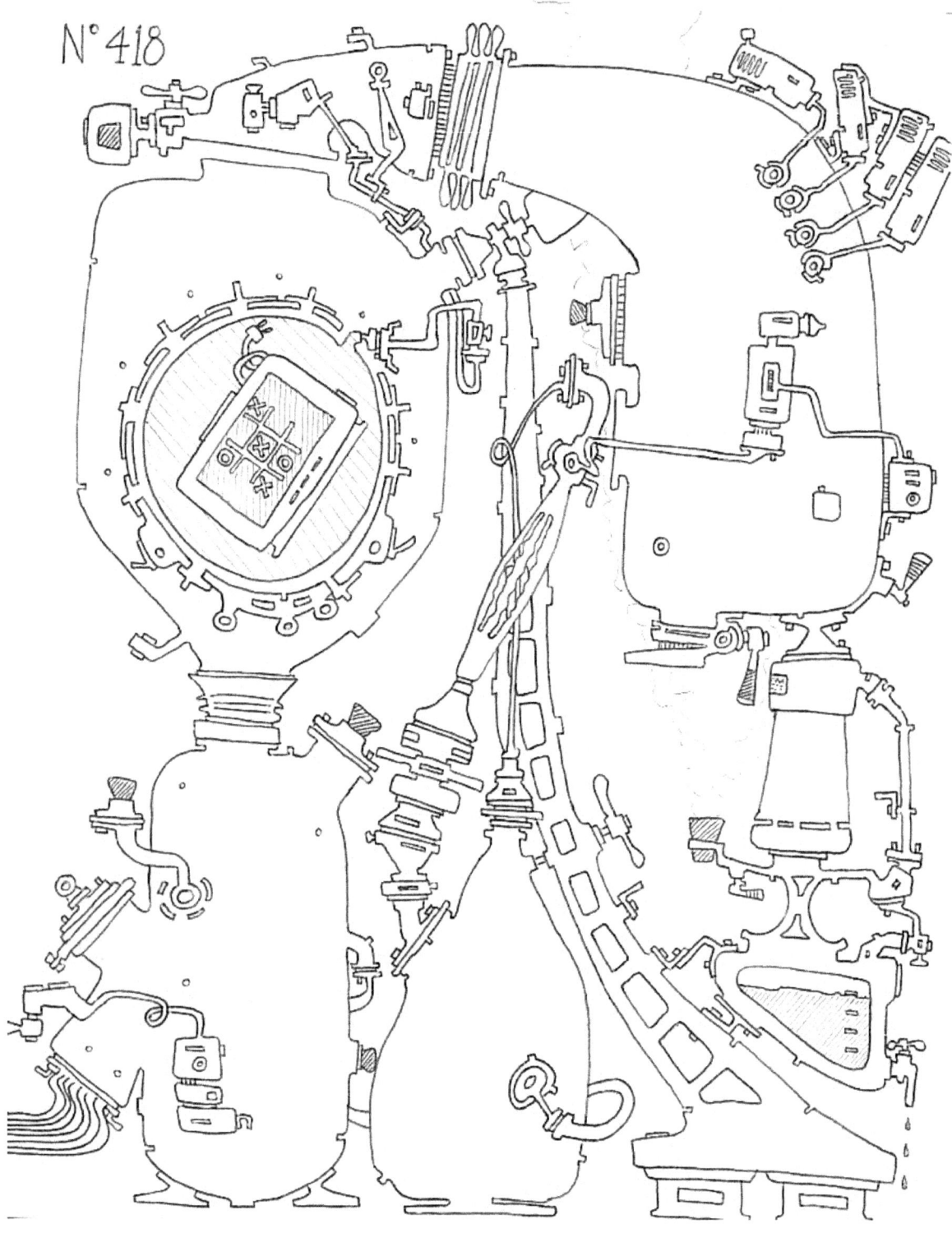

N° 419

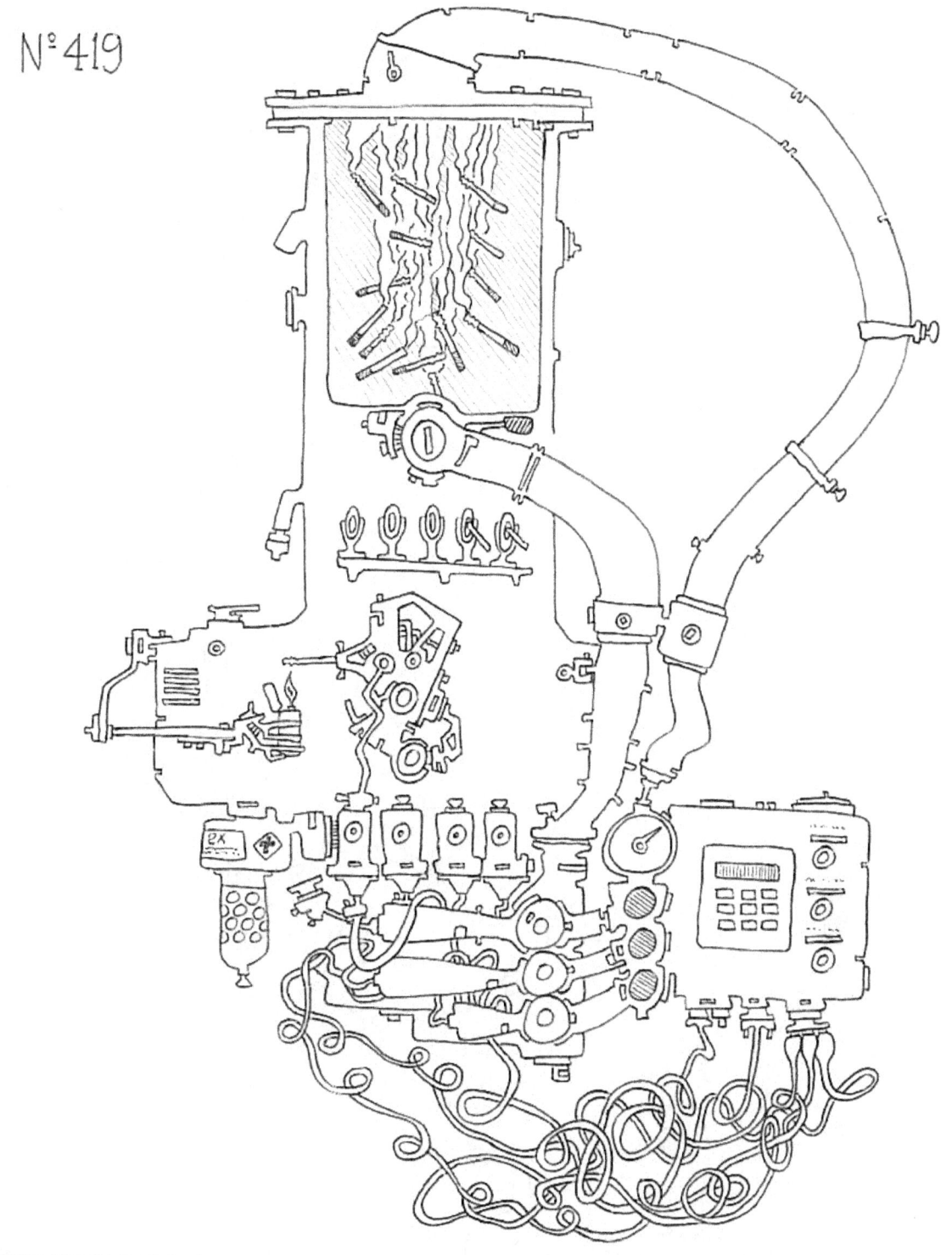

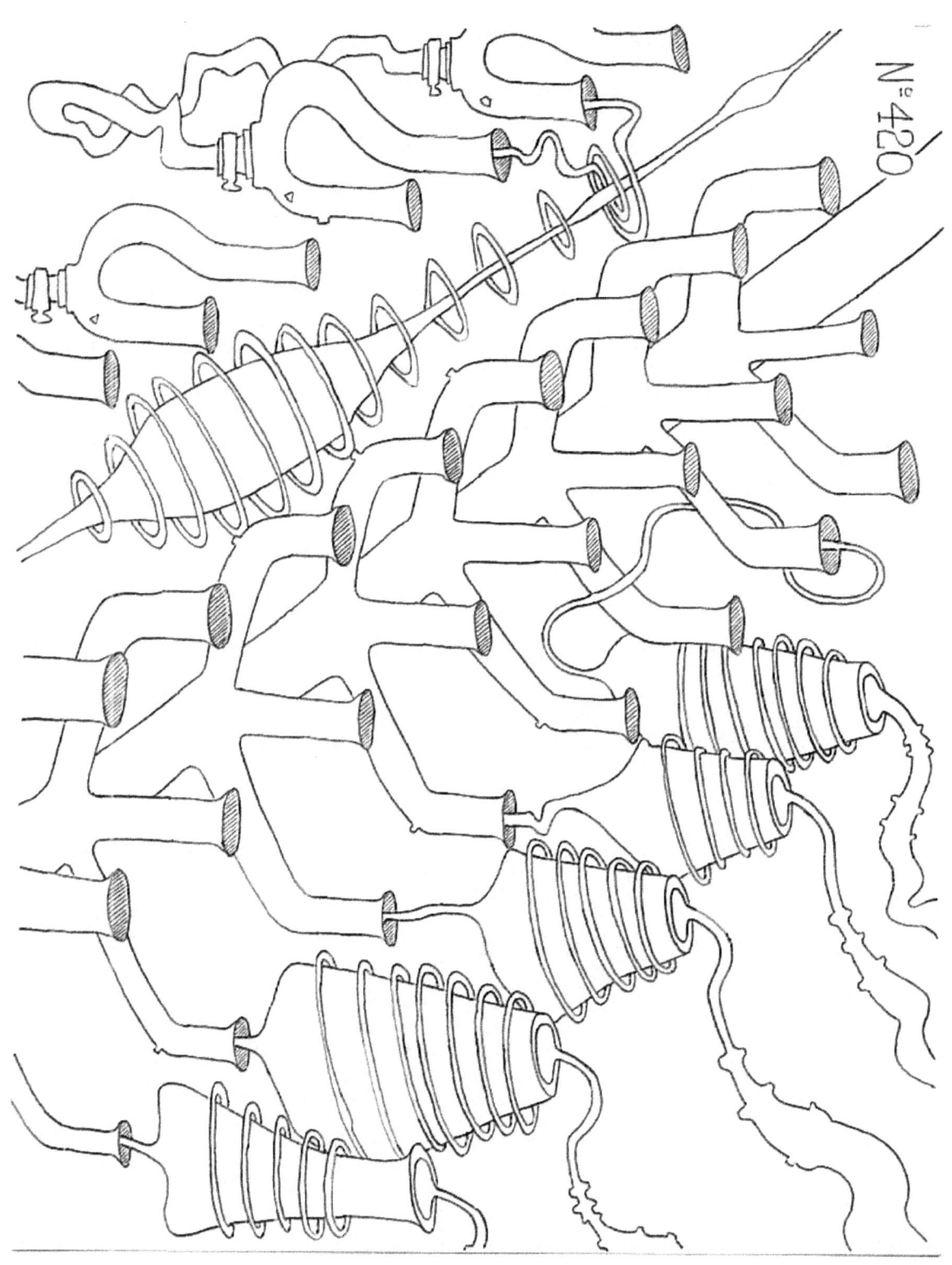

N° 421

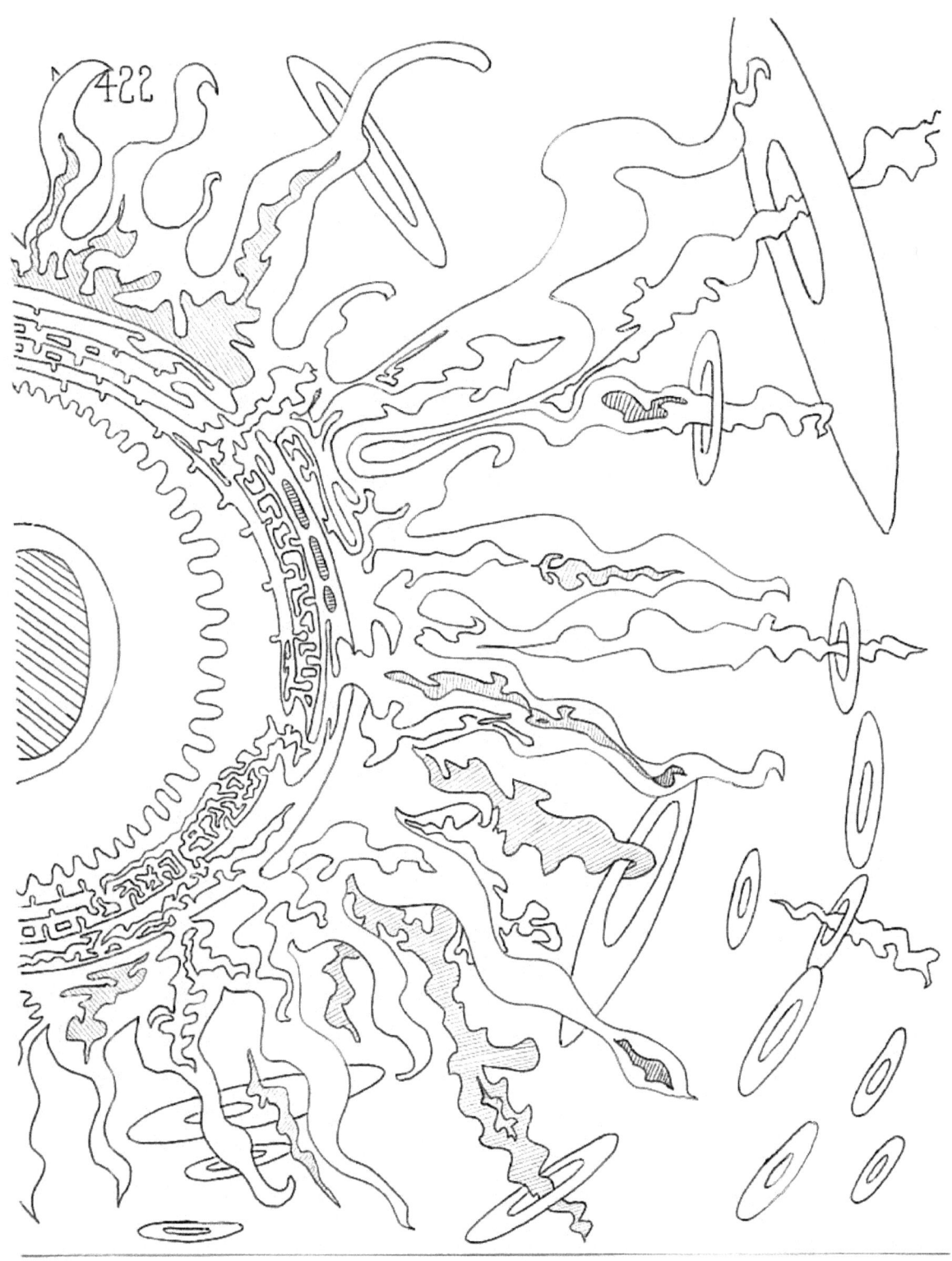

N°423

N° 424

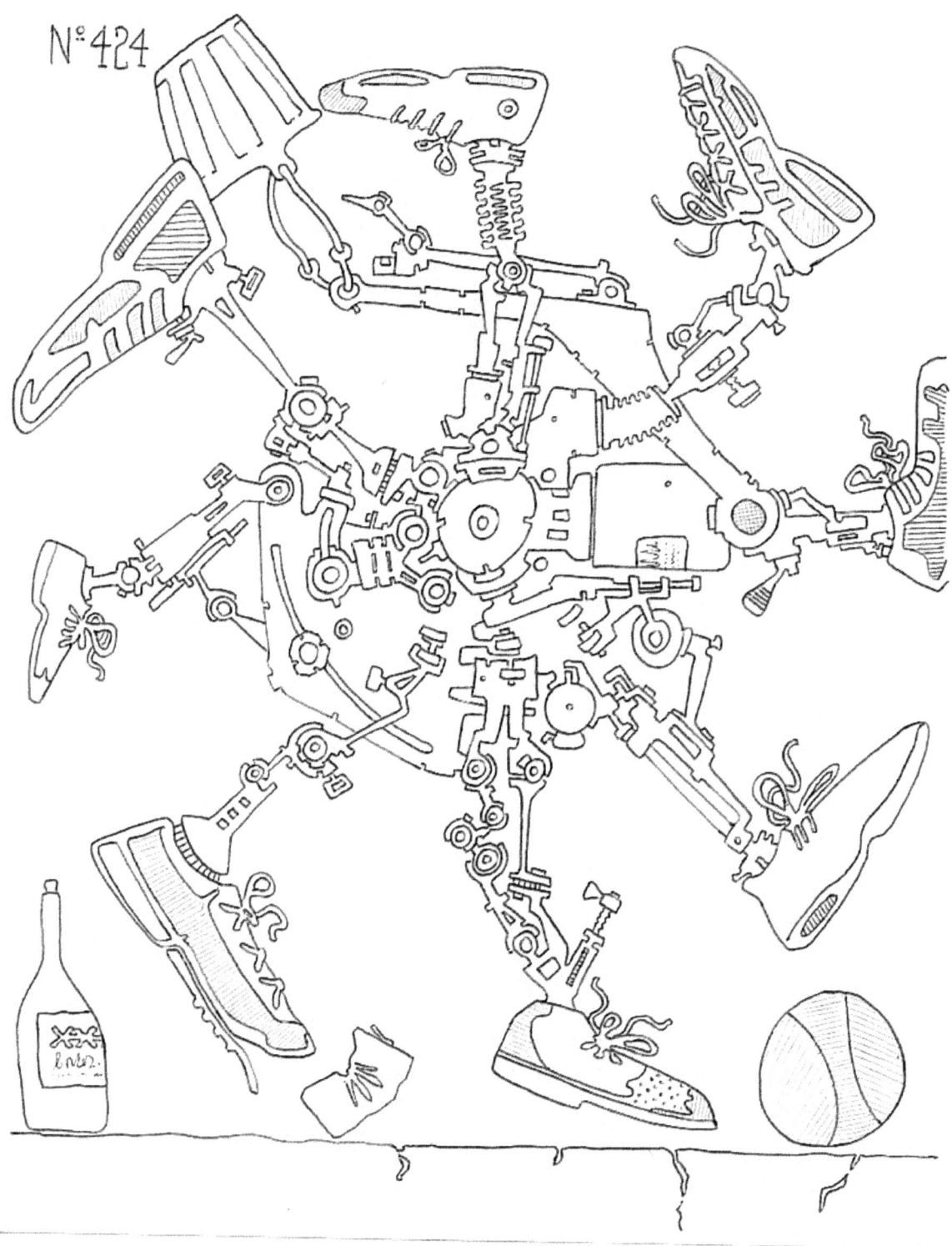

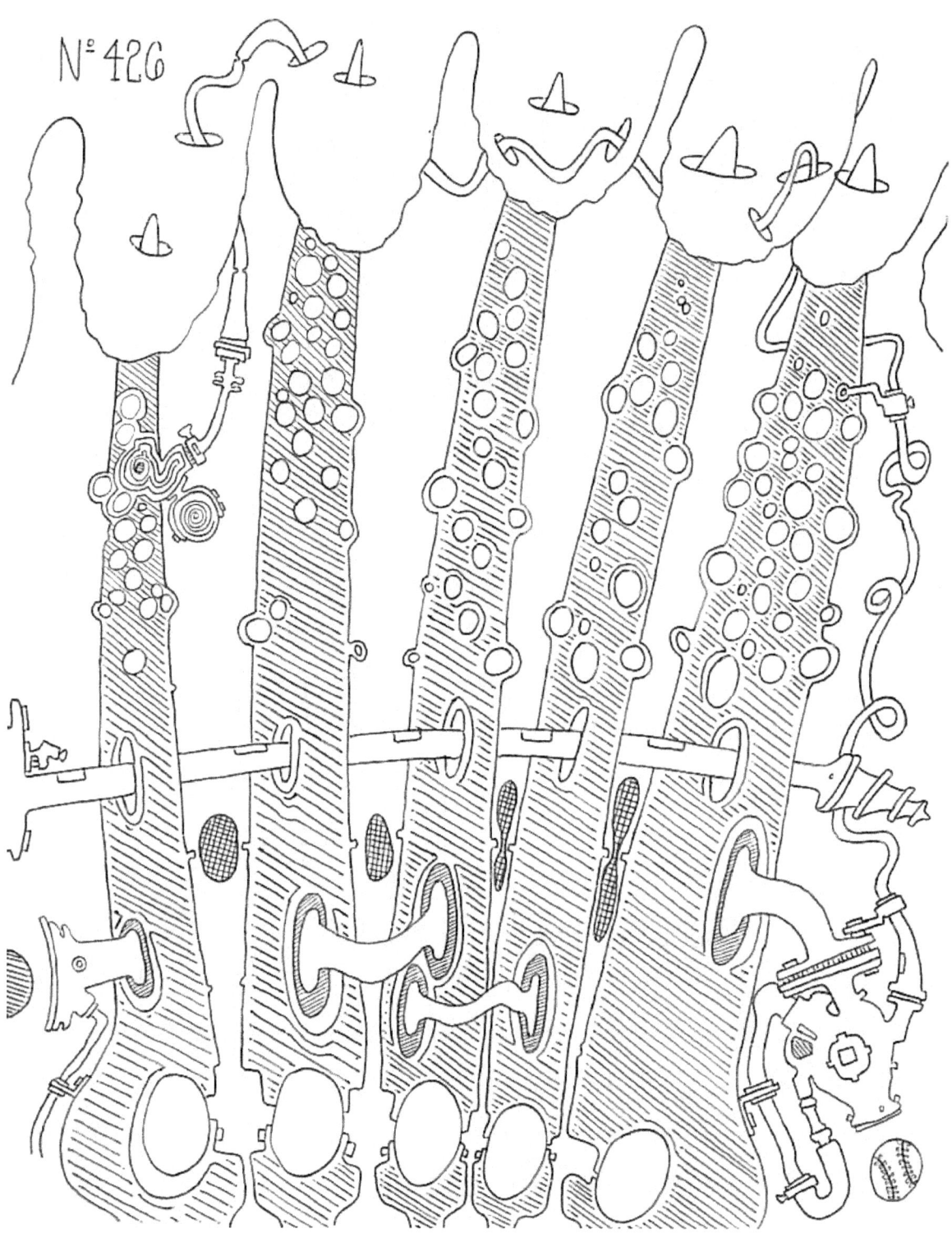

Nº 427

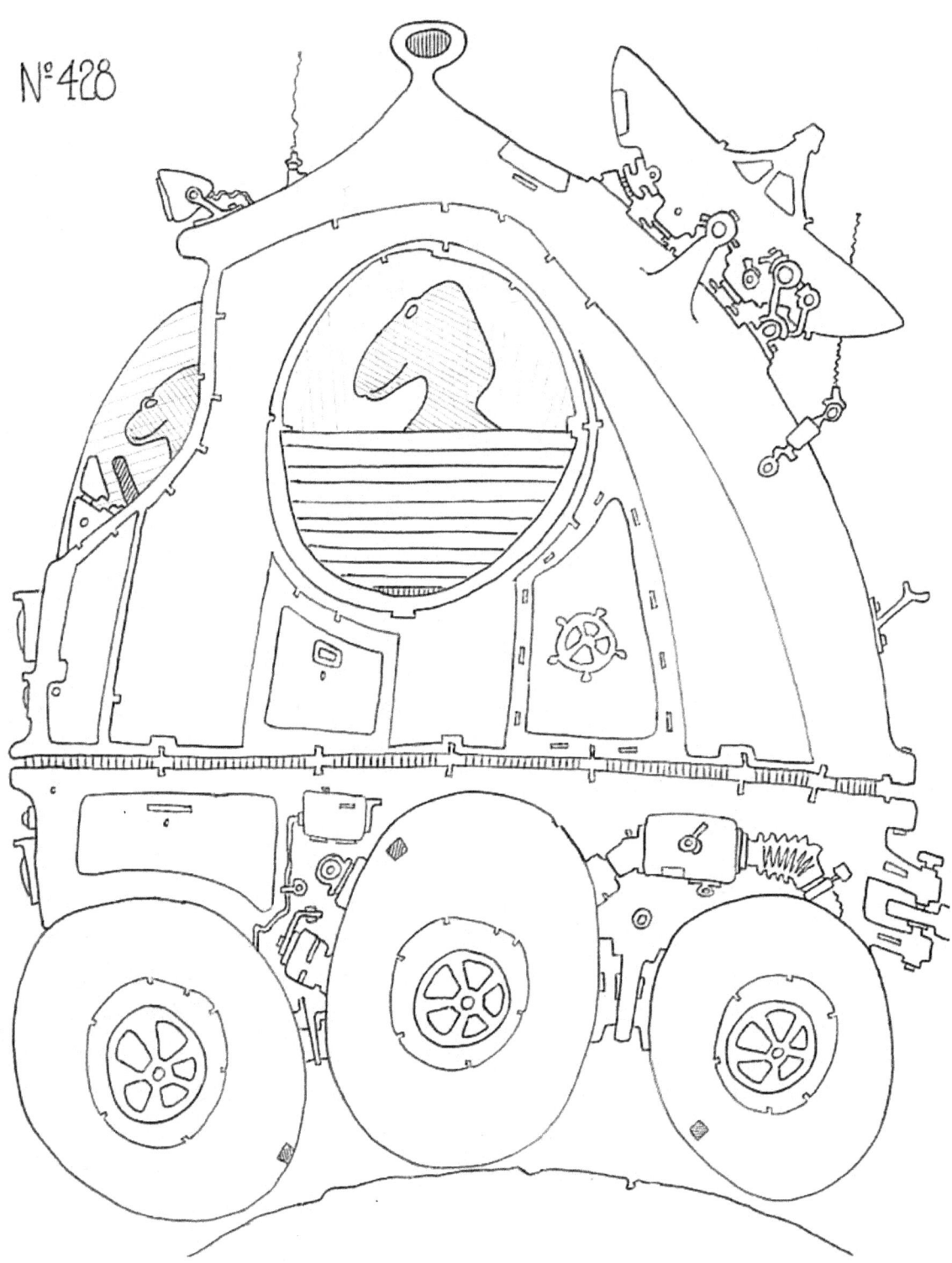

N° 429

N° 430

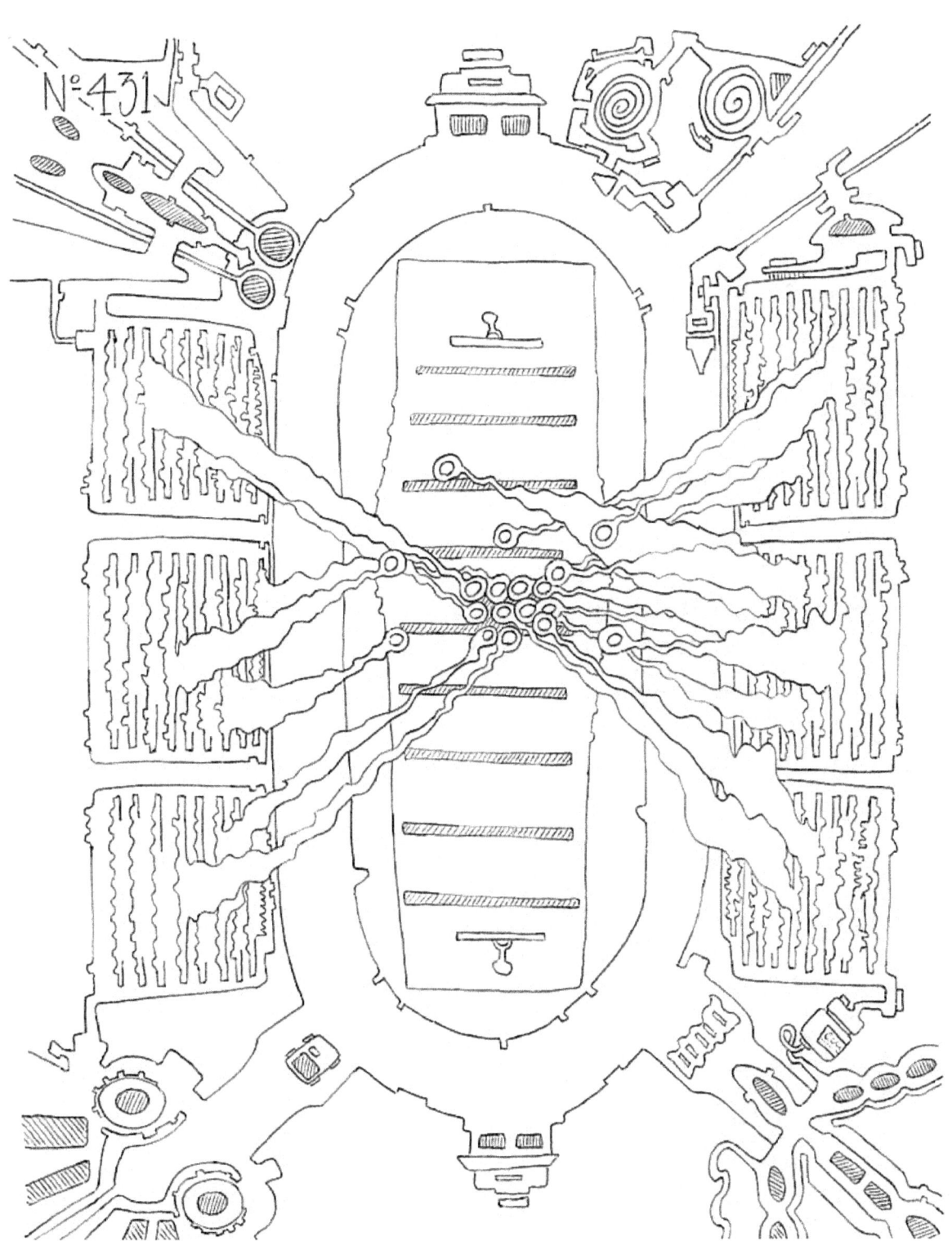

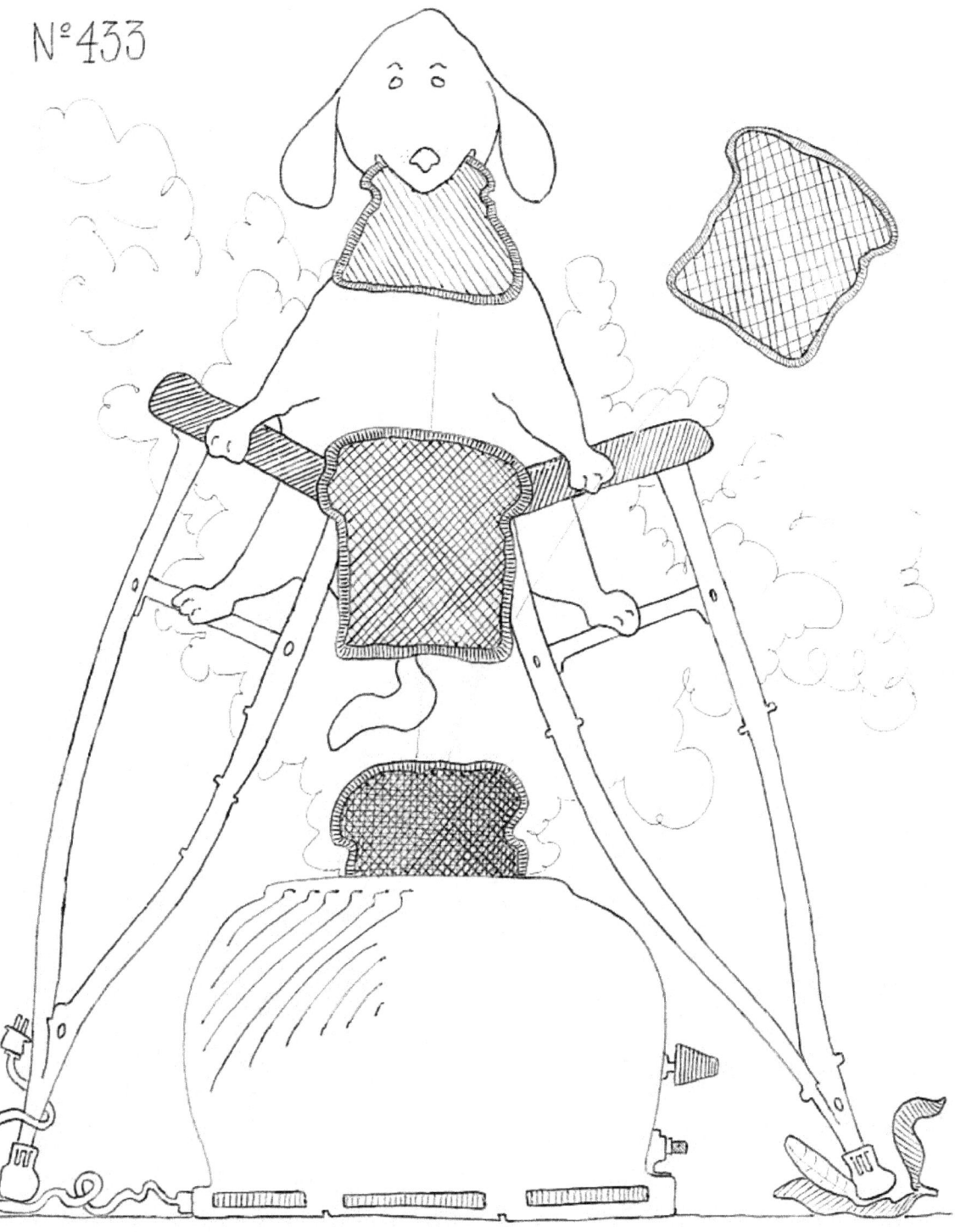

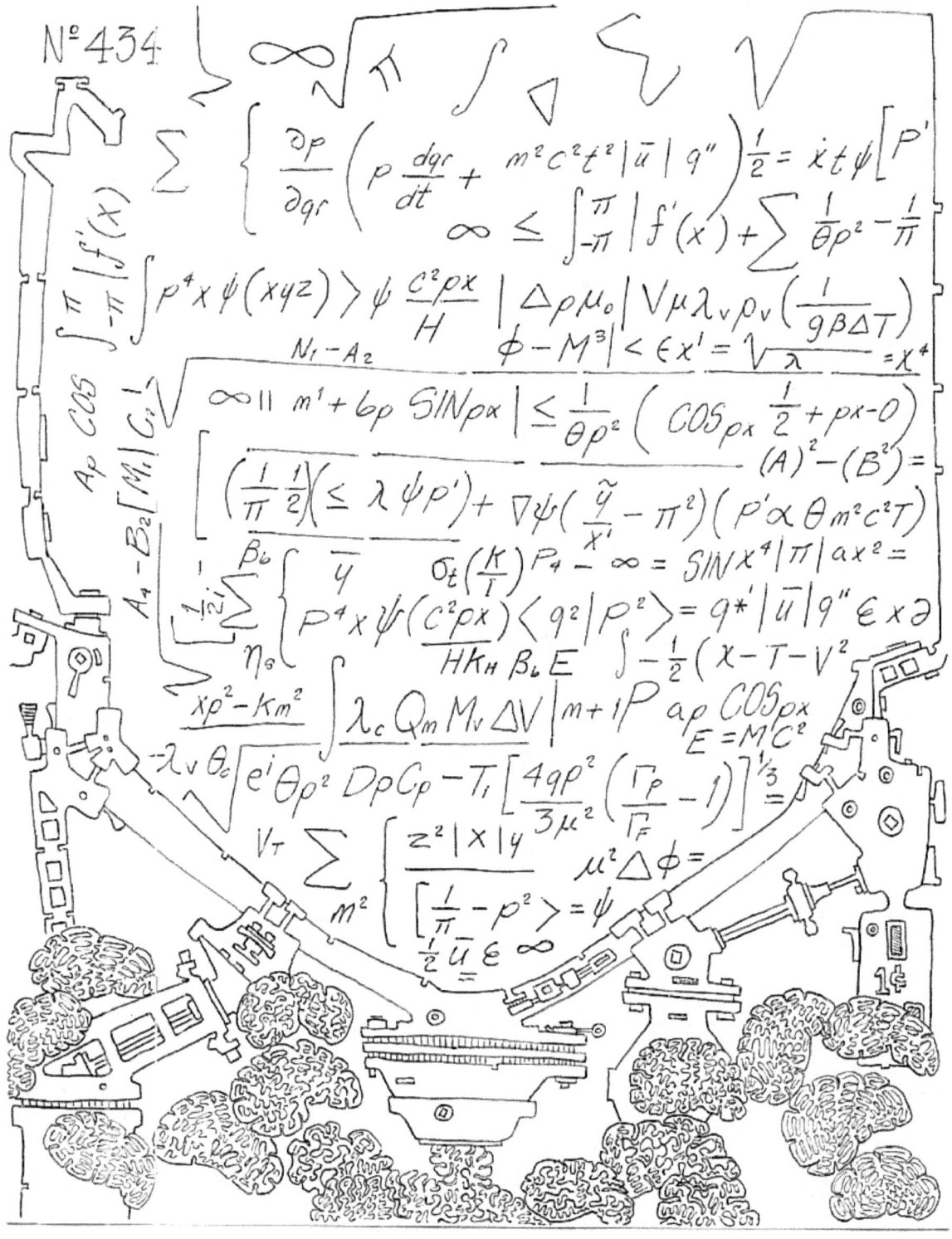

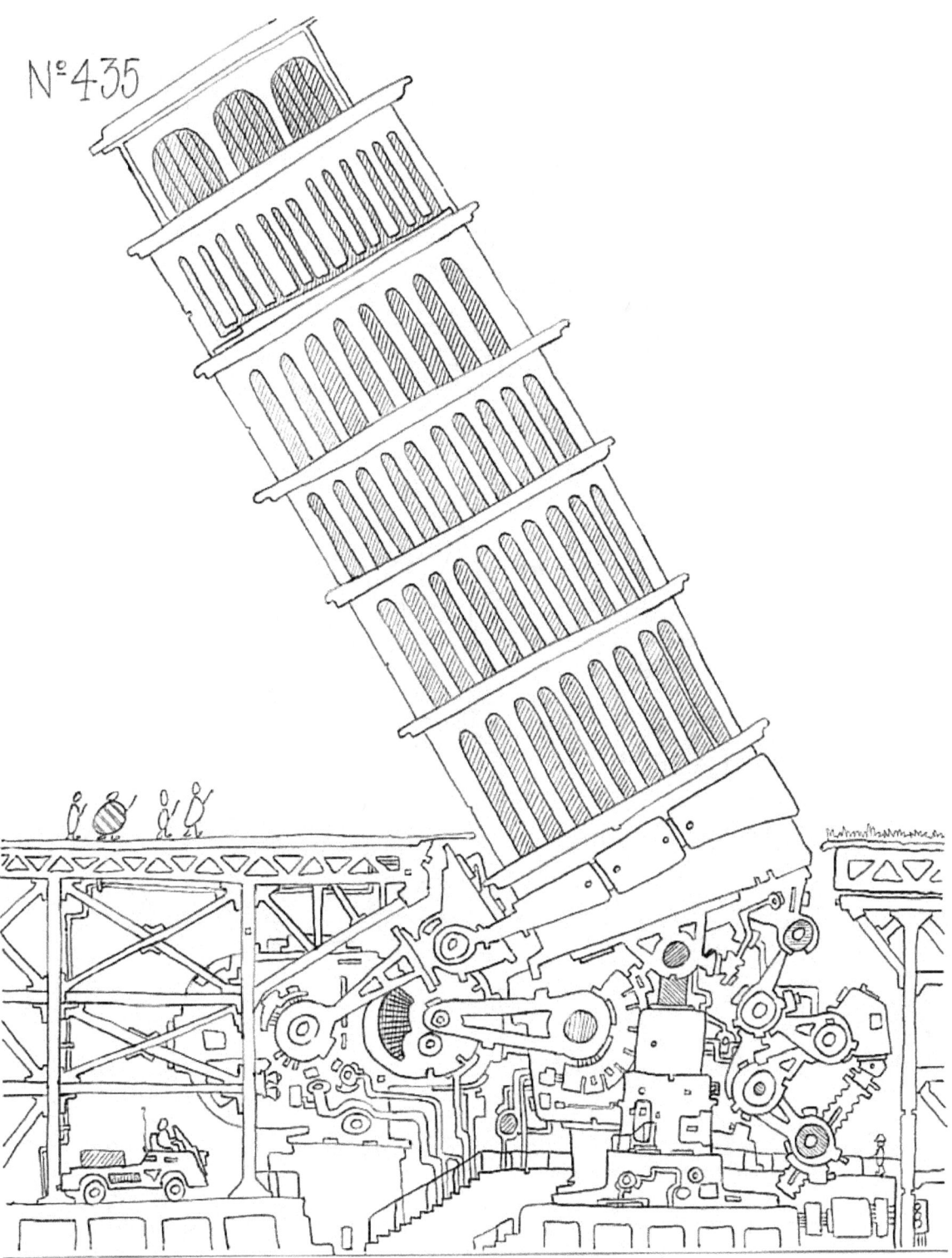

N°437

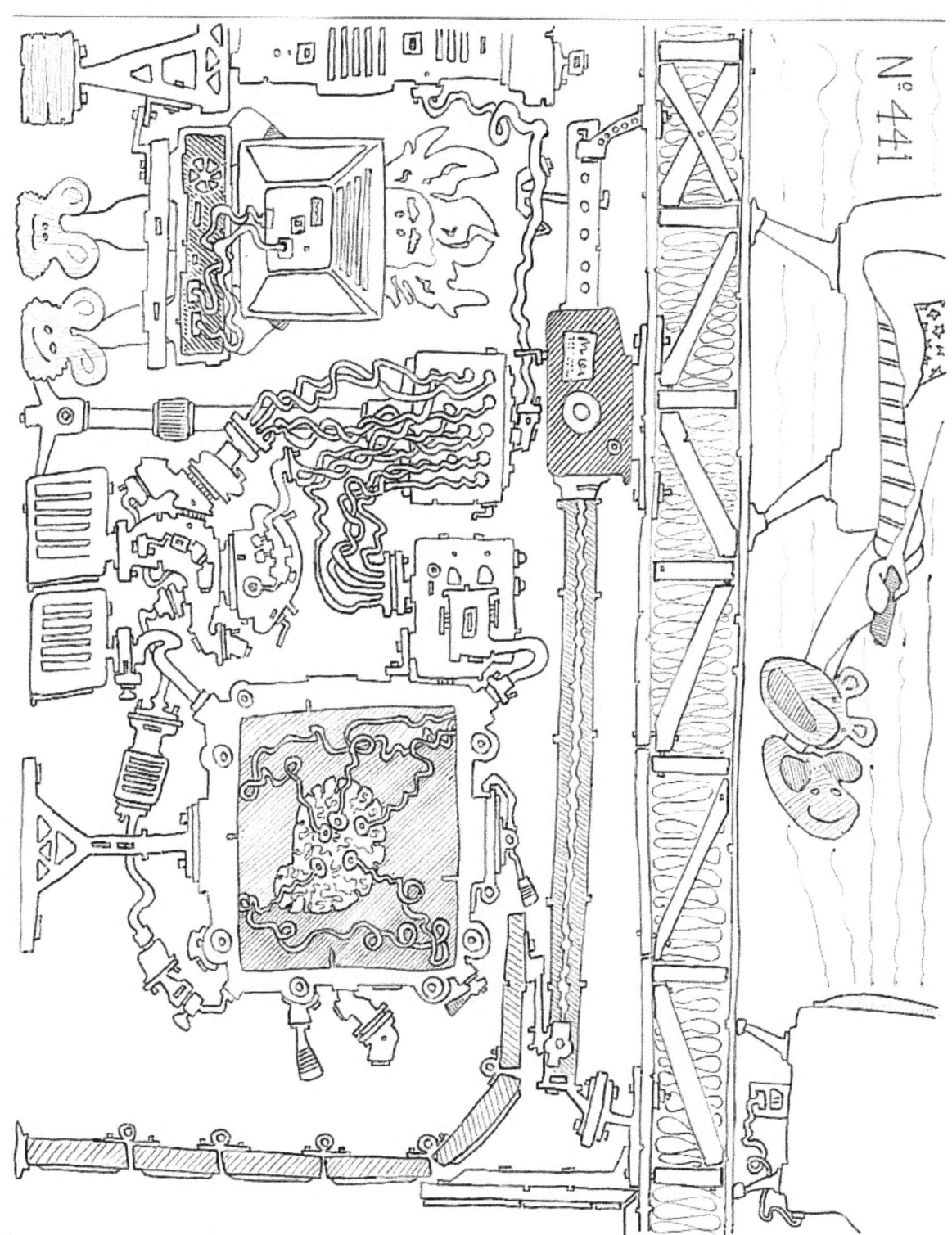

N° 443

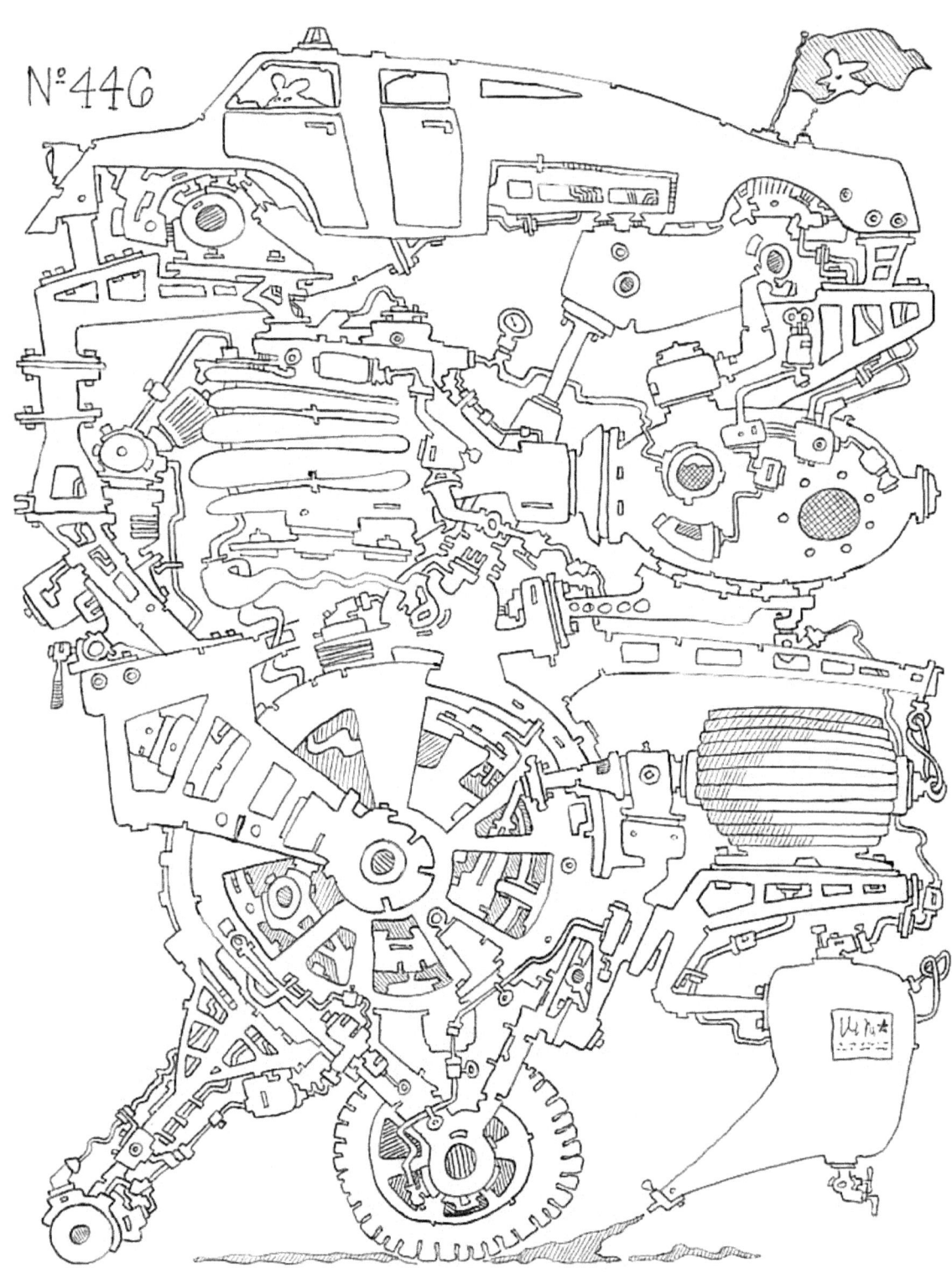

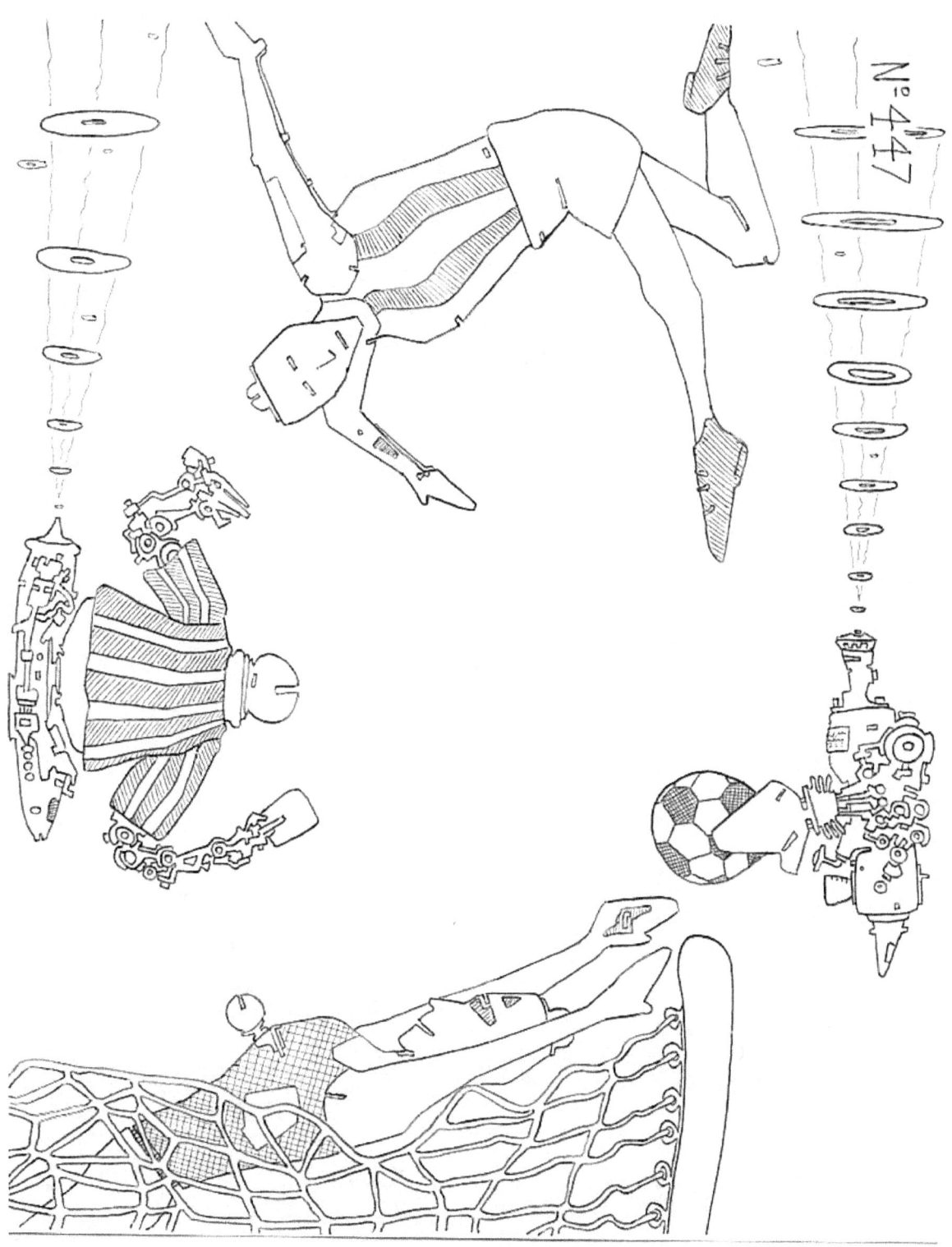

Nº 448

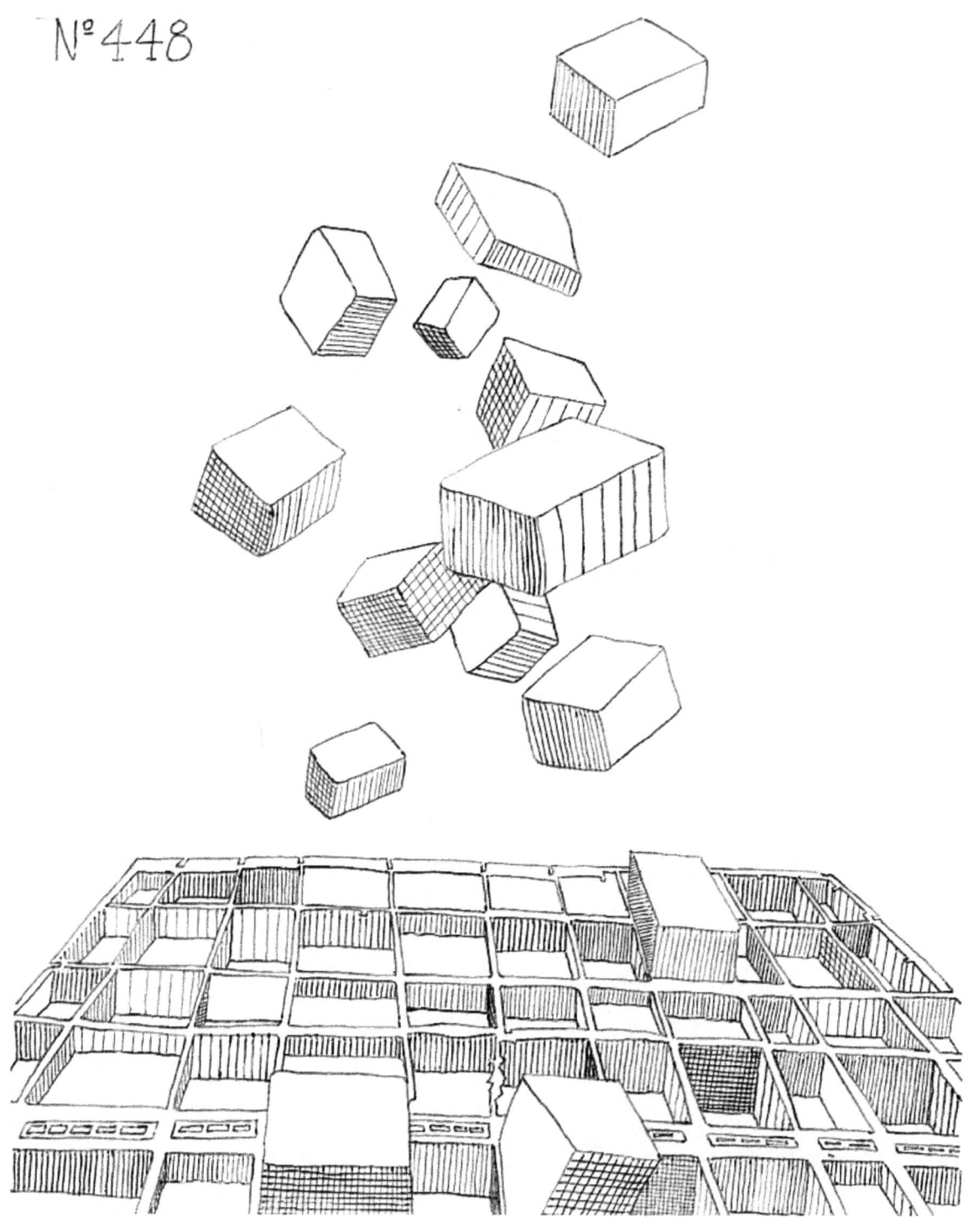

N° 449

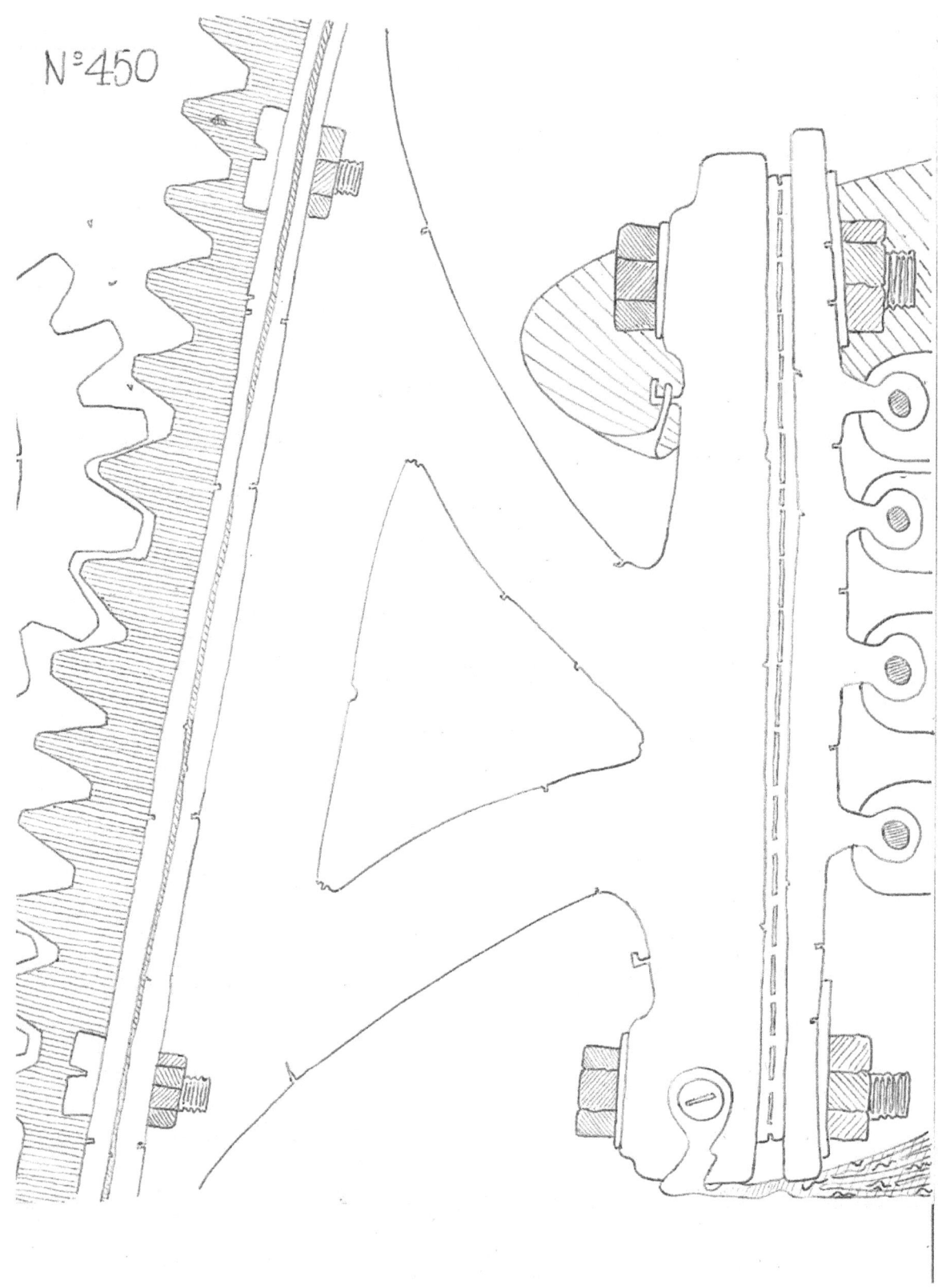

N°450

Nº 453

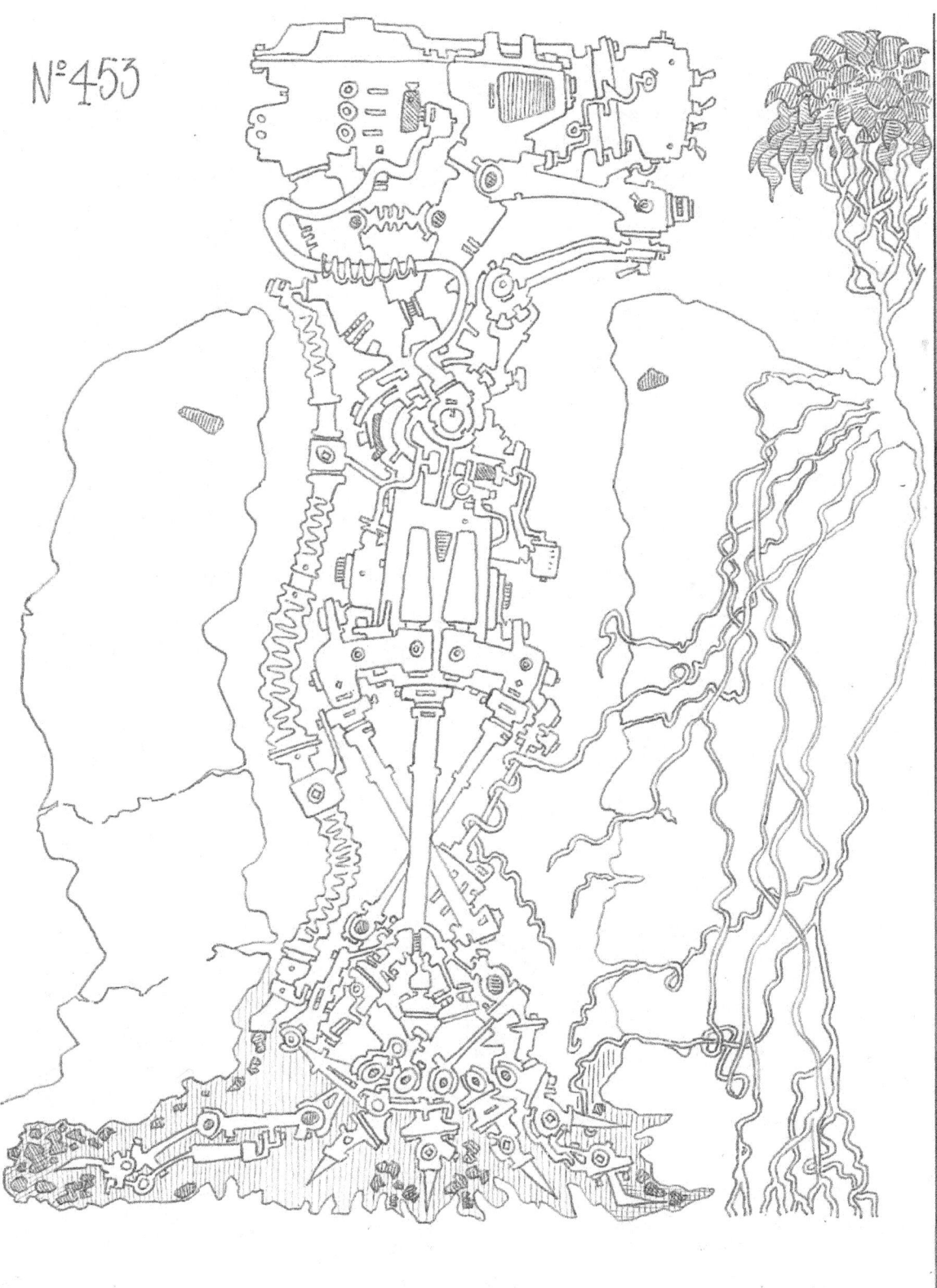

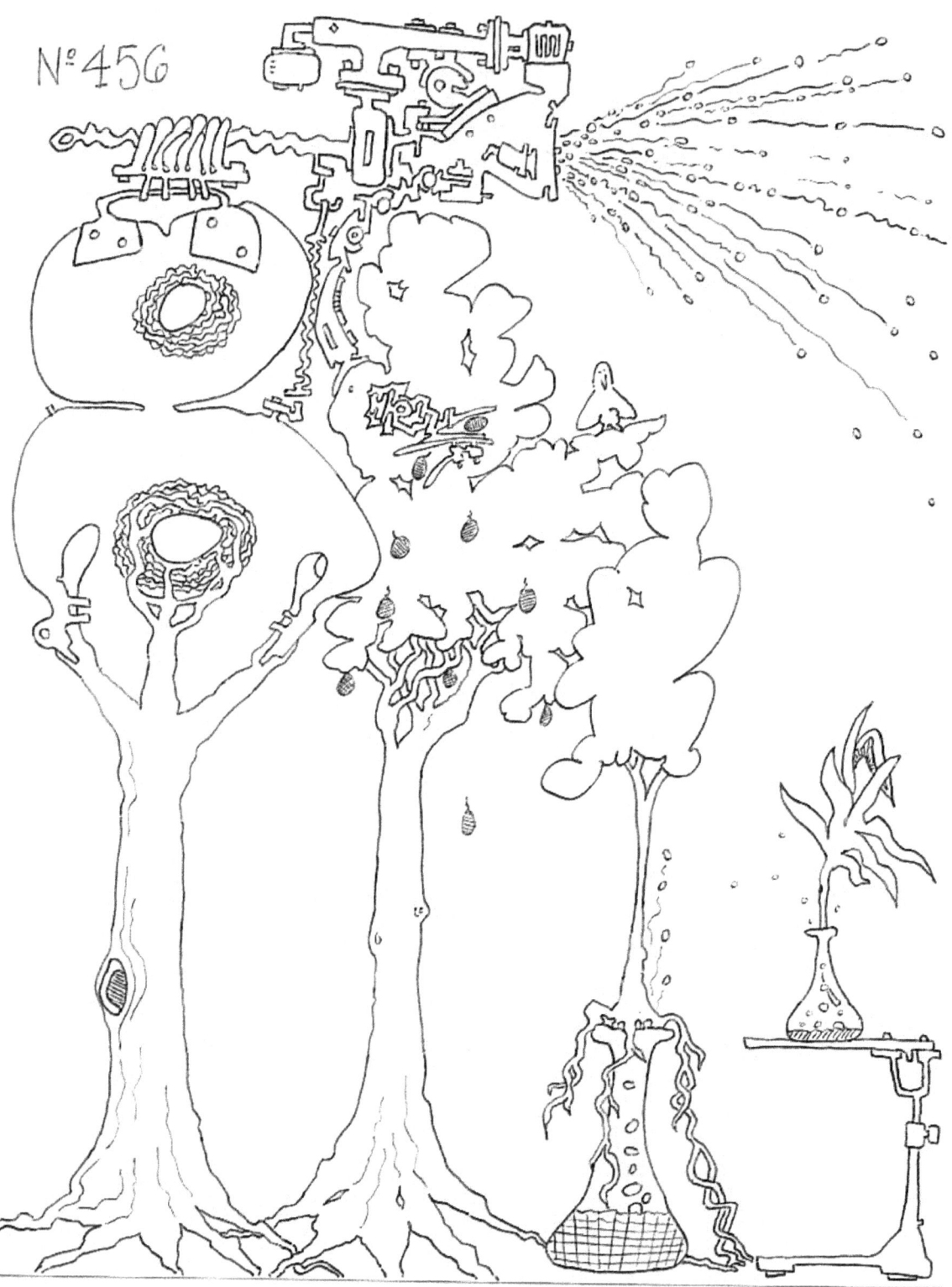

N° 457

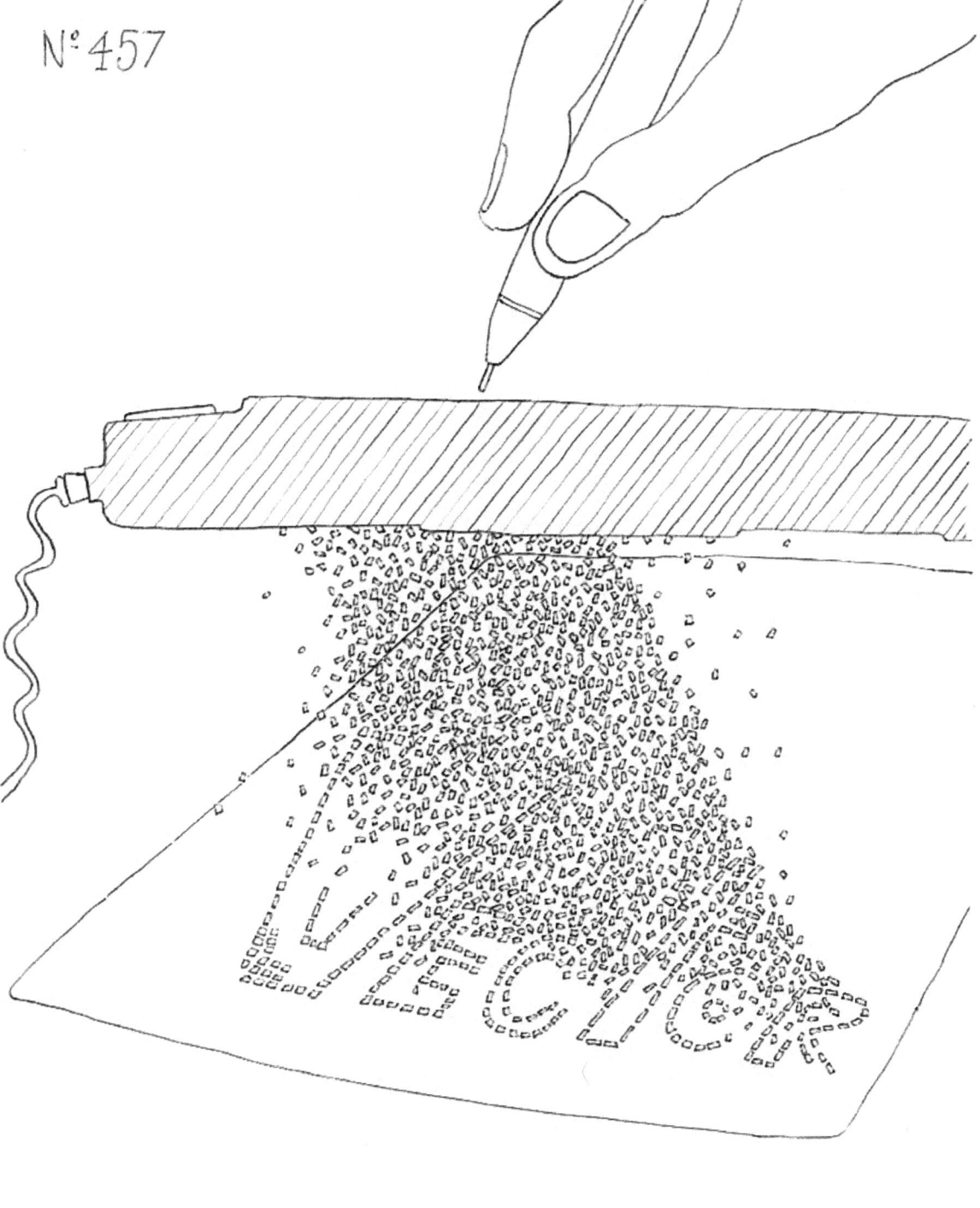

N° 458

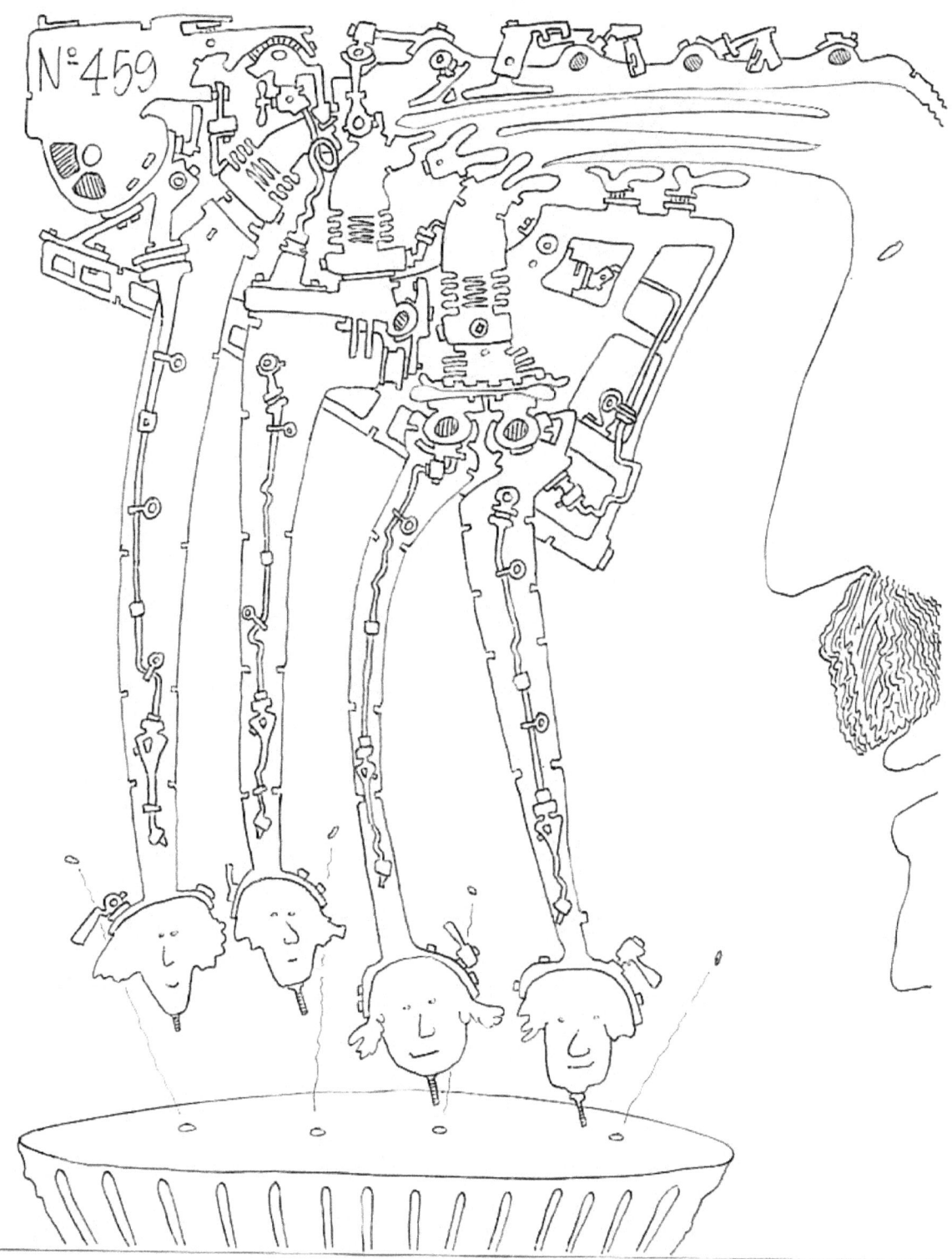

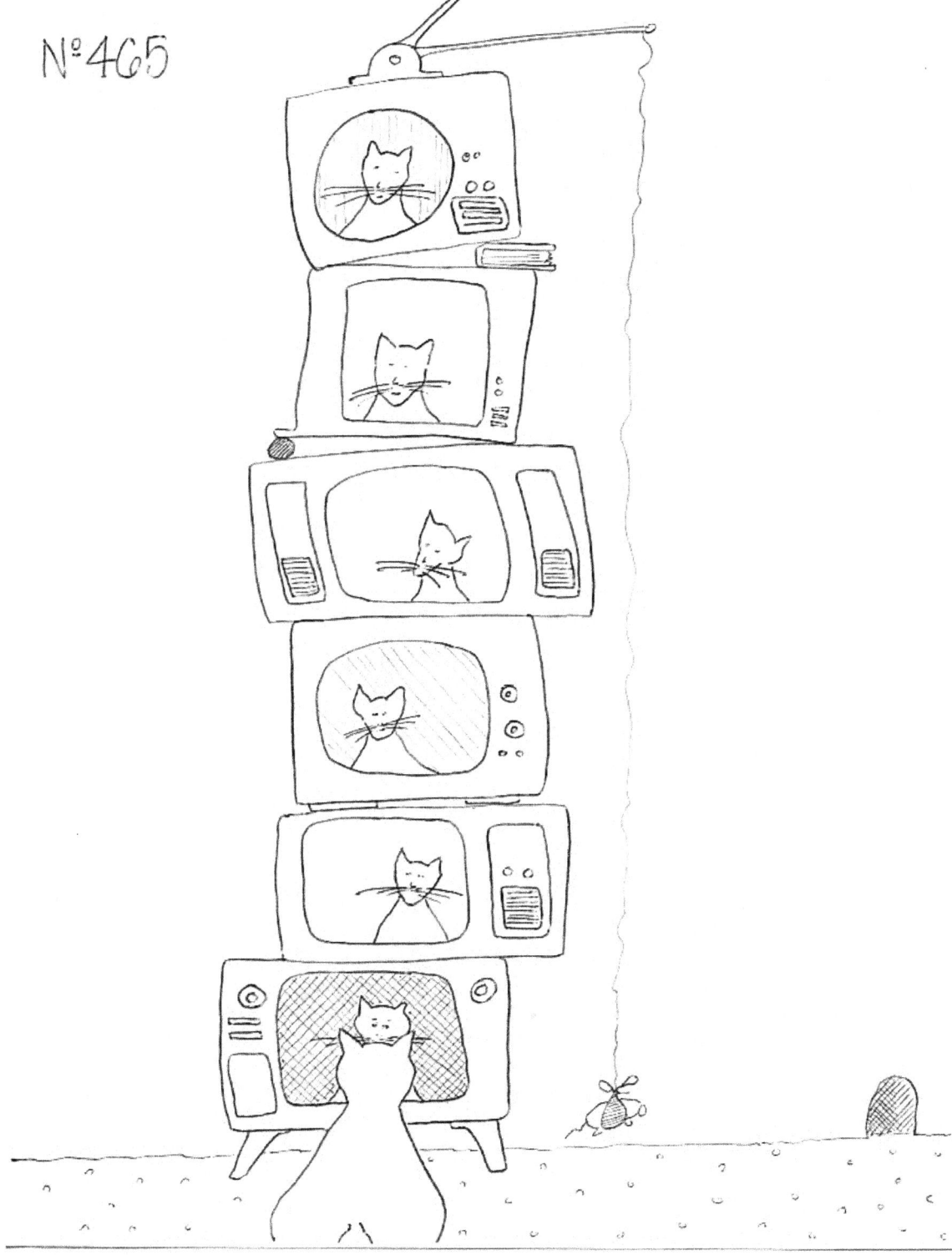

N° 466

N° 407

N° 468

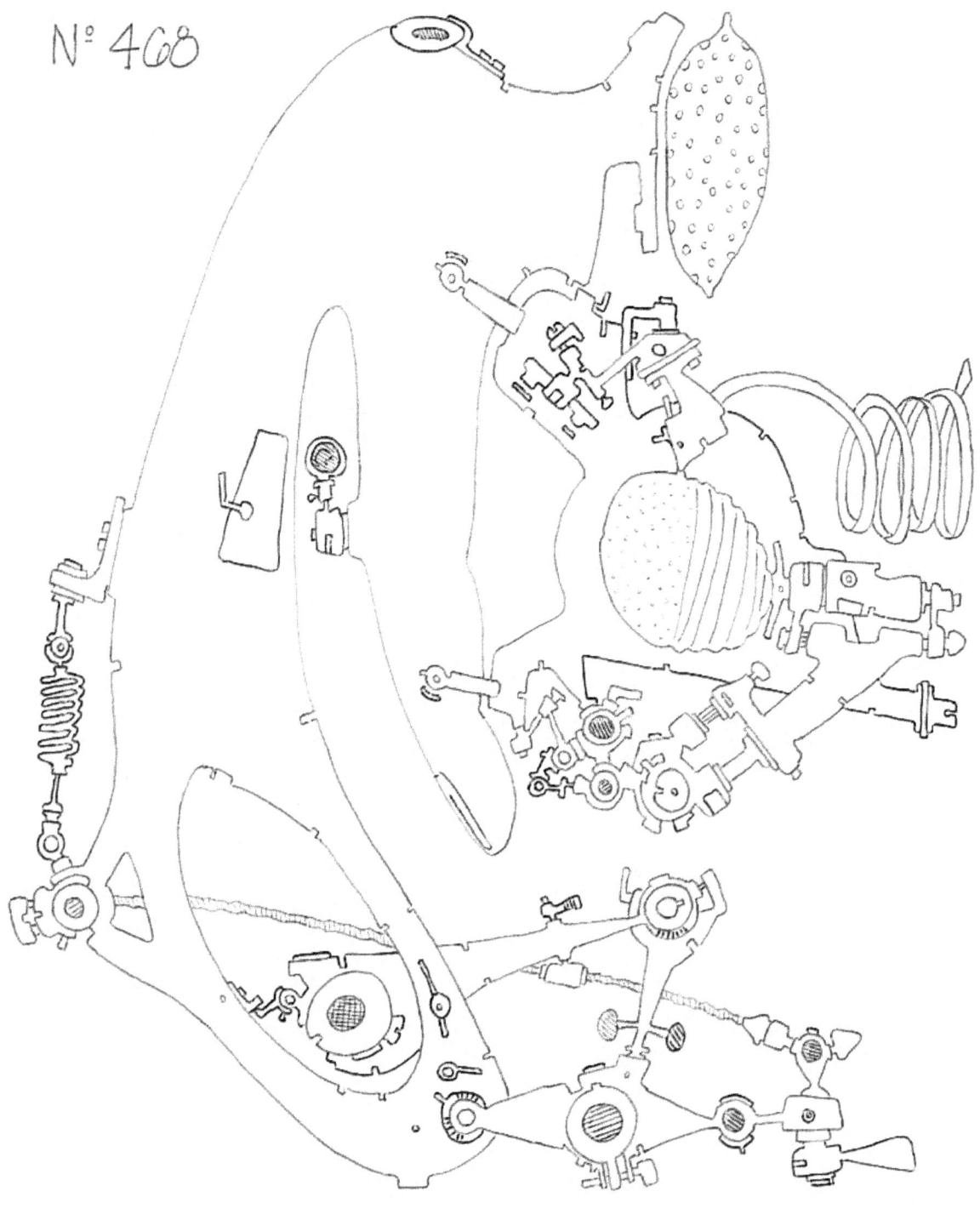

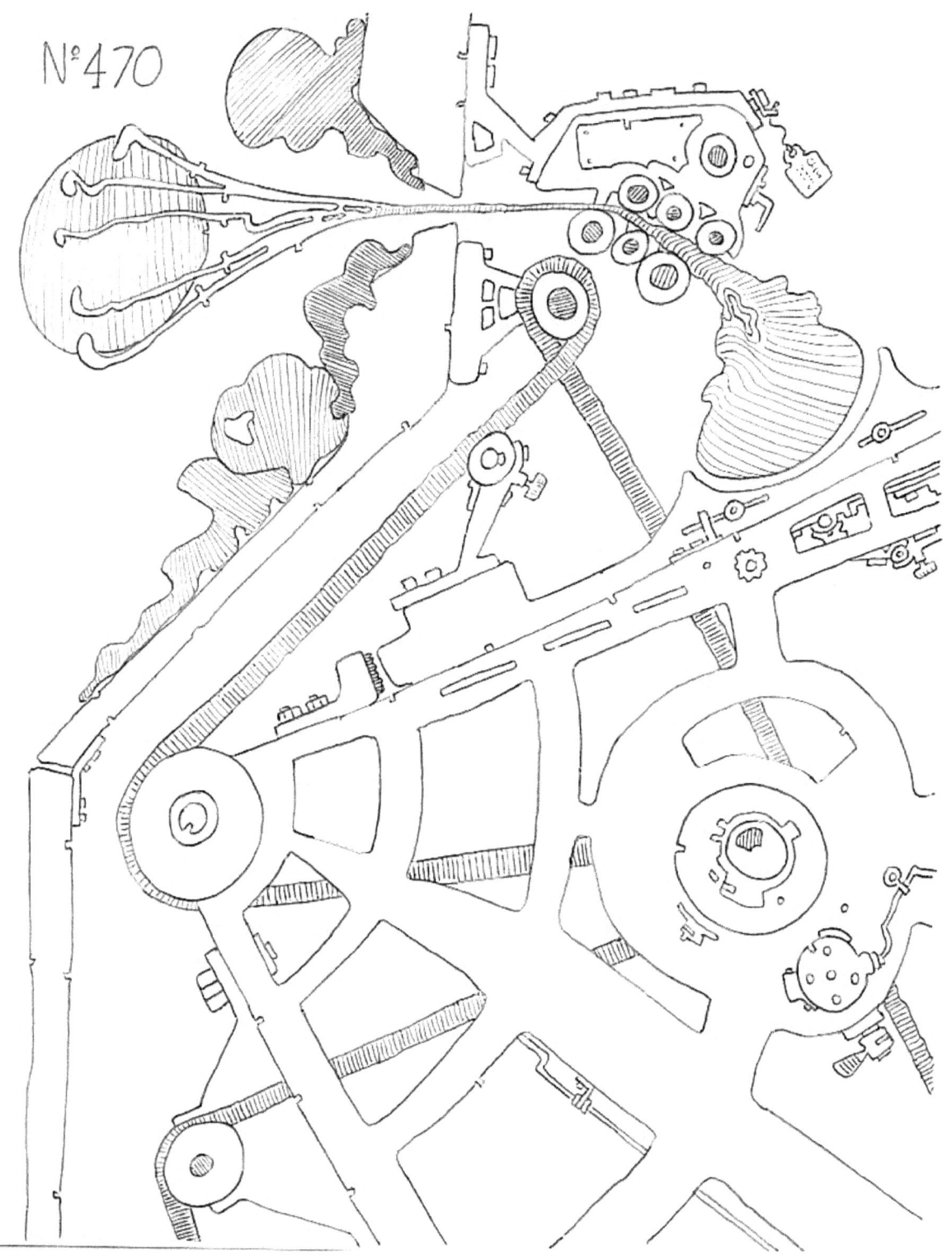

N° 471

N° 473

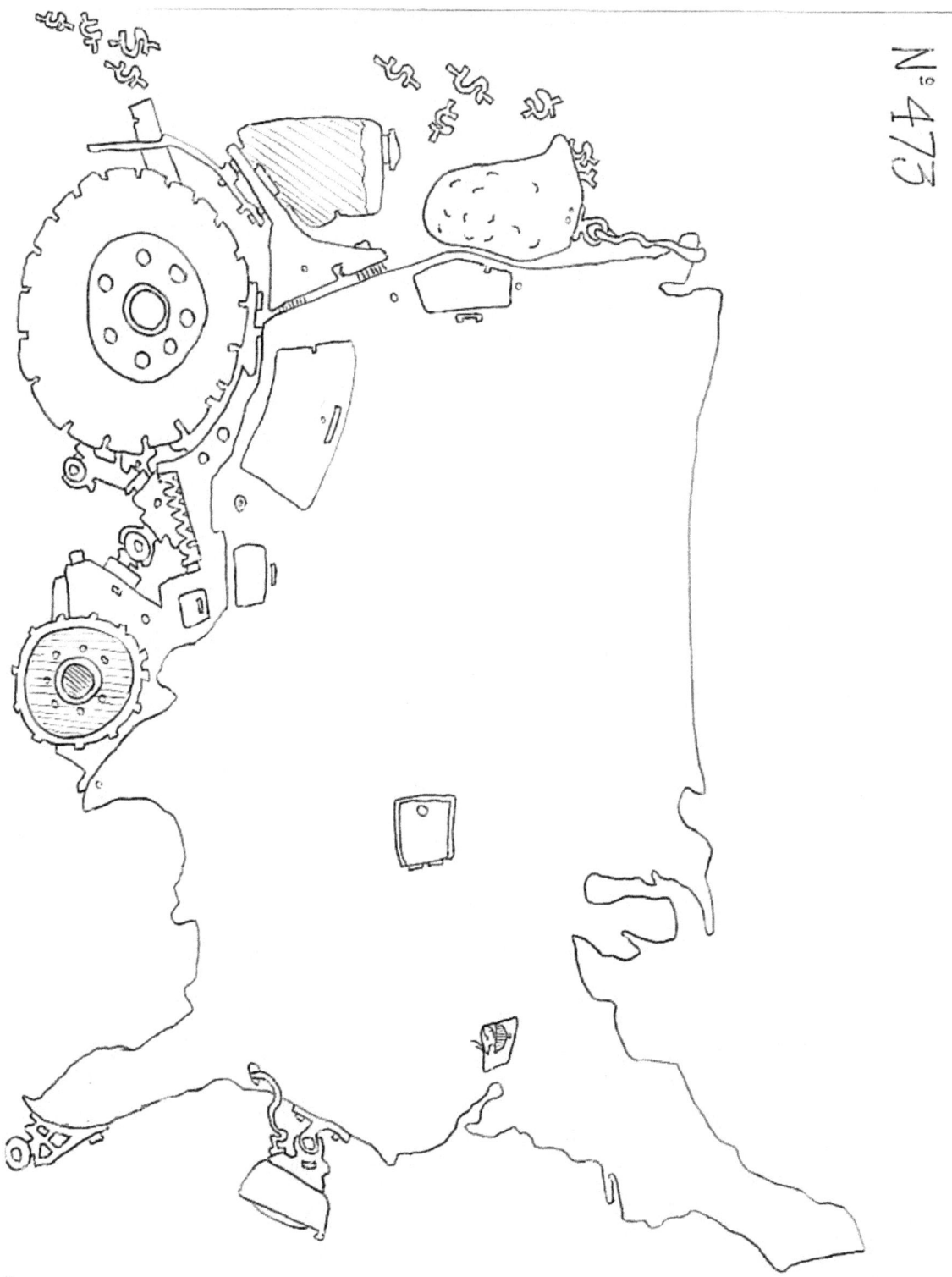

N° 474

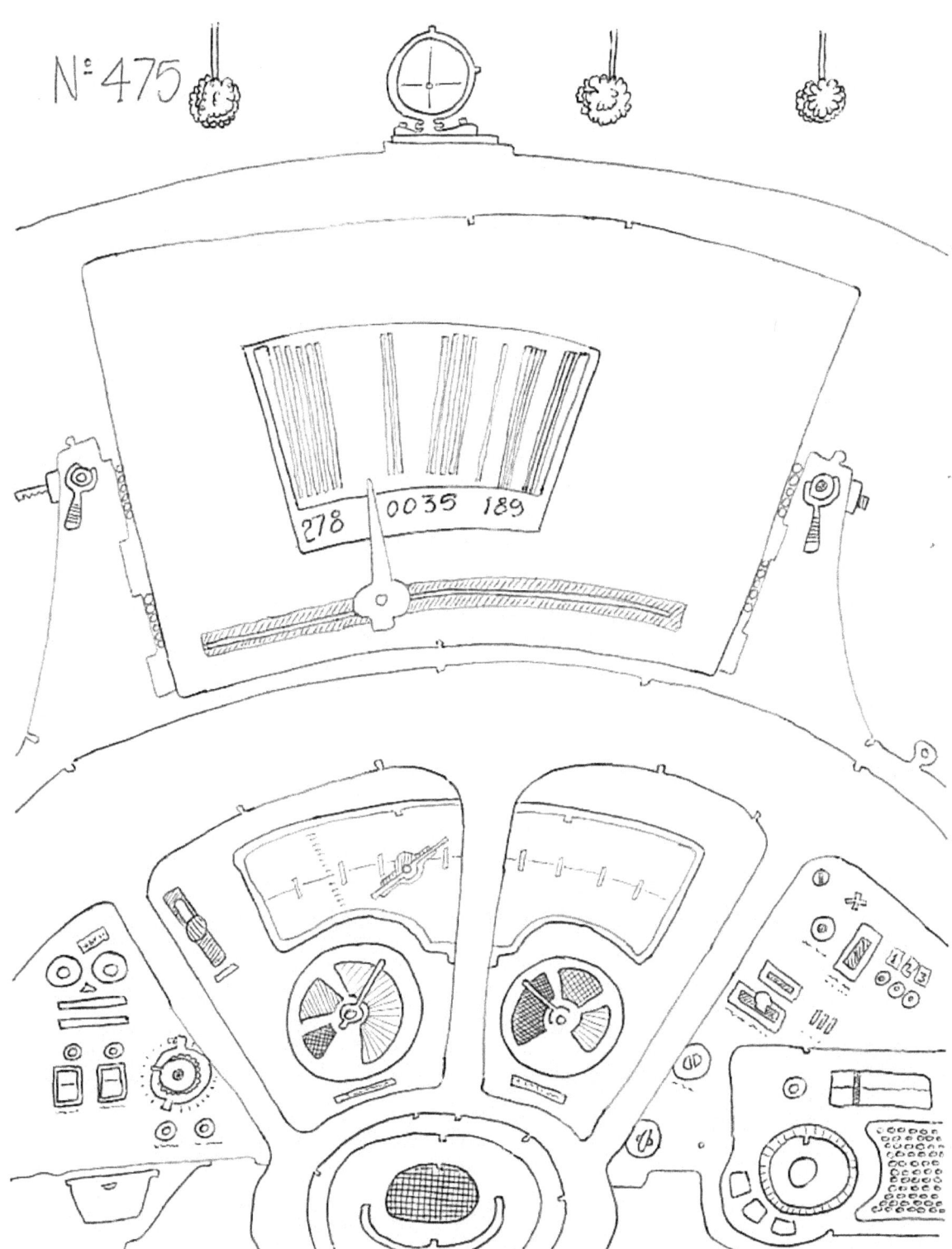

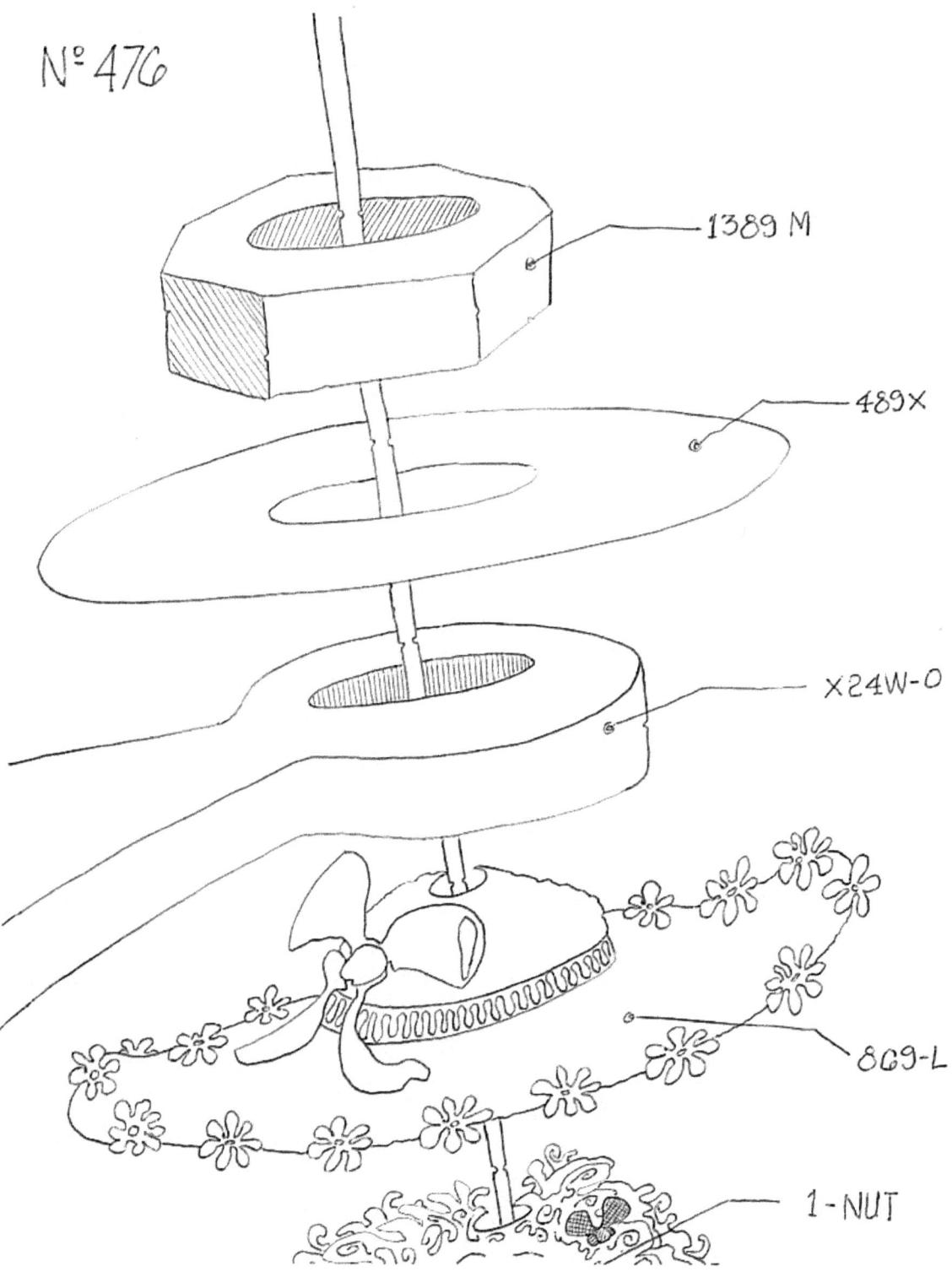

N° 476

1389 M
489 X
X24W-O
809-L
1-NUT

Nº 477

N° 477

Nº 478

N° 479

N° 400

N° 481

N° 482

Nº 486

Nº 488

N° 489

N° 490

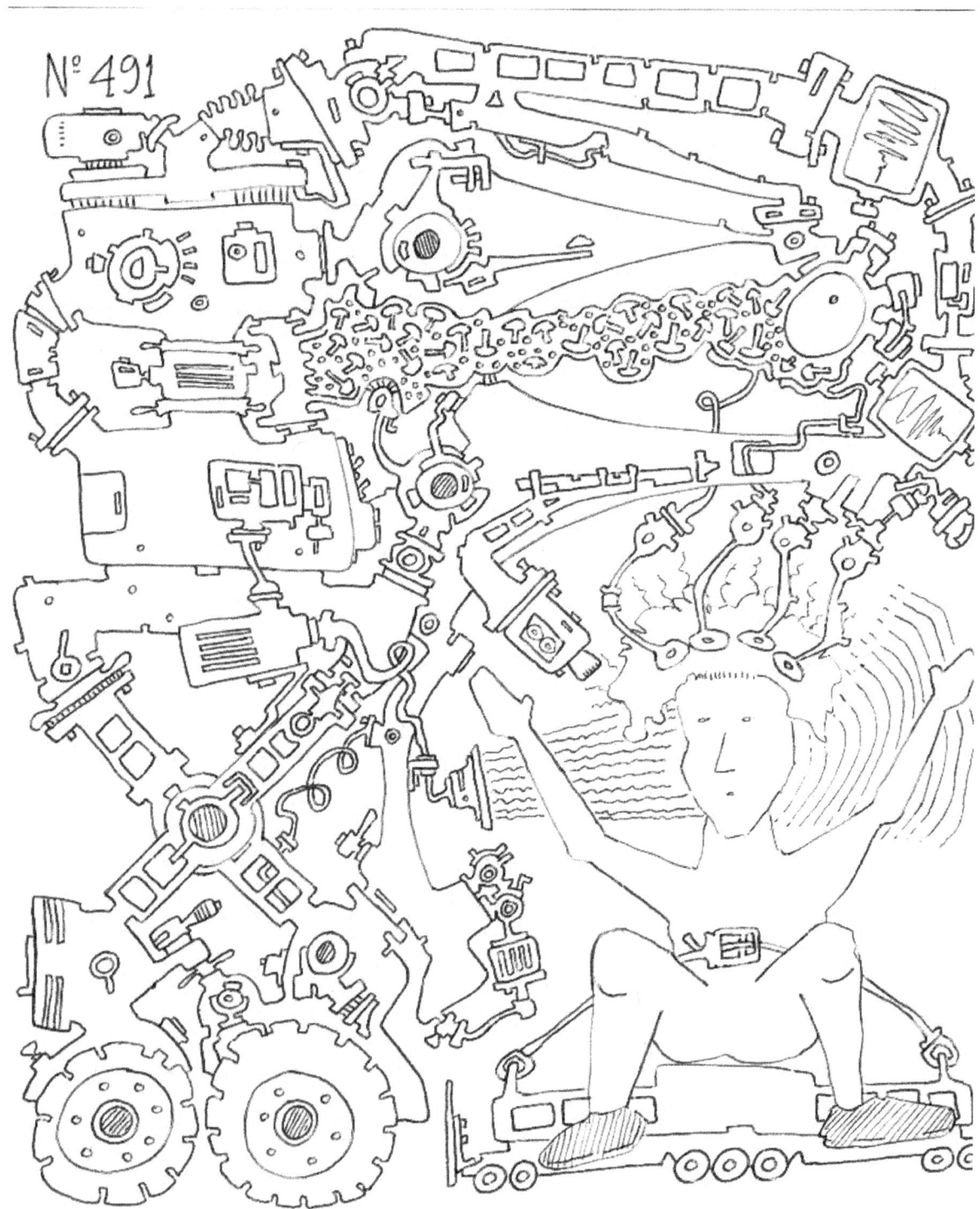

N° 494

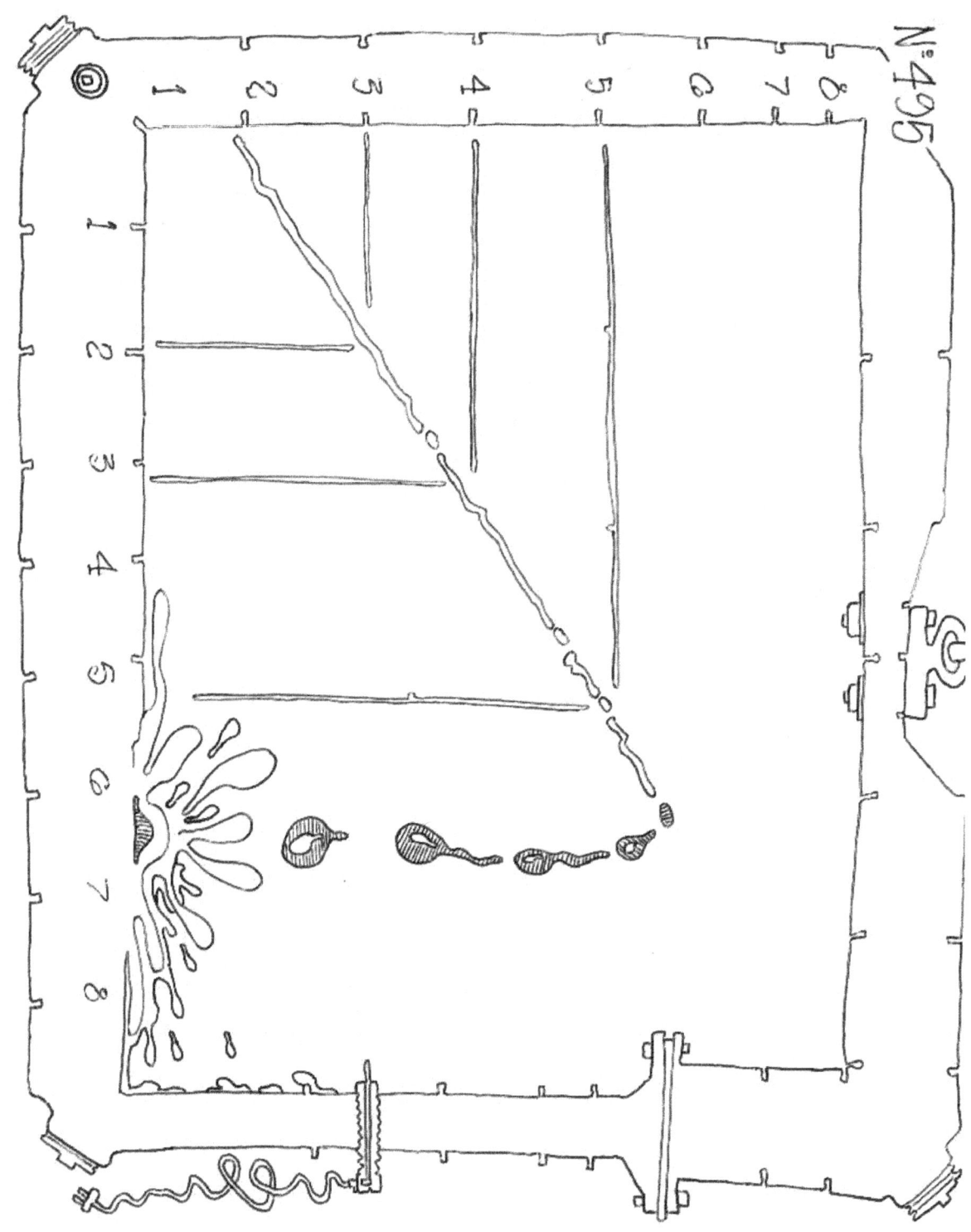

N° 497

Nº 498

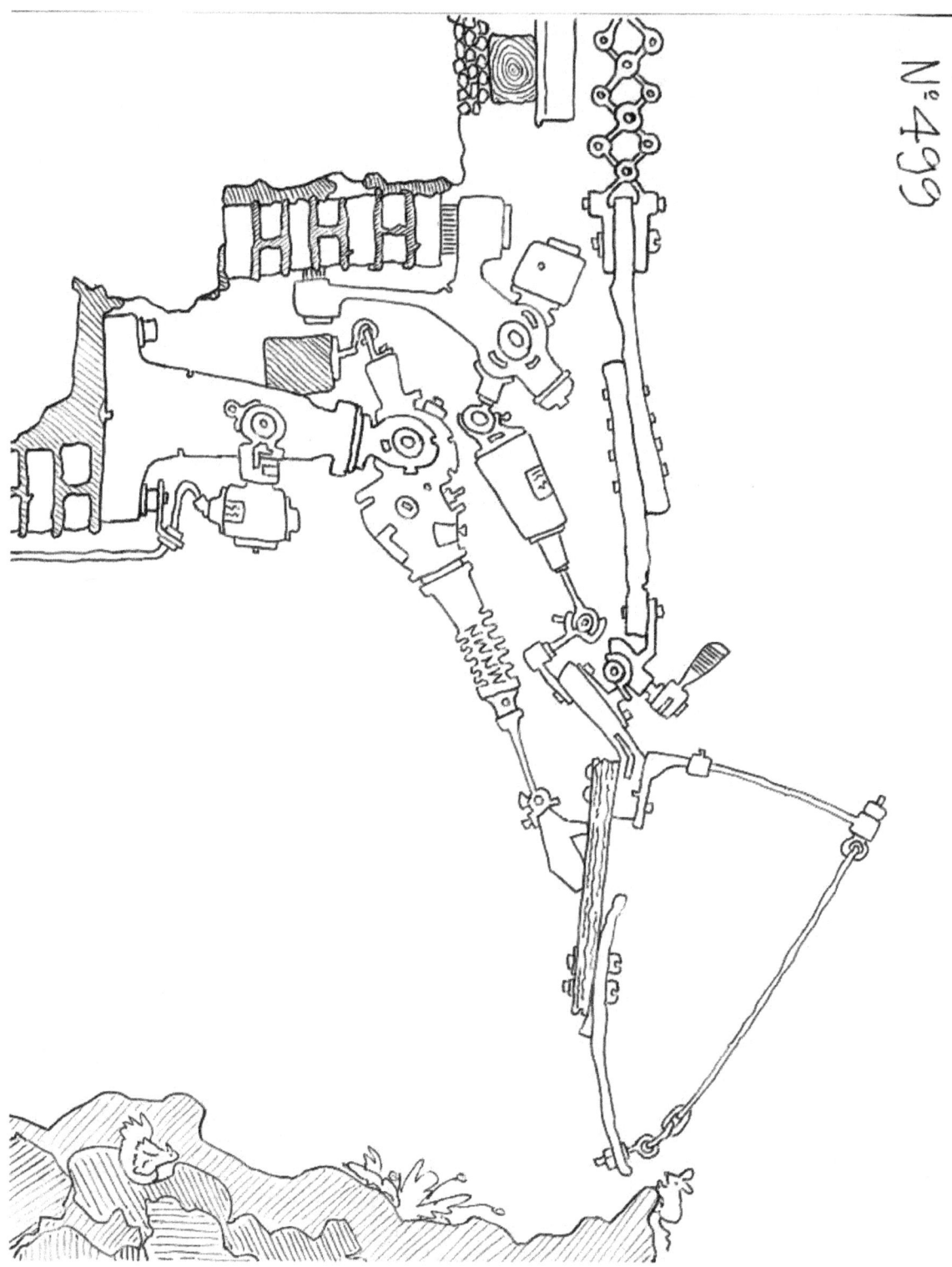

N° 500

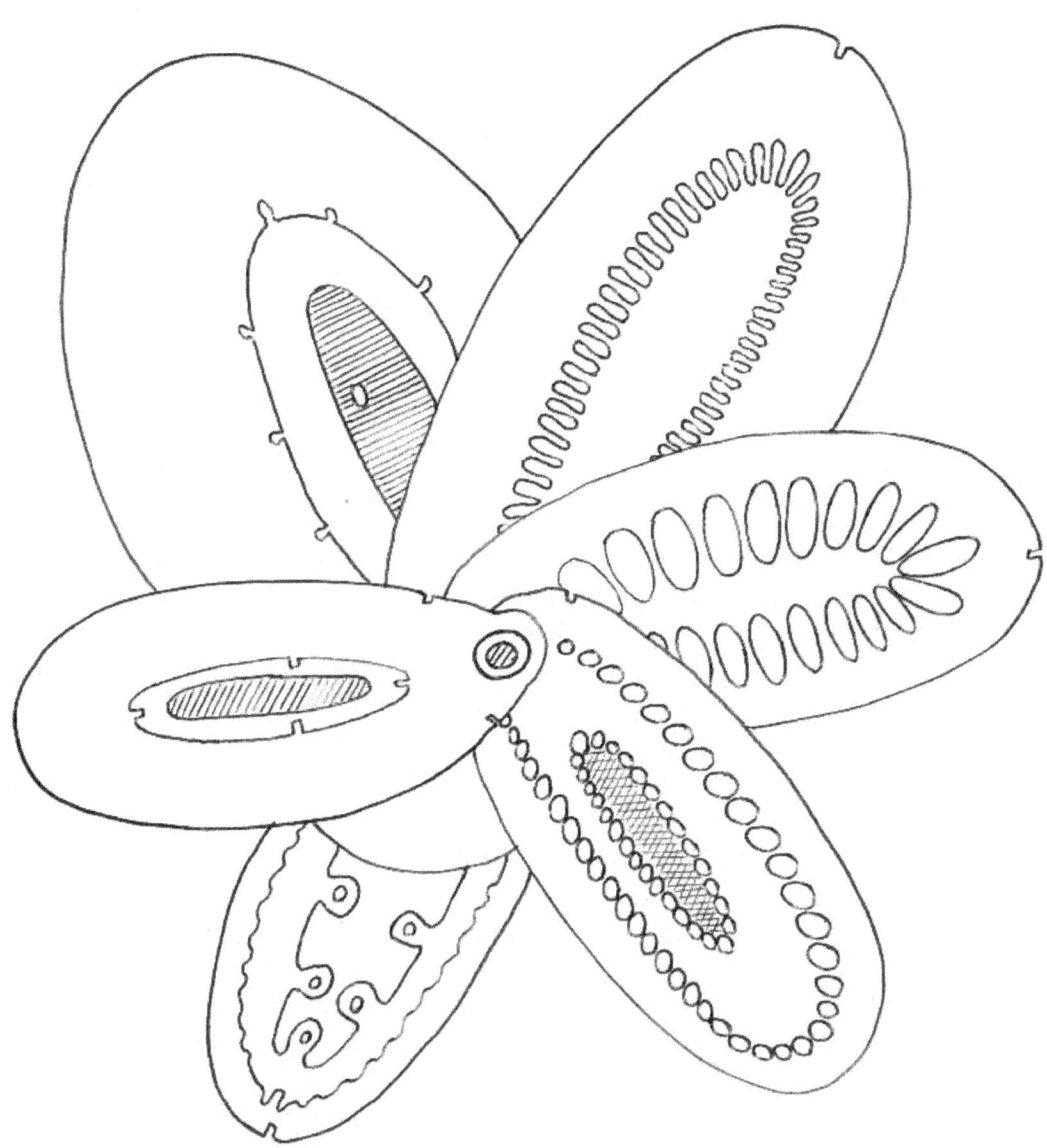

www.ingramcontent.com/pod-product-compliance
Lightning Source LLC
LaVergne TN
LVHW061253060426
835507LV00020B/2305